Designing Effective Speech Interfaces

By Susan Weinschenk
and Dean T. Barker

WILEY COMPUTER PUBLISHING

WILEY

John Wiley & Sons, Inc.

New York • Chichester • Weinheim • Brisbane • Singapore • Toronto

Publisher: Robert Ipsen
Editor: Theresa Hudson
Assistant Editor: Kathryn Malm
Managing Editor: Frank Grazioli
Text Design & Composition: Judy K. Spreng

Designations used by companies to distinguish their products are often claimed as trademarks. In all instances where John Wiley & Sons, Inc., is aware of a claim, the product names appear in initial capital or ALL CAPITAL LETTERS. Readers, however, should contact the appropriate companies for more complete information regarding trademarks and registration.

This book is printed on acid-free paper. ∞

Published by John Wiley & Sons, Inc.

Published simultaneously in Canada.

This publication is designed to provide accurate and authoritative information in regard to the subject matter covered. It is sold with the understanding that the publisher is not engaged in professional services. If professional advice or other expert assistance is required, the services of a competent professional person should be sought.

Library of Congress Cataloging-in-Publication Data:

ISBN 0-471-37545-4

Printed in the United States of America.

10 9 8 7 6 5 4 3 2 1

Acknowledgements

When Terri Hudson, our editor at John Wiley & Sons suggested we do this book we knew it would take a lot of work and research and we were right. But we had help along the way.

So here is our list of acknowledgements and thank yous. Thanks first to Terri for continuing to think of us and for being a visionary editor who keeps at least a year ahead of what people need to/want to read in our field. Our day-to-day editor was Gerrie Cho. She kept us on task and organized. Without her help every day for months we wouldn't have met our deadlines.

Thanks to the experts we interview in the book: Sharon Oviatt, Kate Dobroth, Ahmed Reza, John Karat, Nicole Yankelovich, and Candace Kamm. Their ideas, insight, and previous writings helped us grow in our knowledge and assisted in our synthesizing the information. Thanks to all of our clients who always keep us thinking and add to our experience bank from which we can draw for ideas and examples.

Sally Yeo gave us advice on everything from layout to content to wording. She also did the excellent indexing.

Michael Bryant gave "sound advice!" Judy Spreng was our layout guru. Marge Sumner was our copyeditor, and improved our writing significantly. Linda Rothenberger created many of our graphics, started our project Web site, and kept it up to date. She was also an excellent proofreader. Ted Goff provided our wonderful cartoons.

Special thanks go to our families, Lisa, Peter, Guthrie and Maisie, for putting up with very long nights, lots of working weekends, and stressed-out authors.

C O N T E N T S

Part Four - Best Practices 267

Chapter 11 - Usability Processes and Techniques 269

Chapter 12 - Universal Design 325

Chapter A - A History of Relevant Technology for Speech 335

Chapter B - Glossary 353

Chapter C - Resources................................363

Chapter D - Bibliography 379

Index................................387

Introduction

In 1985 I worked on my first natural language interface. We were building a proof of concept system that would allow top managers at an insurance company to use natural language commands to query a database. If the system didn't know a word that was used, it would come back with a question asking for the meaning of the term it did not know. During an early test one of the users asked, "How much life insurance was sold last year in the Northeast?" The computer questioned us back with, "What is the meaning of life?" How thrilled we were that we had created the first thinking computer!

During the last few months I have talked to many people about this book I was writing. I can't count how many people mentioned the *Star Trek* computer or HAL from *2001: A Space Odyssey* to me when I would tell them the title of the book. For a while I thought it was neat that people could relate to what I was writing about. After all, if I mention the title of my last book, *GUI Design Essentials*, to people who are not in the field of computers I usually get blank, glazed stares. As the same comments continued to come, I started to inwardly groan. But as I write this now, in the thick of the project, I have decided that it is significant. The idea of a talking computer and a computer that understands our speech is something different. It's striking. It's a novel idea that captures people's attention and imagination. At first it seems easy to understand why so many people who had seen *2001* would remember HAL. HAL is the somewhat sinister computer in *2001* who closes the pod doors, leaving the human character floating in space. People remember "him" because he's evil, right? But then, how many evil characters are there in movies? Do we always remember their names? And what about the original computer in *Star Trek*? That androgynous computer was just called "computer." And he/she wasn't sinister at all. Why do we remember that one?

I think it's because speech is something that is uniquely human. Dogs bark, and chimpanzees can communicate with written "language," but only humans talk. To talk is to be human, and HAL and "Computer" stick in our memory because they are computers with uniquely human traits. We are fascinated by this idea, and maybe even repelled by it.

Speaking is so natural to us as humans, that we want to be able to talk to our computers.

No wonder, then, that speech capabilities in computers seem to hold that love-hate, avoidance-attraction aspect for us. Speaking is so natural to us as humans, that we want to be able to talk to our computers. It seems that it would be easier. And we want our computers to talk to us, because listening to information rather than reading it leaves our eyes and hands free to do other tasks. Yet we hesitate. We come up with so many reasons not to embrace the technology.

True, the reasons are plentiful and many are all too valid. The state of speech recognition, and dealing with the errors it produces, are enough to still drive many away. I used speech technology, specifically dictation systems, when I was writing this book. I dictated the phrase "…and manual output, and performance was worse with auditory input and spoken output." When I glanced at the screen, the recognizer had written "and Immanual Kant put an the of paint boatman and Spokane output."

Last week a press release from the University of Southern California proclaimed a breakthrough in speech recognition using neural network technology. The improvements are dramatic. By the time this book is released, using neural networks for speech recognition may have made many of the error handling and recovery issues unimportant. None too soon for me.

But high error rates are not all that is holding us back. I think we worry about losing our uniqueness. We don't want humans to be machines, and we are still uncomfortable with our machines being human-like.

I don't believe that talking to a computer, or listening to a computer, makes us any less human or the computer any more human. We are about to overcome our hesitancy and leap into speech in a big way. What will that transition be like? Will it continue to happen slowly? Or will it snowball?

We are historically very poor at predicting the pace of acceptance of new technologies. In a conversation I had with one of the original creators of the cell phone, he told me that when they developed the first cell phone they thought the total worldwide market was about 100 phones (top CEOs and maybe heads of large powerful governments). T.J. Watson from IBM predicted worldwide computer use at five computers (of course he meant large mainframes). The Internet was confined to a group of scientists for many years. We cannot predict the speed or the direction or the use of new technologies.

We cannot predict the speed or the direction or the use of new technologies.

The uses of speech technologies will be much more social and human than we think.

I suspect, however, that the uses of speech technologies will be much more social and human than we think. When people embrace a technology, they take it into their social situations. People sign on to the Internet to chat with each other, or sell items like a big garage sale. People use their cell phones to call home and talk to children and spouses. Certainly, business and commerce will be targeted for speech applications, as they have already been, but if you want to find the point at which the technology is fully embraced, look for places where speech brings us closer to other people.

Susan Weinschenk

November, 1999

Introduction to Speech Interfaces

In order to understand the current state of speech technology and how to use if effectively, you must be familiar with some basics of speech. Part One: Introduction to Speech Interfaces contains information on speech technologies and human-computer interaction concepts, including

Chapter 1: Basic Concepts. Covers definitions of user interfaces, types of user interfaces, and definitions of speech interfaces.

Chapter 2: Human Factors in Speech Technology. Gives an overview of the field of human factors, covers the basic concepts of human-computer interaction, and summarizes the major human factors issues in speech interfaces. Discusses cost/benefit calculations for usability engineering on speech interfaces.

Chapter 3: The Nature of Sound. Explains sound terminology and technology.

Chapter 4: The Nature of Language. Summarizes what we know about language and communication, including the structure of language, grammar, syntax, and semantics.

Chapter 1

Basic Concepts

"Sorry, I don't know anything. We just
thought it would be really cool to build
this high-tech information kiosk."

> **"There is one thing stronger than all the armies in the world, and that is an idea whose time has come."**
> *Victor Hugo*

This book is about speech interfaces. For this first chapter we will focus on what an interface is, types of interfaces, and what we mean by a speech interface. At the end of this chapter, we describe the individual parts (sections) and chapters of the book.

What Is an Interface?

An interface is the part of technology that people interact with. The interaction between a computer and a user is a two-way interaction. Sometimes the user is giving information to the computer, and sometimes the computer is giving information to the user. This interaction can include hardware components like keyboards, mice, or keypads, or software components such as a screen, window, page, sound, or talking voice. Any technology, computer, or machine also has elements the operator or user never sees or interacts with. In the case of software, code and programming are hidden elements. Since the user only interacts with the interface, the interface is in many ways the embodiment of the product. If a user comments that a particular product is easy to use or hard to use, they are not necessarily commenting on the underlying technology, but usually on the interface.

Designing an interface is no small task. What you consider a "well-designed" interface depends on your perspective. To a programmer, a well-designed interface might mean that the interface works within the technical constraints of the project. To a product manager, a well-designed interface might mean that the interface can be easily changed over time as new versions of the product are developed. To a business stakeholder, a well-designed interface might mean that the interface has more bells and whistles than the competition's product. To a usability engineer a well-designed interface might mean one that is designed with a particular user group in mind. And to the user of the product, a well-designed interface might mean that the product works the way they expect it to. All these perspectives are important, but because our background is usability engineering, we tend toward the last two definitions, and concentrate on them in this book.

As usability engineers we are interested in how to make technology easy to learn and use. We are concerned with how to design products so that people can be as productive as possible with the product, as quickly as possible. The biggest single impact we can have on products is in the area of the interface. Designing to optimize usability means paying specific attention to how the interface looks and acts. This includes

- ensuring that the interface matches the way people need or want to accomplish a task;
- using the appropriate modality (for example, visual or voice) at the appropriate time;
- spending adequate design time on the interface.

Designing to optimize usability means paying specific attention to how the interface looks and acts.

What Are the Types of Interfaces?

There are several types of interfaces. In the past (and still around to some extent) were character-based user interfaces (CHUI), then graphical user interfaces (GUI) became prevalent, and next came Web user interfaces (WUI). In this book we discuss speech user interfaces (SUI).

What Is a Speech Interface?

It seems as if this question, What is a Speech Interface?, would be simple to answer, but it is not. Because it is a relatively new idea to have our technology involve speech, this is a field that is just starting to grow. Like any new field, the definitions and terminologies are not standard. Here are some of the current terms in use, what they usually mean, and how we will apply them here.

Speech Interfaces

The term *speech interface* describes a software interface that employs either human speech or simulated human speech. You can further break down speech interfaces into *auditory user interfaces* and *graphical user interfaces with speech*.

Auditory User Interfaces (AUI)

An auditory user interface (AUI) is an interface which relies primarily or exclusively on audio for interaction, including speech and sounds. This means that commands issued by the machine or computer, as well as all commands issued by the human to control the machine or computer, are executed primarily with speech and sounds. Although AUI may include a hardware component, such as a keypad or buttons, visual displays are not used for critical information. Examples of auditory user interfaces include

- medical transcription software that allows doctors to dictate medical notes while making rounds;
- automobile hands-free systems that allow drivers to access travel information and directions (systems without screens and maps);
- interactive voice response (IVR) systems in which users access information by speaking commands, such as menu numbers, to listen to information of their choice;
- products for the visually impaired that rely only on audio text and cues.

Graphical User Interfaces with Speech (S/GUI)

In this book we discuss AUI, where the user interacts with the software primarily via speech. We also discuss interfaces where speech is part of the interface, but is joined by other interface forms—usually visual—such as a GUI window or a Web page. We call these multi-modal interfaces *graphical user interfaces with speech*, or S/GUI (for Speech/GUI). Examples of S/GUI include

- a wordprocessor that allows users to dictate text instead of or in addition to typing it in;
- Web navigation software that allows users to navigate to and within Web sites by using voice;
- talking dictionaries that speak definitions.

In these S/GUI applications, tasks can

- be completed using speech only, where users issue a speech command or listen to the software speak to them;
- rely on visual or manual GUI aspects, for example, viewing a graphic or clicking on a hyperlink;
- require or at least allow a combination of both a GUI aspect and speech, such as using speech commands to edit a document.

Non-Speech Audio

Some interface elements include audio, but not speech. These interface elements include music and sounds. Some non-speech audio is included in almost all interfaces of any type, including S/GUI, AUI, and GUIs. Examples of non-speech audio include:

- The computer beeps when the user makes an error.
- The user clicks on a map and hears a low tone to indicate that the water to be found at that site is deep in the ground or a high tone to indicate that the water is closer to the surface.

We do not focus on non-speech audio in this book.

Book Focus

In our research of books and articles on speech interfaces we were struck by two aspects of the literature. The first was the lack of information about speech interfaces overall. Second, the literature that does exist is technical in nature and assumes a thorough familiarity with speech technology. What happens, we wondered, when a practitioner in software and interface design needs to work on a speech interface, but is new to the field? This is the point of view we adopted in this book.

We focus primarily on the AUI and S/GUI aspects of the interface, not the underlying programming techniques. Our bias is toward a usability point of view. We cover the basics of speech technology that an interface designer needs to understand in order to construct a usable interface, for instance, the basics of sound and language. We discuss guidelines for effective communication, prompting, wording, and error handling to ensure that the interface is easy to learn and use. We do not discuss writing code for speech recognizers.

Intended Audience

The intended audience for this book includes

- interface designers—those responsible for designing the interface portion of a product that includes a speech component or is primarily speech-based. We assume you are new to designing speech interfaces;

- usability engineers—those responsible for ensuring that a product that includes speech or is primarily speech-based is usable. We assume you are new to speech interfaces;

- developers—programmers and technical people on a speech project who are new to speech interfaces;

- product and marketing managers—those responsible for bringing a project to fruition. Product managers will be interested in what makes a speech interface work, and marketing managers will be interested in what makes a particular project usable and competitive.

We assume that you—our intended audience—are familiar with GUI interfaces, but have had little exposure to the design and development of speech interfaces. Interface design expertise will help you understand some of the underlying principles we discuss, but is not necessary to put the book to practical use. We have included information on human factors, interface design, and usability engineering for readers new to these fields.

While we assume you have a minimal familiarity with speech technology or acoustic areas, we have included summaries to provide critical information about these subjects.

Book Summary

Here is a summary of the book contents. Part One sets the stage with an introduction to the basic concepts of speech interface, sound, and language, and a discussion of how human factors impact these areas. Part Two covers available speech technologies and how to apply them. With these tools in hand, the boundaries and guidelines to using them in interface design are explained in Part Three. Part Four demonstrates best practices and techniques.

Part One

Part One: Introduction to Speech Interfaces contains information on speech technologies and human-computer interaction concepts, including

Chapter 1: Basic Concepts. Covers definitions of user interfaces, types of user interfaces, and definitions of speech interfaces;

Chapter 2: Human Factors in Speech Technology.
Gives an overview of the field of human factors, covers
the basic concepts of human computer interaction, and
summarizes the major human factors issues in speech
interfaces. Discusses cost/benefit calculations for
usability engineering of speech interfaces;

Chapter 3: The Nature of Sound. Explains sound
terminology and technology;

Chapter 4: The Nature of Language. Summarizes what
we know about language and communication,
including the structure of language, grammar, syntax,
and semantics.

Part Two

Part Two: Speech Technology explains the current state of
the field of speech, including

Chapter 5: Speech Technologies. Defines and describes
the main terms in the field, including speech
recognition, speech synthesis, continuous versus
discrete speech, and natural language;

Chapter 6: Computer Software. Surveys the current
state of speech software on the market, both
applications and development tools;

Chapter 7: Hardware. Covers hardware such as sound
cards, microphones, voice cards, and modems that
affect the usability of speech applications;

Chapter 8: Applications of Speech Technology.
Describes how speech applications are being used
today.

Part Three

Part Three: Laws and Guidelines for Speech Interface Design. Provides specific advice for how to improve the usability of speech applications, including

Chapter 9: Laws of Interface Design. Describes 20 laws of human factors that apply to speech interfaces. The discussion of each law includes the human factors research behind it;

Chapter 10: Speech Guidelines. Provides specific guidelines for designing speech interfaces. These guidelines are based on the laws from Chapter 9, and contain the dos and don'ts to follow when designing speech applications.

Part Four

Part Four: Best Practices. Covers best practices in interface design and usability engineering, including

Chapter 11: Usability Processes and Techniques. Describes a comprehensive method for designing applications to ensure they are usable, and the basic usability engineering techniques used in the process;

Chapter 12: Universal Design. Discusses designing for universal design and accessibility.

Throughout the book we include interviews with several industry experts on the topics of speech interfaces:

Kate Dobroth, American Institutes for Research

S. Ahmed Reza, Speech Interface Design

Sharon Oviatt, Center for Human-Computer
Communication, Oregon Graduate Institute of Science
and Technology

Candace Kamm, AT&T Labs

John Karat, IBM T.J. Watson Research Center

Nicole Yankelovich, Sun Microsystems

Human Factors in Speech Technology

"No, I'm not your reflection.
I'm the toaster tutorial window."

> **"Making the simple complicated is commonplace; making the complicated simple, awesomely simple, that's creativity."**
> ***Charlie Mingus***

Mark Sanders and Ernest McCormick (1993) say that human factors refers to "designing for human use." In a broad sense human factors refers to taking the human being (the user) into account during any kind of design, for example, buildings, furniture, tools, computers, machinery. There are two aspects—engineering and human. The first includes the actual design or engineering of the thing, for example, a lawn mower or a chair. What size should it be? How should it work? What features and functionality should it have? That is the design of the "system" itself. On the other side is the human. How well does the item suit the humans who have to use it? Making sure that design takes into account the human aspects is the goal of human factors work.

A Brief History

Human factors refers to taking the human being into account during design.

In a sense, as long as humans have been interacting with their environment there have been human factors considerations. Given the shape, arrangement, and working characteristics of our hands and thumbs, for example, what is the best size and shape stick to use when we want to hit a tree to make the fruit come off? So much of the early human factors "work" was probably not done consciously, and certainly was not called "human factors."

Now a growing group of designers are interested in taking human factors into account. There are hundreds of human characteristics that have been researched, studied, and catalogued, for example, height, weight, size of hands, reaction times on specific tasks, memory, visual perception, sound detection. The list is extensive, and large manuals—for instance, the 2137-page book by Salvendy (1997)—describe these known characteristics in detail.

It is hard to pinpoint when the field of human factors officially began. We have hinted at placing the date somewhere back in our cave days, but most people in the field point to World War II as a pivotal point. Before that, during the early 1900s, there was some research on designing work areas to improve performance and minimize fatigue. But it was during World War II that psychologists and engineers started working together to design equipment that would be easier for humans to learn and use. Expensive and deadly errors by airplane pilots during the war convinced the U.S. and British military it was time to change the equipment. Labs were set up by the government to study and re-engineer equipment to take human factors into account.

It was during World War II that psychologists and engineers started working together to design equipment that would be easier for humans to learn and use

In the late 1940s and 1950s, official human factors organizations were formed, conferences were held, and journals were started. During this time most of the human factors work was done by the military. In the 1960s and 1970s human factors work spread to other industries, for example, medical, computer, car, and office equipment such as copiers and typewriters.

As technology grew more pervasive and sophisticated, so did the possibility of tragic error from using it, and the costs of those errors. During the 1980s and 1990s disasters and accidents highlighted the need for machines to take human factors (and foibles) into account. These disasters included nuclear power plants, x-ray machines, and airplanes. As these accidents mounted, so did the legal costs and liabilities. More organizations and businesses became concerned with designing products with human factors considerations in mind.

Usability engineering grew out of human factors, as did the terms now used, including *interface design, interaction design, human factors specialist,* and *usability specialist.*

During the 1980s computers in general, and computer software in particular, grew in use and complexity. A new branch of human factors blossomed in this period—that of human-computer interaction and, specifically, human factors applied to the design of software and screens. Usability engineering grew out of human factors, as did the terms now used, including *interface design, interaction design, human factors specialist,* and *usability specialist.* The idea is to apply what we know about human factors to the design of computer interfaces, in order to improve user performance, speed, error rate, and satisfaction.

A lot of the work in human factors applied to computer software focused first on character-based legacy systems (CHUIs). Then as interfaces changed, the human factors specialists worked on improving the usability of graphical user interfaces (GUIs). These days, Web interfaces have been added to the mix (WUIs). This CHUI to GUI to WUI trend has occupied human factors specialists over the years, but they do not represent all of the interface/interaction modalities that people have been working on.

Some designers have been working in the emerging technologies. What are the human factors implications of a system that uses virtual reality gloves or headsets? What about using gazing or gesturing as a means to communicate with a computer? Each new and proposed technology brings with it its own set of human factors issues.

Human Factors in Speech

For many years, a group of human factors specialists have studied the implications of speech technology on human-computer interaction. Going back to the 1940s, a body of knowledge has accumulated dealing with how human capabilities intersect with speech technology. For example, what can the human ear hear? How well do people recognize speech? What characteristics of speech make it hard to understand?

In addition to physiological aspects of human factors, there are the cognitive and psychological aspects of humans interacting with speech technology in computers. For example, what constraints must users observe in their speech so that a speech recognizer can understand them? Does constraining their speech make them more or less effective? Does it change the way they work? How do people react to synthesized speech? Do they mind if the computer sounds like a computer? Do they prefer that it sound like a human? How does computer speech affect task performance? Now add to this the aspect of *multi-modality*. Some speech technology involves speech only, but a significant portion of the interfaces being designed with speech are multi-modal. They involve not just speech, but other modes, such as tactile or visual. For example, a desktop dictation system involves speaking to the computer, and possibly using a mouse and keyboard to make corrections. Speech added to a personal digital assistant (PDA) handheld device means that people will be speaking while looking at a small screen while pushing buttons. Research is looking at when people use which modes and how they use them together.

Here, then, are some of the human factors issues surrounding speech technology. These issues, as well as the interviews with experts, are discussed in later chapters on design guidelines.

High Error Rates

Although error rates are improving, speech technologies still make significant errors—speech recognition systems in particular. New work by University of Southern California researchers using neural networks (Berger-Liaw, 1999) may make errors all but obsolete. Neural network technology dramatically improves speech recognition and allows speech recognizers to hear human speech even better than humans do, especially when competing with background noise. Most speech technology in current use does not incorporate neural network technology—and the current speech systems produce many errors. Much work has to be done to help humans to detect errors, and to devise and carry out error strategies. Imagine if every tenth key press you made on your keyboard resulted in the wrong letter appearing on the screen. This would affect your typing and your performance significantly. That describes the state of errors with speech recognition for many systems.

The current state is that speech systems produce a lot of errors.

Note that most of these errors are being made by the system, not the human. We are speaking here from a human factors point of view: how humans react when the system has made an error, not the other way around.

Unpredictable Errors

Besides relatively high error rates, the errors that speech systems make are not necessarily logical or predictable from the human's point of view. Although some are more understandable—such as hearing *Austin* when the user says *Boston*—others seem illogical. When we speak to a computer we do not appreciate the effect that such qualities as intonation, pitch, volume, and background noise can have. We think we have spoken clearly, but we may actually be sending an ambiguous signal. The computer may understand a phrase one time and misunderstand the same phrase another time. Users do not like using unpredictable machines. Users rate unpredictable systems lower in terms of acceptance and satisfaction of speech technology.

Humans do not like using unpredictable machines.

People's Expectations

Humans have high expectations of computers and speech. When they are told that a computer has speech technology built in, they often expect that they will have a natural conversation with it. They expect the computer to understand them and they expect to understand the computer. If this human-like conversational expectation is not met (and it is often not met), then they grow frustrated and unwilling to talk to the computer on its realistic terms.

However, if humans are given realistic expectations of what the computer can and can't say or understand, then they are comfortable constraining their speech to certain phrases and commands. This does not seem to impede performance on task. Using constrained speech is not a natural way for people talk to other people, or even a natural way for people to talk to computers. Nevertheless, within a short time, users can learn and adapt well to constrained speech.

Users prefer constrained speech that works to conversational speech that results in errors.

Some of the most problematic expectations have to do with computers' lack of ability to learn new words. Some users report the expectation that the system would learn new commands—that it would be teachable. In the future, we might want to build in the capability for speech systems to be taught new commands altogether.

Working Multi-Modally

Many tasks lend themselves to multi-modality. For example, a traveler may point to two locations on a map while saying, "How far?" People will use one modality (such as speech alone) followed by another modality (such as pointing with a mouse or pen). In other words, they will switch between modes. Sometimes they use two or more modes simultaneously, or nearly so, for example, pointing first, then talking.

Speech-Only Systems Tax Memory

Because a speech-only system lacks visual feedback or confirmation, it is taxing on human memory. Long menus in telephony applications, for instance, are hard to remember.

Spoken Language Is Different

People speak differently than they write, and they expect systems that speak to them to use different terminology than what they may read. For example, people can understand terms such as *Delete* or *Cancel* when viewing them as button labels on a GUI screen, but they expect to hear a less formal language when they listen to a computer speak.

Users are not always aware of their speech habits. Many characteristics of human speech are difficult for computers to understand, for example, using "ums" or "uhs" in sentences or talking too fast or too softly. Many of these characteristics are unconscious habits.

People Model Speech

Luckily people will easily model another's speech without realizing it. We can constrain or affect the user's speech by having the computer speak the way you want the user to speak. People tend to imitate what they hear.

People tend to imitate what they hear.

The Cost/Benefit of Human Factors

How interested we are in applying human factors depends on several cost and benefit factors. These include 1) the complexity of the technology itself, 2) the user, 3) the role of people in the system, 4) the cost of human labor, 5) the cost of human error, and 6) the competitiveness of the market.

The Complexity of Technology

When a tool is simple, easy to design, and has few parts and a single function, then the engineering of the tool is often close to the needs of the human. A pencil is relatively easy to design, and relatively easy to make usable. With more complicated technology, the engineering of the technology becomes more complicated. This results in designs that optimize the technology, often at the expense of the humans. In his book, *The Inmates Are Running the Asylum*, Alan Cooper (1999) describes his run-in with a camera. All the features and functions built into the camera result in a design that makes it hard for the human to take a picture.

As technology gets more complicated and sophisticated, the gulf between the needs of the technology and the needs of the humans widens. As technology gets more complicated, the attention to human factors should increase. More time and energy should be put into designing it so it will work well for humans—the human factors question. However, there is not a direct relationship between the complexity of technology and the amount of attention paid to human factors. In fact, judging by how hard it is to use many gadgets, the human factors budget for some products seems close to zero. When products become unusable, the consumer/user starts to complain and signals displeasure by not purchasing the product. Eventually, competition or loss of sales may spur the company to pay attention to human factors.

There is not a direct relationship between the complexity of technology and the amount of attention paid to human factors.

The User

When computers were used by "computer scientists" who were specialists in the field, less attention was paid to the human factors of computer systems. The small group of users was technically knowledgeable. But when the technology moved from the specialists to the general public, matching computers and software to the needs of the humans became more important. More users in more varieties were affected, resulting in more human factors problems.

When the technology moved from the specialists to the general public, matching computers and software to the needs of the humans became more important.

Let's consider an X-ray technician who uses several machines, but only uses a particular machine once a week. For that machine, the human factors considerations must be more closely designed and planned than for an often-used machine. Human factors considerations grow in importance as technology is used by a wider range of users.

The Role of People

In the past, when entry-level employees used computer terminals strictly for data entry, human factors considerations were not paramount. When, however, managers within an organization were frustrated by hard-to-use systems, that got attention.

How much attention you give to human factors depends somewhat on how you view the role of the human versus the role of the system. Some technical people, who focus exclusively on technical systems issues, tend to put the needs of the system over the needs of the humans. Those people consider users to be "messy" complications. If, on the other hand, you see the people as important as, or even more important than, the systems they are using, then you put more time and energy into applying human factors.

The Cost of Human Labor

In the book *Cost Justifying Usability* (Bias and Mayhew, 1994), the authors include several formulas for calculating the costs and benefits of usability engineering. These calculations are similar to the costs and benefits formulas that take human factors into account in the design of a product. Many of these calculations are based on labor savings. When the labor market is tight, which it is as we write this book, then saving people time becomes critical. In our interview with Ahmed Reza in this book, he discusses reducing what was once a two-person job into a one-person job. In a labor market where you cannot hire enough people to fill the openings you have, these savings are significant. If applying human factors can save people time or reduce the number of people needed to do a task, then human factors rise in relative importance.

> When the labor market is tight, which it is as we write this book, then saving people time becomes critical.

The Cost of Human Error

People make mistakes. It is unrealistic to assume that they will not make mistakes. At the least, the cost of errors is annoyance. But often the cost of an error can be deadly. In 1989, in the Persian Gulf, a U.S. Navy vessel shot down an Iranian commercial jet, believing it was a military plane. On a radio broadcast that night a Navy official said that all the information the ship personnel needed to make a correct decision was on the computer screens. "But in the stress of the situation," he said, "people could not find the information. We need to do some human factors engineering of our computer screens."

If the cost of errors is high, then the cost of human factors engineering seems smaller in comparison.

In the 1980s we worked with a client who called for human factors engineering after losing $7 million overnight when an experienced commercial real estate appraiser filled out a hard-to-use online form incorrectly.

If the cost of errors is high, then the cost of human factors engineering seems smaller in comparison.

The Competitiveness of the Market

Figure 2.1 shows a bell curve that relates competitiveness to time and attention paid to human factors.

There is pressure to bring product to market quickly, even at the expense of human factors.

If an industry or organization does not feel competitive pressure—if they feel their market share is safe—then they may not put a lot of resources into human factors design issues. If, however, they feel pressure from competitors, they may look to human factors engineering as one area to gain competitive advantage. This pressure fuels human

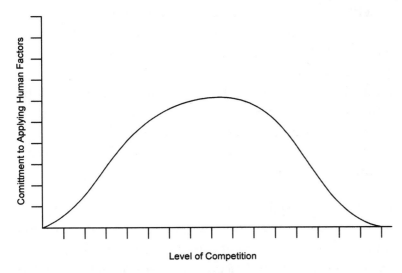

Figure 2.1 Competition vs. commitment to human factors.

factors work until the stress of the competition becomes too high, at which point there is pressure to bring product to market quickly, even at the expense of human factors.

Cost-Benefit Calculations

We can calculate the costs and benefits of applying usability engineering to incorporate human factors into the design of a specific product. Let's demonstrate through an imagined scenario.

We have a telephony speech application that processes requests from customers. The average revenue per customer is $50. If we use human factors to improve the prompting of the system, we anticipate we will have two benefits: first, we will induce potential customers to become actual consumers of our product, and second, we will be able to process more customers in a day. Let's assume a rate of ten calls an hour. By improving prompting, we can raise that to 12 calls per hour. Based on a 16-hour day, we now handle 32 additional callers per day. If our sell rate on customers is 25 percent, we will have added eight customers per day for a total of $400 per day additional revenue.

If our system is selling seven days a week, then $400 per day is $146,000 a year, and $1,460,000 over a 10-year period. If the design improvement used $25,000 in design resources, then we will recoup our investment in about two months.

Let's take a different scenario—a command-and-control industrial application. There are 1000 users who use this application at several plants around the world. The users work 230 days per year at an average wage of $18 per hour, including benefits. Let's assume that by applying human factors to the speech system we are able to save each user a minimum of 60 seconds a day. Each user saves 60 seconds or $.30 per day. Multiplying by 1000 users gives us $300 per day in savings. $300/day times 230 work days, gives us $69,000 a year, or $690,000 over a 10-year period. If the improvement to the human factors of the system cost $25,000, the company will recoup its investment in less than five months.

There are plenty of reasons to do human factors work, including the fact that it is worth the cost.

These numbers are purposely conservative. If, in the latter example, we are able to save people two minutes a day, the resulting gain is doubled.

There are plenty of reasons to do human factors work, including the fact that it is worth the cost.

Interview with John Karat

Research Staff member

IBM T.J. Watson Research Center

Undergraduate degree in
Mechanical Engineering from
Lehigh University

Ph.D. in Cognitive Psychology
from University of Colorado

John Karat is a senior research staff member at the IBM T.J.
Watson Research Center. He has an undergraduate degree
in Mechanical Engineering from Lehigh University, and a
Ph.D. in Cognitive Psychology from the University of
Colorado. In this interview John talks about his research at
IBM on speech technology.

Tell me about your background.

I started with IBM with a group in Austin, Texas, that was
developing our common user access guidelines and was
with that project until it moved to Boca Raton, Florida.
Then I went to the research division.

*Tell me what areas of speech interfaces you have been
specializing in.*

I'll tell you how I came into working with speech interfaces.
It wasn't something that I've always or continuously done
in my career. I became interested in the design of
interactive systems, and what I, as a behavioral scientist,
could contribute to making technology work better for
people. Working for a technology company there are a
whole lot of folks running around doing research in

making better technology, but they're not necessarily focused on the use of that technology.

When I first came to the research division we had the User Interface Institute, which was a central gathering place for the behavioral scientists within IBM's research division. Within the group there were people focusing on theory development. And then there were people focusing on advancing human-computer interaction by working on projects and technologies. The projects people were learning by working on projects and by reflecting on what it was that you were doing and trying to relate that to better technology for people. I was part of the latter focus rather than the grand theory focus.

We attached ourselves to projects. In 1992, while IBM was struggling trying to make profits rather than losses, one of the things the folks in the research division were asked to do was have their projects be tied to commercial return. We have a large and active speech recognition group but they had never turned out a product. They turned out people who left IBM and turned out product, but they had not turned out product themselves. They were strongly encouraged to connect what they were doing to product development. A group was formed with a mission to develop a product based on IBM's research technology within one year. I joined that project as a user interface design specialist. What we set out to do ended up as IBM's first desktop speech recognition product called, VoiceType, which came out in December of 1993.

A group was formed with a mission to develop a product based on IBM's research technology within one year.

My speech recognition involvement began with trying to figure out what to do with that technology. We were free at first to look at any type of application that would be based on speech technology and figure out what it was that we wanted to build. We focused on large vocabulary, isolated words, meaning that you had to put pauses between words. We were also focusing on speaker dependence, meaning that it didn't function very well at all unless you enrolled in it. Some of my work was exploring what might speech be good for, and after that it focused on how we create the interface to a dictation system where people dictate and correct text.

After that product was released I went on to another area of work, electronic patient records.

I came back into the area last year when we were looking at using speech for a wider range of multi-modal applications. I came back to do an evaluation of what was the state of the art for large vocabulary speech recognition systems. It was enlightening.

In designing the VoiceType system we knew where there were some weak spots. Recognition rate aside, providing a correction model that is as effective as typing a correction, or mouse and keyboard correction, was going to be a significant challenge. We didn't think we got it with the first version of the project, and doing the study comparing competitive systems now, verified that nobody's got it yet.

Continuous is certainly better than isolated, and all the systems do that. All the systems are modeless so you can dictate words and you can dictate commands and the systems do a pretty good job of telling whether you intend it as text or a command. And for all of the systems the command languages are not all that hard to learn, although throughput is still not that good. Throughput is the overall time it takes people to create a correct piece of text: to enter something, go back and correct it, and be satisfied with their product. Our experiments show that except for a small percentage of people who stay with the product for a long time, people are more effective with keyboards and mice.

Research continues to try and look at what to do about that, how to make speech a more effective input mechanism for text compared to keyboards. Some of this is driven by the fact that we don't think we will always exist in a world where the only interactive devices are those that can have keyboards with them. Smaller devices with smaller displays call for new input mechanisms, such as graffiti. Speech is an obvious candidate in that space.

With 30 years of research behind us, we've not been able to put out a system that the general public instantly latches on to. But, I don't expect anybody to conclude that speech recognition isn't going to work. We'll continue working on the problems, now largely because the technology is driving us to do this. Five years ago the edict came down that IBM should come up with a commercial product in speech recognition because it was done with the feeling that we've been doing this research for a long time, we haven't got anything to show for it, we've got to find out if there is any market for this or get out of funding the research project market.

While there wasn't a commercial success, the technology has changed, making it unlikely that anyone will pull the plug on our speech recognition research.

Are you saying that's because of this idea that the technology is going to need it?

Pervasive computing calls for it more. There is a gleam in folk's eyes that says you aren't going to put an effective keyboard on handheld devices. Graffiti is fine for small quantities of text, but speech recognition is likely to be able to provide more effective input mechanism for that class of devices than a lot of other contenders. The expectation of the direction of the technology is largely behind the continued or renewed optimism.

> Smaller devices with smaller displays call for new input mechanisms, such as graffiti. Speech is an obvious candidate in that space.

> Graffiti is fine for small quantities of text, but speech recognition is likely to be able to provide more effective input mechanism for that class of devices than a lot of other contenders.

The field is sort of funny. I don't know if these people believe their own press. It makes me cringe to look at product boxes that say 140 correct words per minute, where it's 140 correct and 20 wrong, and a lot of time in that minute of going back and correcting that 20. There are a lot of ways to mislead the public by hyping. I don't think that does justice for the field when people experience buying product that turns out not to be as good as they thought it was.

How is this motivation that is coming from the new technology affecting your work? Is it just giving it renewed interest? Or are you actually starting to do some different work because you know you're headed toward these devices without keyboards?

We're looking at different things. We're looking at speech interfaces in different environments, for example, in automobiles, and on smaller devices that don't have keyboards as an option. For IBM this means looking at the more integrated speech pictures. We've done work on speech recognition, but nothing on the synthesis side. There's been this newer emphasis on speech as not just an input technique, but also as an output technique. What does it mean to play in that domain?

There's a new kind of model of architecture that's being explored. You have information that can be presented on a variety of devices. Let's look at the characteristics of those different classes of devices and look at effective input and output techniques and assume that they may be different for the different classes. How I present information on a screen and a keyboard and on an office system that has a 17-inch monitor is a separate class, and most of my current work is in that space.

How I present information on a screen and a keyboard and on an office system that has a 17-inch monitor is a separate class....If I'm trying to get that same data over a phone, how would I do that?

If I'm trying to get that same data over a phone, how would I do that? How do we present information with speech synthesis and take commands or input data over a telephone?

The engine guys made a lot of progress on continuous, and now they want to look at algorithms for noisier inputs. Being able to dictate over a telephone has been harder than direct dictation to your desktop system because the quality isn't as good. The information that goes into a handheld is not going to be that good.

What are some of the interface design issues that you are facing or anticipating?

There are always some that are expected. One is how to deal with mis-recognitions. There is fundamentally a different set of errors that happens with this technology than happens with keyboard and mouse technology. If I hit the A key on a keyboard I never get a Q. I might get something besides an A because I did something wrong, but I understand I did something wrong. When I send a note to a colleague and I say "We have to work on formal steps" and the note comes as "We have to work on oral sex"— it's a problem. It's not because I said something wrong. It's not the kind of thing I can anticipate.

What the system hears compared to what I say isn't deterministic, so you're always going to have this problem of how to deal with errors and how to help people understand where the errors might have been, how to help them correct them once they have occurred. This is an interface challenge that is not solved. If you look at the commercially available speech recognition products, nobody has solved that to any good extent. It takes longer to correct something with a speech recognition system than it does with a mouse and keyboard system. On the order of

---

There is fundamentally a different set of errors that happens with this technology than happens with keyboard and mouse technology. If I hit the A key on a keyboard I never get a Q.

It takes longer to correct something with a speech recognition system than it does with a mouse and keyboard system.

ten seconds per correction rather than one second of correction. Which causes people to put them on the shelf in large numbers after they've used them a little bit.

Here's where we think we'll make progress: It looks like experienced people learn to do things multi-modally, even though the boxes say put your keyboards and your mouse away and talk to the system. To be effective and productive you quickly learn that there are some things you just do better by pointing to them with a mouse than trying to get the focus of attention on that word using speech. Sometimes it's faster to type that correction than re-dictating it 40 or 50 times and getting embedded in error loops and having files accidentally deleted when curse words are recognized as commands.

Experienced people learn to do things multi-modally.

We in the research community had focused for a while in making a speech-only interface that worked well, but the challenge now is speech as one of a number of input techniques. How to integrate speech with other things is a big interface challenge.

The challenge now is speech as one of a number of input techniques.

In the early days we thought there would be command language problems. People can be saying text or issuing commands. We thought that having them know what they are allowed to say would be a problem. I'm not convinced that that's all that big a problem. If you compare the command languages across the products, some will say "Delete this" and others "Delete that." But if you just have one and you're interacting with it, everyone has done a decent job at creating a command language that's easy enough to learn so that forgetting the command language doesn't seem to be a big problem.

The big difficulties continue to be: How do you deal with the fact that the stuff makes mistakes?

People adjust to new styles of creating text fairly easily.

When you are typing you detect your errors much more quickly than with speech recognition.

If you're in a room with 500 people who are trying to take notes by whispering into their palm pilot – what's that going to do?

Another issue we weren't sure about that doesn't seem to be a big deal is the composition process. If I dictate something, it appears on the screen with a lag compared to when I'm typing something. People adjust to new styles of creating text fairly easily. I no longer consider that as a major barrier to the acceptance of the technology. It's different and calls for different error correction mechanisms, and errors are harder to correct. We've looked at people typing and how often they make errors when they type and how quickly they correct those errors. Error rates for typing are similar to speech recognition error rates for a broad class of typists, but when you're typing you detect your errors much more quickly than with speech recognition. If I hit the wrong key I have a sense that I have done it, or I'm monitoring what's going in as I create it, so I can see the errors. But the speech strategies don't have to be equivalent to the typing strategies in order to make progress. They have to be easier, but it may be OK if they are different.

John, why do you like being in this field?

It's exciting because it offers a real potential for people to interact in fundamentally different ways with technology. And it's complex enough so that it has interface design challenges and interaction design challenges that I think are going to be difficult for years.

We haven't begun yet to get to a place where you have good speech recognition on your PalmPilot. If you're in a room with 500 people who are trying to take notes by whispering into their Palm Pilot—what's that going to do? We're just starting to think intelligently about how speech is going to fit in with other speech input and output techniques so that we get a good marriage of the technology and potential application. For me it's good and exciting because it offers new potentials that aren't trivial to figure out. Once upon a time I may have just believed that speech is right because it's a more natural way of communicating. About three-fourths of the way through our comparative systems study I counted a half dozen people who told me they didn't like speech because typing was more natural for communicating with devices. The first time I heard that I was shocked, but then I realized that if we're communicating with devices, there may be other ways that are more natural. I've always liked to take on things that I don't expect to be solved in my lifetime, just so that I don't have to change careers.

So you're saying this is going to take awhile?

The algorithm people have been working on this for 30 years and we can say we aren't there yet. Really effective speech communication with devices still needs a natural language environment. Command recognition systems do have some natural language components to them, but they aren't really natural language understanding. That technology is a long way off.

What do you think about the state of tools for interface designers and programmers?

Abysmal but getting better. Folks like Dragon and IBM have always tried to provide tools so others can integrate the technology. But it's access to technology that doesn't work all that well. My belief is that the problem is not the tool, but that the technology breaks. There's still this hard work to do—what makes good applications for this technology. We were naïve in thinking that just having speech technology available would result in a worldwide storm of keyboards being thrown out windows, and the trampling of mice. It's not happening. There are problems with the tools but it's not impossible. The real hurdle is: What are the right applications?

> If we're communicating with devices, there may be other ways that are more natural.

> Then there's the whole family of output and dialog. We can expect improvements on the synthesis side.

> We were naïve in thinking that just having speech technology available would result in a worldwide storm of keyboards being thrown out windows, and the trampling of mice.

What advice would you give to interface designers or programmers just starting out in this?

Don't jump into speech technology unless you are really convinced that it's the right technology for the type of application you're trying to build. And the right technology is still a hands-busy environment where someone can't really use their hands and you can provide a tool that can make it work. This is a niche market, because for the most part people have available hands. If you're trying to develop a system for someone who's handicapped or is in an activity where they are using their hands, then it's possibly the right technology.

The right technology is still a hands-busy environment where someone can't really use their hands and you can provide a tool that can make it work.

The next thing to consider is, what would be the impact of errors? If the impact of errors is deadly or critical, then even though you have good technology you are risky going forward. Think for example about an intelligent assistant for a surgeon. The surgeon is in a hands-busy environment, but if errors are going to cause someone to die, then you shouldn't move forward.

If the impact of errors is deadly or critical, then even though you have good technology you are risky going forward.

If I were new to this but believed that speech could help differentiate my product, I would try to do something and gain experience. The technology is getting better, and it's getting better faster than I thought it would. We've gotten to modeless and continuous and sort of speaker independence faster than I thought we would, and I have every reason to believe we'll get better. I'd get some experience with this now because the handheld devices are going to make it a better market over the next five years than it is today.

Summary

Speech technology brings with it its own set of human factors problems. If we are to successfully implement speech interfaces, we must deal with these human factors issues in design, as well as understand the medium in which we are working. This chapter covered the human factors issues. The next two chapters describe the basics of speech: sound and language.

The Nature of Sound

"I'm sorry, you'll have to upgrade to first class if you want to use our ISDN line."

"Look with thine ears."
William Shakespeare's King Lear (Act 4, Scene 6)

Speech technology revolves around the physics of sound. Speech is a particular type of sound and therefore inherits the universal characteristics of *sound* in a scientific sense. Sound is defined as "a vibration in an elastic medium at a frequency and intensity that is capable of being heard by the human ear" (Isaacs et al., 1996). The "elastic medium" we are most concerned with is air. A vibration, such as that caused by the movement of human vocal chords that produces speech, travels through the air, and reaches our ears by physically striking our eardrums. Our ears then send an electronic signal to the brain. That message is perceived as sound. Sound may also be received by a microphone and then electronically processed in any of several ways related to the development of speech software, such as recording or broadcasting. This chapter covers the nature of sound, including its measurement and properties.

Measurement of Sound

Sound travels at a speed of 1130 feet per second (called the speed of sound). It travels through the air in a manner similar to waves traveling across the ocean surface. As sound travels, it contracts and expands, disturbing the air pressure around it. The contractions are called compressions and the expansions are called rarefactions. This is because the contractions compress air particles while the expansions cause the air particles to be more rare in that physical space. These compressions and rarefactions form a sound wave, or *sine wave* named after the trigonometric function. The sine wave is typically represented as a graph showing increases and decreases in atmospheric pressure over time, as shown in Figure 3.1. The center line of the graph represents normal atmospheric pressure. Compressions, the increases in pressure, are called *peaks*. Rarefactions, the decreases in pressure, are called *troughs*. The distance between a peak and a trough is a single wavelength, also known as a *cycle*.

Frequency

The number of cycles a wave completes in one second is called its *frequency.* An example of a 4-cycle wave is shown in Figure 3.2. The shorter a wavelength is, the higher its frequency. The longer the wavelength is, the lower its frequency. Frequency is measured in *hertz*, which means cycles per second. This is abbreviated as Hz. One thousand hertz is one *kilohertz*, abbreviated kHz. The range of sound, or vibrations the human ear is capable of hearing, is between approximately 20 and 22,000 Hz. Vibrations below this range are called *infrasounds* and above it are called *ultrasounds*. The average human voice has a frequency of 5kHz.

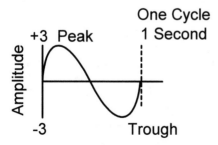

Figure 3.1 A wavelength.

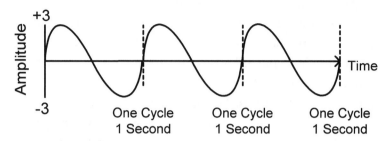

Figure 3.2 A 4-cycle wave.

Sounds Eponymous

The decibel is named after Alexander Graham Bell, the inventor of the telephone. Bell's contemporary Heinrich Rudolph Hertz was the first person to artificially produce electromagnetic waves and is honored by his own scientific unit of measurement.

The pitch of a sound can also be measured. *Frequency* and *pitch* are technically synonymous, but pitch is usually discussed in the context of sounds made by musical instruments and described in units other than kHz. The higher a sound wave's frequency is, the higher its pitch. The lower the frequency, the lower its pitch. From a standpoint of personal experience, humans understand pitch, such as low sounds and high sounds, more easily than frequency. However, computers and electronic devices don't typically think musically, so we need to understand frequency as well. Table 3.1 illustrates ranges of frequencies and the types of musical instruments you would hear in each range. (An audio equalizer for a home stereo is typically divided into similar frequency ranges.)

Frequency range	Example of musical instruments in this range
20-200 Hz	Bass, tuba
200 Hz-10kHz	Saxophones, violins, clarinets, trumpets, guitars, flutes, piccolos
10kHz-20kHz	Above the range of most musical instruments

Table 3.1 Frequency Range of Musical Instruments

Amplitude

Amplitude is the scientific term for the loudness of a sound. The loudness of a sound is determined by the size of its wavelength. In Figure 3.3, sine wave A has a larger wavelength than B; therefore, it is said to have greater amplitude and is perceived as being louder.

A large wavelength has a greater impact on air pressure than a smaller one. Human ears respond to this impact on air pressure by perceiving changes in the intensity of the sound pressure level (SPL). The sound pressure level is the range between the threshold of sound, or softest sound heard by the human ear, and the threshold of pain, or loudest sound we can hear without experiencing pain. However, scientific measurement of the SPL does not accurately reflect human perception of sound because we respond to changes logarithmically, not linearly. Therefore, a more reasonable measuring unit called the decibel, abbreviated dB, is typically used to describe amplitude.

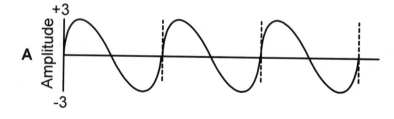

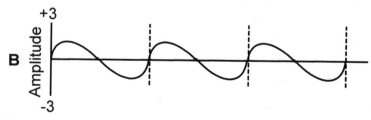

Figure 3.3 A comparison of amplitude.

The decibel is actually a ratio used to describe the change in loudness. Using decibels, the threshold of sound, or absolute quiet, is measured as 0 dB. The threshold of pain is about 130 dB. Table 3.2 lists different decibel levels and the sounds they are associated with.

Decibel Trivia

- A one-decibel change in sound pressure is impossible for most people to detect.
- The average human hears loudness differences in 3 dB increments.
- To double the perceived loudness, the sound pressure level must be increased by 10 dB.

Adapted from Sound Check: The Basics of Sound and Sound Systems *by Tony Moscal*

Other Properties of Sound

In addition to frequency and amplitude, sine waves have several other properties that contribute to the human perception of sound. These properties include *phase, timbre,* and *envelope*.

Phase

When two sine waves occur simultaneously, they interact with one another and create a composite sound wave. If the two waves have exactly the same amplitude and frequency, the composite wave will be the sum of the amplitudes—in other words, twice the volume. For example, having two audio speakers instead of one provides double the volume. However, altering the frequency or amplitude of one sine wave would put them "out of phase."

Decibel Level	Sound
130 dB	Emergency siren; threshold of pain
120 dB	Jet airplane
110 dB	Jackhammer
100 dB	Heavy thunderstorm
90 dB	Motorcycle
80 dB	Lawn mower
70 dB	Heavy traffic
60 dB	Loud conversation
50 dB	Average office
40 dB	Average household
30 dB	Quiet conversation
20 dB	Whisper
10 dB	A pin dropping
0 dB	Absolute quiet; threshold of hearing

Table 3.2 Decibel Level of Certain Sounds

Timbre

The timbre of a sound is its tonal character, sometimes called its tone color. Most sounds are not pure, or single, sine waves. Most sounds are composite waves comprised of a *fundamental wave* (the sound's lowest frequency) and additional frequencies called *harmonics*. Additional frequencies change the human perception of tonal character and thus the perception of the overall sound. For example, consider a man singing a single musical note. His voice has a specific frequency. If he is joined by a woman singing the note in unison, the composite sound would have the same frequency, but the timbre would be perceived as different.

Envelope

Because sounds occur over time, or for only a specific duration, they are said to have an envelope. The envelope of a sound is a graph that describes the *attack, decay, sustain,* and *release* of the sound. The attack is the point in time when the sound begins. At that point in time, the sound rises from silence to its maximum volume. It then decays slightly and has a period of sustain where the volume is held before it finally releases back into silence. Compare the sound of the single honking of a car horn to that of an ambulance siren. The two sounds could have a similar sine wave, but very different envelopes.

How Humans Hear Sound

Since the definition of sound that we are working with is any "vibration" that "is capable of being heard by the human ear" we should have some familiarity with how sound is actually heard. As discussed earlier in this chapter, any sound wave with a frequency between approximately 20 and 22,000 Hz that strikes our ears is perceived as sound. We previously said that a sound wave reaches human ears and physically strikes the eardrums. Then, our ears send an electronic signal to the brain and the message is perceived as sound. We can delve more deeply into this process by discussing the physiology of hearing.

Anatomically, the human ear has three parts: the outer ear, the middle ear, and the inner ear. The process of hearing begins when a sound wave is physically captured by the outer part of the human ear.

The outer, or external, portion of the ear is shaped in such a way that it funnels sound waves further into the ear. The hole in our outer ear is the beginning of the auditory canal. When a sound wave travels through the auditory canal, it resonates and the sound pressure level is increased by many decibels. At the end of the auditory canal is the eardrum, which marks the beginning of the middle ear.

The eardrum, also called the tympanic membrane, is a flexible membrane that vibrates when struck by a sound wave. A series of three bones, called the ossicles, touches the inside of the tympanic membrane. The ossicles vibrate in sympathetic response to the vibrations of the tympanic membrane. These small bones move in conjunction with one another in a manner similar to levers or engine pistons and carry the sound vibration to the inner ear. The muscles attached to the ossicles function as a guardian to the inner ear. They flex in response to loud, potentially harmful sounds and reduce the amplitude of the sound by as much as 20 dB. However, because this flexing motion has latency of approximately 35 to 150 milliseconds, the ear may not be able to protect itself against extreme explosive or percussive sounds.

The inner ear, formally called the cochlea, is a snail-shaped organ filled with fluid. When the ossicles vibrate, they force the fluid of the cochlea through the coil. This movement transfers vibrations through a membrane called the basilar membrane and the organ of Corti. The organ of Corti contains nerve endings which convert the vibrations into an electronic signal. The electronic signal is a neural impulse, which is carried to the brain by the auditory nerve.

Summary

Any vibration in the air that is capable of being heard by human ears is defined as sound in a scientific sense. In human-computer interaction we are concerned with the impact of speech sounds as well as non-speech sounds. In this chapter we looked at the nature of sound. In the next chapter we look at the nature of language.

The Nature of Language

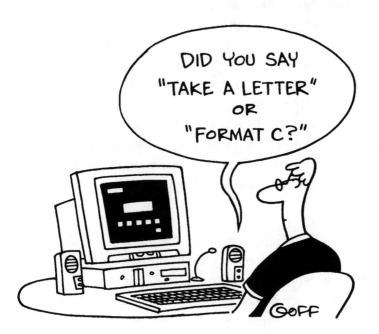

"The limits of my language indicate the limits of my world."
***From Wittgenstein's* Tractatus Logico-Philosophicus**

As humans, our capability to receive any form of communication is based on our sensory organs: the ears, eyes, skin, nose, and taste buds. The reception of communication through a single sensory organ is referred to as a *modality*. Each of us has five modalities, directly related to our senses. They are auditory/vocal, visual, tactile, olfactory, and gustatory. The study of how humans perceive communication through these sensory organs is called the science of *semiotics*. Specifically, semiotics provides a theoretical approach and related techniques for analyzing the structure of all forms and meanings of signals and signs in human communication received via these modalities.

Figure 4.1 shows the branches of semiotics and illustrates the relationship between our communication modalities. As human factors professionals, the more knowledge we have about each modality, the better we can design systems for our users. In the design of speech user interfaces we are primarily concerned with the auditory/vocal modality. A greater comprehension of this modality comes from understanding the process of verbal communication and the structure of language.

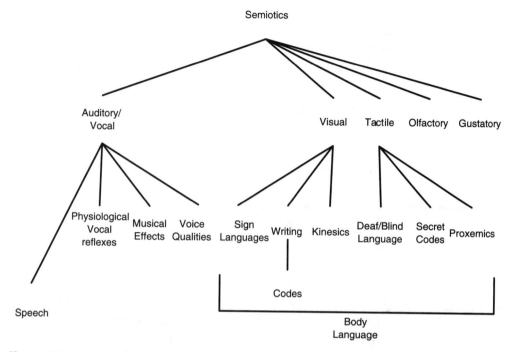

Figure 4.1 Aspects of semiotics.

Adapted from *The Cambridge Encyclopedia of Language*, Cambridge University Press, 1987

The Verbal Communication Process

Communication is a process that involves a message, sender, receiver, and channel. The message is the information being transmitted. In verbal communication between people, the words used to convey the message are actually only a part of what is eventually understood. Nonverbal communication such as body language between humans actually carries a large part of the message. However, in human-computer interaction using speech user interfaces, we have certain constraints and can only work with the verbal aspects of communication. Although computers sometimes make us smile and sometimes make us frown, they cannot yet interpret any meaning from our body language or other nonverbal communication. The sender is the person sending the message. The receiver is the person who receives the message. In the case of human-computer interaction the sender or receiver may be a computer. The medium used to transfer the message is called the channel. Channels can include the telephone, the written page, a face-to-face meeting, or even a computer.

The goal of communication is to achieve a shared understanding of the message, meaning that both the sender and receiver understand the message in exactly the same way.

The communication process has six stages: conception, encoding, transmission, reception, decoding, and feedback. This process can be illustrated at a fundamental level by the transmission model shown in Figure 4.2.

Conception

The communication process begins when the sender conceives a thought. The sender has an idea or message they wish to convey to someone else. The origin of human thought is a controversial subject. Linguists subscribe to theories that language precedes thought and perception while cognitive psychologists posit that the categories of thought influence the categories of language.

> The goal of communication is to achieve a shared understanding of the message, meaning that both the sender and receiver understand the message in exactly the same way.

> "Abstraction is exclusively human."
>
> *Moshe Feldenkrais*

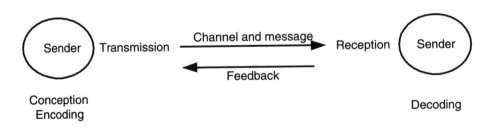

Figure 4.2 The transmission model of communication.

It is generally accepted that humans experience both verbal and nonverbal thought. One theory to explain rational thought from a verbal paradigm is the theory of linguistic determinism, which postulates that language determines how we think. This is a theory dating back to the late eighteenth century. Although the relatively new field of psycholinguistics has adapted and refined this theory to deal more with perception and memory, we can use the basic definition of linguistic determinism to help understand the process of communication.

People think in terms of objects and taking actions on those objects. If we accept that language determines how we think, then the word for an object defines a person's basic concept of that object. This is represented in language by the presence of nouns. If you are thinking of a clock, you don't mentally experience the phrase "thing which tells time," you simply think of the word "clock."

> People think in terms of objects and taking actions on those objects.

The presence of verbs represents our thought process regarding taking actions on objects. If you want to wind the clock, your mental experience isn't the phrase "turn little handle in back of thing which tells time," your mental experience is a simple phrase, "wind the clock."

If, as linguistic determinism states, people think in terms of language, then communicating a thought begins with conceiving a message based on specific words, then determining how best to convey those words to others. To organize those words into a coherent package, the sender must encode the message.

Encoding

During the encoding stage of communication, the sender chooses the specific words, phrases, and sentences that convey the most precise meaning of the message. The sender considers the intended meaning of the message, but also chooses specific words based on an assumption of how the receiver will understand those words. Therefore, part of encoding includes making assumptions about the receiver's decoding abilities. Poor assumptions about the receiver's decoding can be a source of miscommunication.

Encoding is affected by the sender's perception, attitudes, beliefs, values, personal experience, emotional and physical state, behavioral patterns (genetic and learned), as well as communication abilities. These characteristics act as a filter to the message and have a profound impact on the meaning of the message and the quality of the communication. These same characteristics are also mirrored by the receiver in the decoding process. This filtering of meaning based on human characteristics is described in the study of communication by the System/Process theory. This theory states that the meaning of a message is the response it elicits from the receiver, regardless of the sender's intention.

Transmission

"The ability to express an idea is well nigh as important as the idea itself."

Bernard Baruch

After encoding a message, the sender selects a channel and transmits, or broadcasts, the message. The quality of communication is affected by the appropriate selection of a channel, the quality of the channel, and the timing of the transmission.

A sender must select an appropriate channel based on the content of the message. If you decided to quit your job or propose marriage, you could choose to transmit that message through a letter, an e-mail, a telephone call, or a face-to-face meeting. The face-to-face meeting would likely be the most appropriate channel because of the importance of the message. However, if you simply wanted to communicate to several people what time to arrive for a dinner party, a written channel might be most appropriate.

Each transmission occurs in an environment. The environment affects the quality of the channel. The term "noise" is used to describe anything in the environment that interferes with transmission. This may literally mean physically-generated noise, or sounds, interfering with the transmission of verbal communication. This would perhaps cause the sender to increase the amplitude of the transmission. However, noise can also refer to other interferences. Suppose you were trying to tell someone something important but they were so thoroughly engaged in reading a book that they ignored you. The book could then be classified as a source of semantic noise that had an impact on your transmission. In human-computer interaction there are many potential sources of noise. People and equipment in working environments create physical noise. Other software applications may create semantic noise that interferes with the transmission of a message from your application. For example, error messages from the operating system or a virus-checking program may supersede your application at any time. Also, human attention spans have limits and must be a consideration. Users may create internal semantic noise that interferes with their work. It is important for an interaction designer to consider the potential sources of noise and design accordingly.

Communication can fail if the timing of the transmission is poor. In order for the communication process to be successful, the receiver must be ready to receive. If a sender transmits a message when the sender is not ready to receive, the result can be failed communication or miscommunication. For example, if you are speaking a command to your computer to print a document while the

---

"It is a luxury to be understood."

Ralph Waldo Emerson

computer is still "booting up," it will not receive your transmission and the communication will have failed.

Reception

Reception is perhaps the simplest stage of the communication process. This is the stage where the receiver acquires a transmission. This is simply a physical act. No interpretation of meaning is involved.

Communication can be received in one of two ways, *synchronously* or *asynchronously*. This relates to the selected channel. Synchronous communication occurs when the sender and receiver are communicating directly with one another at the same time, such as a face-to-face meeting or a phone call. Asynchronous communication occurs when the receiver actually receives the message at a different point in time than when it was transmitted. E-mail and voice mail are examples of asynchronous communication.

Decoding

Decoding is similar to encoding. It is affected by the perceptions, attitudes, beliefs, values, personal experiences, emotional and physical states, behavioral patterns, and communication abilities of the sender and receiver. Based on these personal characteristics, a receiver may automatically limit or exclude input from the message, which poses a challenge to the parties involved in the communication process. Decoding is also affected by the manner of reception and noise in the environment.

In decoding, the receiver filters the message and determines whether or not it comprehends the message. If the receiver believes that it comprehends the message, it then decides how to interpret it. The receiver then decides what to do with the information found in the message. This is where personal interests and emotional response become a factor in communication and when feedback is prepared.

Feedback

Feedback is a transmission regarding the message that was just received. This instigates a role-reversal and the person or machine that was the receiver now becomes the sender. Without feedback the communication process breaks down. Feedback provides the element that allows communication to become a complete cycle. It gives the receiver an opportunity for clarification or to gather additional information.

"A man cannot speak but he judges and reveals himself. With his will, or against his will he draws his portrait to the eye of others by every word."

Ralph Waldo Emerson

The Structure of Language

Language is "a system of rules which relate sound sequences to meanings" (Hayes, et al., 1997). The rules regarding sound sequences and their meanings are described in the field of linguistics. Within linguistics there are structural systems that are pertinent to the field of human-computer interaction. Human-computer interaction also shares a common foundation—cognitive psychology—with another area of linguistics, that of *psycholinguistics*. Psycholinguistics is concerned with issues of language comprehension and is considered in this chapter. Figure 4.3 illustrates the relationship between these systems. Each system is defined and described in this chapter.

"Language is the interpreting system of all other systems, linguistic and non-linguistic."

Emile Benveniste, Semiotics: An Introductory Reader

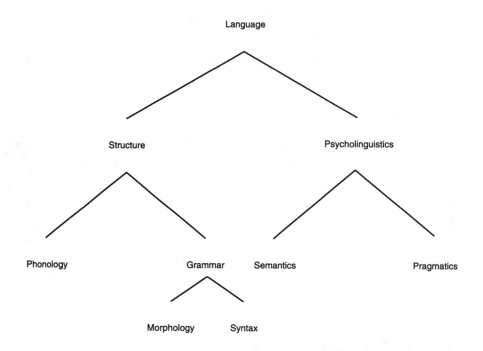

Figure 4.3 Systems of language.

Structural Systems

The two primary structural systems of language are *phonology* and *grammar*. These structural systems provide us with ways to analyze human language. Phonology is the study of language sounds and how they are created by humans. Grammar combines *morphology* and *syntax* to arrive at a set of rules regarding the technical structure of language. Morphology is the study of word structure, while syntax is the study of sentence structure. These structural systems provide important information for the input and output of speech in computer systems through speech recognition and speech synthesis. In addition, familiarity with the terminology and concepts fundamental to each system will assist those who are new to speech interface design in understanding the relevant human factors literature and working with the software development team members who provide technical or linguistic expertise.

Phonology

Phonology answers two questions. First, "What are the speech sounds in a language?" And second, "How are they combined in meaningful ways?" For our purposes, we will discuss the speech sounds of American English, but the rules of phonology could be applied to other languages, or even other dialects of English.

Speech Sounds: When we are speaking in our native language, or in a second language we are fluent in, we nonchalantly create speech sounds every day. We no longer have to think about how to create these sounds. If you can imagine for a moment a child learning how to talk, you can empathize with the difficult process they go through. As they attempt to mimic sounds made by adults in their environment, they contort their mouth and vocal chords until finally they produce a speech-like sound. You may have even experienced this in your adult or young-adult life in the process of learning a foreign language.

As adults, we would represent those sounds in a code, by thinking of or writing down individual words. However, this act of spelling words (called *orthography*) is a convention that provides only minimal detail about the actual sounds represented. Grade school teaches us that the smallest units of sound, or language, are vowels and consonants. From an orthographic standpoint this is true, but there are many variations of pronouncing these letters that we take for granted. These are variations we have simply assimilated into our knowledge of the world. They aren't typically discussed or notated. For example, the letter *t* has a certain sound in the word *hat*, but a different sound in the word *action*. Even though the *t* is notated exactly the same in both instances, you wouldn't have to consciously think about pronunciation, you would just make the appropriate sound.

Phonetics: Phonetics is the area of phonology that notates all of the variations in pronunciation of vowels and consonants. Phonetic notation is based on how we actually use sounds to create words. In phonetics, the primary unit isn't a letter, it is a phoneme. Phonemes are combined to form *syllables*. Syllables are then combined to form words. Figure 4.4 shows how a word is broken up into syllables and then further divided into phonemes.

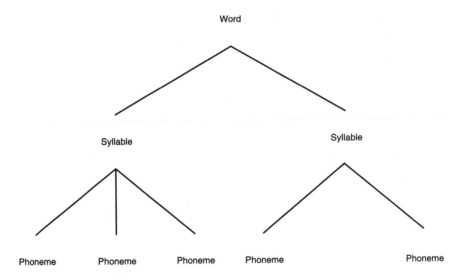

Figure 4.4 Hierarchy of phonology.

Tables 4.1 and 4.2 show the majority of speech sounds in the English language. The English alphabet is divided into consonants and vowels. Table 4.1 provides the consonant phonemes and Table 4.2 the vowels. The phonetic representation for each phoneme, or speech sound, is listed next to the corresponding letter of the traditional alphabet. Examples of words that represent the indicated sound are given. Because of the inadequacies of the English alphabet to denote sound, you will see that some pronunciations require combinations of orthographic letters to represent the single speech sound. For the same reason, some orthographic letters are associated with multiple sounds. Note that this table assumes American English with a Midwestern dialect. There are other American dialects that could be considered, such as dialects from the Eastern or Southern states, but they are beyond the scope of this text.

Orthographic Letter(s)	Phoneme	Pronunciation
p	/p/	pig
b	/b/	bobble
t	/t/	tip, stop
d	/d/	deep, filled
k, c	/k/	kids, cattle
g	/g/	gap
f, ph	/f/	fit, phase
v	/v/	vintage
th	/θ/	thief, ethics
th	/ð/	that
s	/s/	sip
z, x	/z/	zebra, xylophone
sh	/ʃ/	ship, wish
s	/ʒ/	vision
h	/h/	happy
ch	/tʃ/	cheer

continues

continued

Orthographic Letter(s)	Phoneme	Pronunciation
j, dge	/dʒ/	jump, fudge
m	/m/	might
n	/n/	night, happen
ng	/ŋ/	ring
l	/l/	lime, poodle
r	/r/	ready
y	/j/	yes
w	/w/	win
wh, w	/ʍ/	which, witches

Table 4.1 Consonant Phonemes

"England and America are two countries divided by a common language."

George Bernard Shaw

Orthographic Letter(s)	Phoneme	Pronunciation
i	/i/	pit, wish
e	/ɛ/	met
a	/æ/	ash
u, oo	/ʊ/	put, look
u	/ʌ/	hut
a	/ɑ/	pot
au, o	/ɔ/	caught, broth
a, e	/ə/	sofa, item
ee, ea	/I/	bee, bead
a, ei	/e/	mate, weight

Orthographic Letter(s)	Phoneme	Pronunciation
u, oe	/u/	rude, shoe
o, oa	/o/	toe, boat
oy	/ɔj/	toy
ou	/aʊ/	out, house
y, ie	/ai/	my, pie

Table 4.2 Vowel Phonemes

Deconstructing Phonemes: A *phoneme* is a single distinctive speech sound of a language. It is an abstract unit created and used by linguists and psychologists to analyze language, communication, and human thought. The phoneme is the linguistic equivalent of the atom in the field of physics. Changing the phoneme of a word changes its entire meaning. For example, the difference between *fat* and *vat* is a single (and subtle) sound. Changing that sound, or phoneme, changes the meaning of the word.

Each language has a finite body of phonemes, typically 30 to 40. The English language has approximately 38 phonemes (Syrdal, 1995). As you've seen in the previous tables, about two-thirds of the sounds in English are consonant phonemes and one-third are vowel phonemes. English includes phonemes that are not found in other languages. Similarly, other languages contain phonemes not found in English. For example, the English *th*, as in *this* or *thieve*, is not a sound that makes a phonemic difference in German. However, language is a dynamic process and global communications have increased the likelihood of languages adopting sounds from other languages. Typically though, when they do, they will modify the sound and integrate it with their language so that

The phoneme is the linguistic equivalent of the atom in the field of physics.

Language is a dynamic process and global communications have increased the likelihood of languages adopting sounds from other languages.

ultimately it becomes an unnoticeable part of the fabric of the language, not a borrowed sound.

Since phonemes are determined by the speech sounds of a language, discussing them requires a discussion of the physiology of producing human speech. In fact, the classification of phonemes is related directly to the manner of producing the sound.

Human speech is produced by a person pushing air from the lungs, through the larynx and glottis, into the oral cavity, and out though the mouth and/or nose. The precise manner of how the air is expelled distinguishes the sound and thus classifies it as one type of phoneme or another.

Articulation. The tongue causes an expulsion of air from the oral cavity (see Figure 4.5). This procedure is called articulation. The tongue articulates a sound by striking either the hard palate, the soft palate, or the teeth, thus stopping or changing the direction of the air passing through the oral cavity. Articulation is aided by the lips, which work in coordination with the tongue. Their position can subtly or drastically change a speech sound.

To experience the effect of articulation, try this exercise. Position the palm of your hand two or three inches in front of your mouth. At a loud (or even average) volume, speak the word *poodle* followed by the word *noodle*. You can feel the air striking your hand in the first case but not the second. The sounds are very different as a result of the difference between articulations.

Voice. In addition to articulation, the other distinguishing characteristic of a speech sound is referred to as voice. Each speech sound can be classified as either voiced or voiceless. Here's another exercise. Place your hand on your throat at the larynx (sometimes called an Adam's apple). Speak the

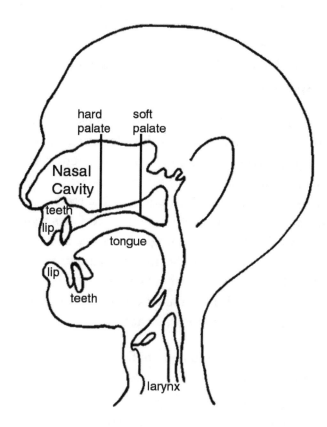

Figure 4.5 The physiology of articulation.

word *hiss* and hold the *ss* sound. Now speak the word *fuzz* and hold the *zz* sound. In the second word, your vocal chords vibrated as you spoke the *z* consonant. Thus, that sound is said to be voiced. In the first case, your vocal chords did not vibrate when you spoke the *s* consonant, so that sound is said to be voiceless.

Categories of phonemes. Several physiological phenomena affect the classification of phonemes. First is the manner of articulation, meaning whether or not the air is stopped to begin the sound, as in *poodle*. Second is the position of articulation, meaning where the tongue is positioned at the precise time of articulation. For example, notice the difference in the position of the tongue when you say the word *told* and then the word *gold*. In the former, articulation is accomplished by the tip of the tongue on the soft palate near the teeth. In the latter, the back of the tongue is responsible for articulation.

There are six categories of consonant phonemes. They are: stops, fricatives, affricatives, nasals, liquids, and glides. The three categories of vowel phonemes are: short, reduced, and long. The manner of articulation, position of articulation—such as on the lips (labial) or the teeth (dental)—and voice are the pertinent characteristics that determine a sound. These physiological characteristics combine in complex ways to determine the category of a phoneme. Fundamentally, consonants are formed by obstructions of the vocal tract while vowels are formed by varying the shape of an open vocal tract.

- *Stops* are consonant sounds where the airflow is halted during speech, such as in the words *pit* or *pop*.

- *Fricatives* are sounds created by a narrowing of the vocal tract, such as the initial consonants in *fit* or *sit*.

- *Affricatives* are complex sounds that are initially a stop but become a fricative, such as *ch* in the word *chill*.

- *Nasals* are similar to stops, but are voiced. For example, the initial consonant in *might* or *night*.

- *Liquids* are produced by a complexity of phenomena with the tongue raised high such as in the words *like* or *rut*.

- *Glides* are consonant sounds that either follow or precede a vowel. They are distinguished by the segue from a vowel and are also known as semivowels. Examples include the initial consonants in the words *yet*, *wool*, and *wick*.

Vowels are distinguished by the tongue's position at the top, middle, or bottom of the mouth. Short vowels are formed with the tongue at the top of the mouth and include the sounds made in *bib* or *win*. The *a* in *coma* represents a reduced vowel sound with the tongue in the middle of the mouth. Finally, long vowels are formed with the tongue position at the bottom of the mouth, such as in *beak* or *bay*.

Long vowel phonemes also include diphthongs. A diphthong is combination of vowel sounds, such as in the word *toy*. See Table 4.3 for further examples of consonant and vowel phonemes.

Allophones. In the exercises where you placed your palm in front of your mouth, you felt the effect of the "puff of air" striking your hand. If a phoneme has a variation based on that "puff of air," then it is classified in further detail. The sound is said to be in a subclass of phonemes called an allophone. For example, the /t/ sound of the *t* consonant has several variations, one as in the word *teal* and one as in the word *steal*. Furthermore, in a word containing two *t* consonants, such as *letter*, there is a third variation, or allophone.

Phonemic Category	Orthographic Letter(s)	Phoneme	Pronunciation
Consonants			
Stop	p	/p/	pig
	b	/b/	bobble
	t	/t/	tip, stop
	d	/d/	deep, filled
	k, c	/k/	kids, cattle

Continues

continued

Phonemic Category	Orthographic Letter(s)	Phoneme	Pronunciation
	g	/g/	gap
Fricative	f, ph	/f/	fit, phase
	v	/v/	vintage
	th	/θ/	thief, ethics
	th	/ð/	that
	s	/s/	sip
	z, x	/z/	zebra, xylophone
	sh	/ʃ/	ship, wish
	s	/ʒ/	vision
	h	/h/	happy
Affricative	ch	/tʃ/	cheer
	j, dge	/dʒ/	jump, fudge
Nasal	m	/m/	might
	n	/n/	night, happen
	ng	/ŋ/	ring
Liquid	l	/l/	lime, poodle
	r	/r/	ready
Glide	y	/j/	yes
	w	/w/	win
	wh, w	/ʍ/	which, witches
Vowels			
Short	i	/ɪ/	pit, wish
	e	/ɛ/	met

Phonemic Category	Orthographic Letter(s)	Phoneme	Pronunciation
	a	/æ/	ash
	u, oo	/ʊ/	put, look
	u	/ʌ/	hut
	a	/ɑ/	pot
	au, o	/ɔ/	caught, broth
Reduced	a, e	/ə/	sofa, item
	ee, ea	/i/	bee, bead
Long	a, ei	/e/	mate, weight
	u, oe	/u/	rude, shoe
	o, oa	/o/	toe, boat
	oy	/ɔj/	toy
	ou	/aʊ/	out, house
	y, ie	/ai/	my, pie

Table 4.3 Articulatory Categories of Phonemes

Coarticulation. When we speak, we usually do not isolate each sound. Most phonemes in practical use have "neighbors." Those neighbors actually affect the articulation that produces a sound. For example, speak the word *bookcase*. If you were to say *book*, then pause and say *case*, there would be two /k/ phonemes spoken.But, in the natural pronunciation of the word *bookcase*, there is only one /k/ sound. This is referred to as *coarticulation*. One of the challenges in designing speech recognition software comes from the coarticulation of neighboring words. For example, people typically pronounce the phrase "don't you" in casual conversation as a phrase that sounds more like "don't chew."

One of the challenges in designing speech recognition software comes from the coarticulation of neighboring words.

Suprasegmental phonemes. There are sounds that augment phonemes called suprasegmental phonemes. These sounds occur over, or during, other phonemes. Suprasegmental phonemes include intonation, stress, tone, and juncture. These sounds may ornament the segmental phonemes, but they are essential to communication. For example, consider the word *what*. In a neutral pronunciation it can mean *that* or *which*. However, simply by changing the intonation, as in "what?," it becomes an interrogative.

International Phonetic Association (IPA): The International Phonetic Association (IPA) is world's largest organization for phoneticians. It was established in 1886 and its goal is to provide a notational standard for the phonetic representation of all languages. The phonetic alphabet gives linguists, psychologists, and human factors professionals a common and refined tool for discussing the sounds of speech. The phonetic alphabet is reprinted here with permission and can be found on the World Wide Web at www2.arts.gla.ac.uk/IPA/ipa.html.

	Bilabial	**Labiodental**	**Dental**	**Alveolar**	**Postalveolar**
Plosive	p b			t d	
Nasal	m	ɱ		n	
Trill	ʙ			r	
Tap or Flap				ɾ	
Fricative	ɸ β	f v	θ ð	s z	ʃ ʒ
Lateral fricative				ɬ ɮ	
Approximant		ʋ		ɹ	
Lateral approximant				l	

	Retroflex	Palatal	Velar	Uvular	Pharyngeal	Glottal
Plosive	ʈ ɖ	c ɟ	k g	q ɢ		ʔ
Nasal	ɳ	ɲ	ŋ	N		
Trill				ʀ		
Tap or Flap	ɽ					
Fricative	ʂ ʐ	ç ʝ	x ɣ	χ ʁ	ħ ʕ	h ɦ
Lateral fricative						
Approximant	ɻ	j	ɰ			
Lateral approximant	ɭ	ʎ	L			

Vowels

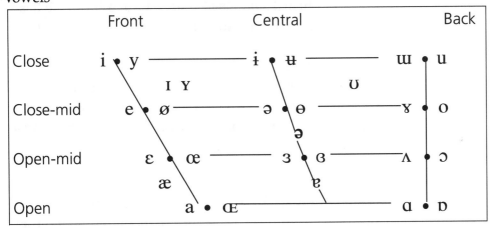

Figure 4.6 The International Phonetic Alphabet.

The International Phonetic Association, Revised 1993, Updated 1996

Grammar

While phonology studies classes of sounds, *grammar* studies classes of words. In addition to classifying words, grammar describes the patterns of words and their relationships to other words. This is typically referred to as sentence structure. A grammar of a language also defines principles based on the analysis of those patterns.

Within grammar, there are two distinct areas, *morphology* and *syntax*. Morphology refers to the structural system of words and syntax to the structural system of sentences.

Morphology: Just as every language has phonemes, all languages contain *morphemes*. A morpheme is a combination of phonemes that creates a single distinctive unit of meaning. It is the minimum unit of meaning in a language. Morphemes are combined to create words, then words are combined to create sentences. The morpheme is similar to the phoneme in that it is an abstract unit created and used by linguists to analyze and describe language.

Each morpheme in a word has a function and contributes meaning. As an example, in the word *unfriendly* there are three morphemes: *un, friend,* and *ly.* Each morpheme has meaning independent from the others. *un* means "not," *friend* has self-evident meaning, and *ly* means "in the manner of." Furthermore, the morphemes cannot be divided into any smaller unit that is meaningful. Each morpheme can be proved to be independent because it functions in other words. For example, *un* in *untied, friend* in *befriend,* and *ly* in *kindly.*

The fact that a unit cannot be divided into further meaningful units is what defines a morpheme. If you consider the word *hat,* you'll notice that it has no internal structure on a grammatical level. It can't be divided into any more meaningful units. You could break it apart phonetically into /h/, /æ/, and /t/, but isolating those three units does not contribute to the meaning of the word.

Sounds do not necessarily denote meaning in words. Admittedly, there are onomatopoeic words that imitate the sounds we hear. For example, in the United States we say that a cow says *moo.* However, in French a cow says *meure.* Similarly, if sounds were equivalent to meaning, then all

---

Sounds do not necessarily denote meaning in words. Admittedly, there are onomatopoeic words that imitate the sounds we hear. For example, in the United States we say that a cow says *moo.* However, in French a cow says *meure.*

languages would have the same words for things. *Hat* has meaning in English because we have given it that meaning. In France, to have someone interpret the same meaning, you wouldn't say *hat* (making the sound /hæt/), you would use the word *chapeau* (making the sound /ʃɔpo/). Therefore, a word can be defined as the combination of sound and meaning.

Understanding morphemes is what allows us to interpret words that are new or unfamiliar to us. In the nonsense word *antipseudochocomobiles*, you could probably provide a morphological analysis quickly. The word (even though it doesn't exist) means "against false chocolate vehicles." This nonsense word also illustrates the relationship, and difference, between morphemes and syllables. It is an eight-syllable word but has five morphemes. Actually, this is a little tricky because there are four obvious units of meaning, but the –*s* at the end denotes plural, providing a fifth morpheme.

Concatenating morphemes to create a word, such as the nonsense word above, is a formal technique called *agglutination* and is used by many languages, as students of German are probably aware. It is important to us in not only understanding new or unfamiliar words but also in adding to the language. Language is dynamic and organic. It is constantly changing. Thus, through techniques such as agglutinating we occasionally have new words become an accepted part of the language, such as bathroom (bath room), brunch (breakfast lunch), motel (motor hotel), or infomercial (information commercial).

Categories of morphemes. A word is comprised of one or many morphemes. There are two primary categories of morphemes: *bound* and *free*. Basically, free morphemes are independent words. A bound morpheme, although it has inherent meaning, requires another morpheme to become a word. For example, in English all prefixes and suffixes are bound morphemes. Consider the word *hats*. The suffix *s* has a meaning of plural, or many, but an *s* alone in a sentence would have no meaning. On the other hand, the morpheme *hat* is independent and requires no additional morphemes. It is a complete word.

In addition to bound and free, there are several subcategories of morphemes. Bound morphemes include affixes (prefixes and suffixes), bound bases, and contracted forms. An *affix*, such as the prefix *re*, must be combined with a base morpheme, such as *build*, making the complete word *rebuild*. Therefore, a base is an independent morpheme to which other bound morphemes are attached. A base can be bound, such as *build* in the word *rebuild*, or free. *Contracted forms* are bound morphemes that are shortened when combined with another morpheme. For example, the morpheme *will* is contracted in *we'll*, the shortened form of *we will*. Free morphemes are divided into two categories, *open-class words* and *closed-class words*. Open-class words include nouns, verbs, adjectives, and adverbs. Closed-class words include conjunctions (*and, but, or*), articles (*the, a, an*), demonstratives (*this, that*), prepositions (*in, at, on, to, from, by*), comparatives (*less, more*), and quantifiers (*some, all, none*).

Categories of words. Every word in the English language can be categorized into a lexical category. These categories are: nouns, verbs, adverbs, adjectives, and prepositions. Typically, these categories are referred to as the "parts of speech" that are taught in primary and secondary school English classes. From a morphological standpoint, what is important about the parts of speech is an analysis of meaning within and across the categories.

Meaning changes as morphemes are changed. For example, *cat* is a noun. Adding a morpheme, the suffix *s*, changes the meaning from one *cat* to many *cats*. This also creates a change in word category, from noun to plural noun. With a few exceptions for irregular nouns, such as *mouse*, all nouns share this characteristic of pluralization. Adding a suffix *s* changes the meaning for *cat, rat, hat, clock, sock, book, car, pen*, etc. But, this characteristic it is not shared by other word categories, such as adjectives. If you add the suffix *s* to *hungry*, you don't get *hungrys*. Therefore, the categories of words are differentiated on a morphological basis.

This morphological principle is of primary interest to the designer of speech user interfaces and can be traced from phonology through morphology to semantics. A change in phoneme (sound) creates a change in morpheme (thus a change in lexical category), which creates a change in meaning as shown in Table 4.4. This is how people interpret changes in meaning when they hear changes in sounds.

Word	Phonemes	Morphemes	Meaning
Hat	/hæt/	hat	One hat
Hats	/hæts/	hat s	More than one hat

Table 4.4 Example of Morphological Change Affecting Meaning

Syntax

Speaking a complete sentence is an exercise in creativity. No speaker of a language, not even a native speaker, has memorized every sentence in their language. A reference book containing every sentence of a language cannot exist because the nature of language is infinite. To speak and understand an infinite number of sentences we learn a

"The structure of every sentence is a lesson in logic."

J.S. Mill

finite set of rules and principles that serve us for an entire lifetime's worth of communication. The linguistic subfield of *syntax* is the study of those rules and principles.

In grade school we are given information by rote about addition, subtraction, multiplication, and division. After a time, we cease to worry over the answers to simple arithmetic problems, we simply generate them. Ultimately, we are able to use that information to perform algebra and solve an infinite number of algebraic problems. In a similar manner, we become highly competent in our ability to perform linguistic operations. Yet, by the time we reach adulthood, how many of us could describe the rules we use in conversation on a daily basis? In a certain sense, it doesn't really matter if we can explain the rules or not, as long as we can still perform the operations. However, the designer of a speech-based interface must understand the structure and rules of generating grammar-based speech, unlike a child acquiring a first language, because the speech recognition model must anticipate novel and infinite constructions.

> The designer of a speech-based interface needs to understand the structure and rules of generating grammar-based speech...because the speech recognition model must anticipate novel and infinite constructions.

Competence/Performance: Linguists describe a person's knowledge of a language, including tacit knowledge, as their competence, or linguistic capacity. Their ability to use that knowledge in speech is described as their performance. If a fluent speaker one day wakes up with a case of laryngitis, they haven't lost their language competence but they are unable to perform. As speech interface designers, we are involved in development of the linguistic capacity and performance of speaking machines.

Syntactic Structure: An understandable sentence has a structure that is logical. How do we judge whether or not the structure of any given sentence is logical? In practice, we make intuitive judgments. One of the goals of the linguist and the cognitive psychologist is to develop rules that explain our intuition. The rules that we might typically think about when contemplating what constitutes an acceptable sentence structure are prescriptive grammatical rules. These rules are taught to us in English classes and are formulated as statements that tell us how to speak or write. For example, "Always end a sentence with a period or other terminal punctuation" might be a prescriptive grammatical rule. To analyze whether or not any given sentence is acceptable, linguists use *generative rules*. Generative rules are based on the practice of native speakers and what have been determined to be the patterns of acceptable sentence construction. These patterns occur at two levels of structure, known as surface structure and deep structure.

Surface structure rules, also known as phrase structure rules, define the phrases in a sentence, such as noun phrases, verb phrases, and prepositional phrases. Using these rules, grammarians have developed categories of sentences. Certain categories of sentences have different surface structures but are related in meaning. For example, consider the following sentences:

The boy walked the dog.

The dog was walked by the boy.

The first sentence is classified as an active sentence while the second sentence is passive. They have different surface structures, but intuitively we know that they mean the same thing. The rules that postulate how these types of sentences are related are called deep structure rules. These rules are also referred to as transformational rules because their proofs are based on transforming sentences from one category to another.

Phrase structure rules. An analysis of surface structure divides a sentence into phrases. The essential phrases in a complete sentence are a subject and a predicate, also called a noun phrase and a verb phrase. Examine the following sentence:

The old man bought a new car.

Intuitively dividing the sentence, you would likely split it into the following phrases:

The old man	bought a new car
Noun phrase	Verb phrase

You might also consider subdividing the verb phrase into a verb followed by a noun phrase.

The old man	bought	a new car
Noun phrase	Verb	Noun phrase

A technique often used to conduct surface structure analysis is Immediate Constituent Diagramming, shown in Figure 4.7. These tree-like diagrams identify the major constituents of a sentence (noun phrase and verb phrase), then continue to subdivide the sentence until each word is identified as a specific part of speech.

After you have identified the parts of a sentence, you can use phrase structure rules to determine whether or not it is an acceptable sentence. Phrase structure rules are sometimes referred to as rewrite rules because a sentence is determined to be acceptable if it can be rewritten as another complete sentence according to these rules.

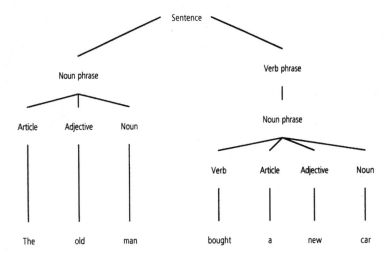

Figure 4.7 Immediate Constituent Diagramming.

The reason that the terms "phrase structure rules," "surface structure," and "rewrite rules" are all used for the same purpose is because syntax is an area whose contributions have come from several disciplines. Therefore, many theorists have attempted to use their own terminology in an effort to distinguish their work from that of others. The seminal work in this area is *Syntactic Structures*, written by linguist Noam Chomsky and published in 1957. Chomsky was also responsible for the creation of generative notation, as shown in Table 4.5. In generative notation, the arrow symbol means "can be rewritten as." Also, generative notation encloses optional items in parentheses. If these items were left out of the sentence, the sentence would still be considered grammatically correct.

The rules in Table 4.5 represent only a handful of the phrase structure rules, but they provide us with enough information to illustrate how such rules work. Examine the words in the sentence previously diagrammed:

The old man bought a new car.

Phrase Structure Rule	Generative Notation
A sentence can be rewritten as a noun phrase plus a verb phrase.	S→NP+VP
A noun phrase can be rewritten as an article plus an adjective plus a noun.	NP→(art)+(adj)+N
A noun phrase can be rewritten as a pronoun.	NP→pron
A verb phrase can be rewritten as a verb plus a noun phrase.	VP→V+NP
A verb phrase can be rewritten as a verb plus a prepositional phrase.	VP→V+prep
A prepositional phrase can be rewritten as a preposition plus a noun phrase.	Prep phrase→prep+NP

Table 4.5 Phrase Structure Rules

The sentence is comprised of the following words categorized into the appropriate part of speech:

> Articles: *the, a*
> Adjectives: *old, new*
> Nouns: *man, car*
> Verb: *bought*

Using phrase structure rules, we can substitute other words (shown in bold in the following list) for the appropriate part of speech and generate a new, grammatically acceptable sentence using the structure from the original sentence. This technique is called generation and is illustrated in Figure 4.8.

Articles: *the, a, **that, an***

Adjectives: *old, new, **young, orange***

Nouns: *man, car, **woman, dress***

Verb: *bought, **wore***

That young woman wore an orange dress.

Figure 4.8 Applying phrase structure rules to generation.

Phrase structure rules are effective for analyzing the syntax of many, even most, sentences. However, they are inadequate for completely describing the syntax of the English language due to its complexity and irregularity. Transformational rules are capable of a more comprehensive grammatical description and also serve to demonstrate relationships in meaning between sentences. This is referred to as the deep structure of language.

It is at this point that the dividing line between linguistics and cognitive psychology is drawn. Linguists have further developed Chomsky's original theories of syntactic structure. However, cognitive psychologists have refuted the transformational rules in favor of other theories. The field of human-computer interaction is largely based on cognitive psychology. While cognitive psychology has not researched the transformational rules themselves, it has investigated and contributed to the body of work regarding language comprehension. In that body of work, it has borrowed from the linguistic subfields of semantics and pragmatics in an effort to explain the relationship between language and cognition.

Language and Cognition

Psycholinguistics refers to the relatively new field pioneered by practitioners of cognitive psychology. They are heavily involved in relating language structure to the psychological processes involved in encoding, speaking, decoding, and comprehending language. Exploring and understanding this relationship between language and cognition involves issues of perception, lexicography, semantics, and pragmatics.

Consider the verbal communication model presented in Figure 4.2. Part of this process involves transmission, reception, and decoding. When we listen to someone speak, our task is to comprehend what they are saying. We hear speech simply as an acoustic signal. To comprehend a message, the listener first receives the transmission (a function of auditory perception), then decodes the message (a function of cognition). To decode the message, however, they must first strip noise from the acoustic signal.

Noises in an acoustic signal are called *invariants* and include literal noise, such as extraneous environmental sounds, or non-phonemic speech sounds, such as coughs, "umms," or "ahhs." There are many acoustic cues that help a listener filter invariants. The suprasegmental phonemes (intonation, stress, tone, etc.) contain many of these cues. These suprasegmentals are articulatory features that provide acoustic cues in the form of variations in pitch, duration, and intensity. These variations help provide meaning in coordination with lexical information. Once noise has been stripped from the acoustic signal, the listener maps the phonemes to morphemes that are part of their lexicon.

The English lexicon is the total stock of all morphemes in the language. Individual adults have personal lexicons ranging from 50,000 to 100,000 words (Miller, 1995). The meaning of a message is interpreted based on our individual lexicon, acoustic cues, and syntactic cues derived from sentence structure. The study of meaning is the area of *semantics*.

Semantics

Acoustic and syntactic cues are important to accurately interpreting meaning. If someone tells you that they recently saw a movie that was "interesting," you could interpret it to mean that they were genuinely interested in the film. However, if they said it in a sarcastic manner, you would be given acoustic cues that would prompt you to interpret just the opposite. This is the difference between a literal and nonliteral meaning.

Syntactic cues provide valuable information to assist in meaning, even if they add phonological complexity. Compare these sentences:

> The girl whom the boy loved was gone.
>
> The girl the boy loved was gone.

The sentences are the same with one exception. In the second sentence the pronoun is deleted. Although it is a shorter sentence and has less phonological complexity, it does not include an important syntactic cue. Therefore, it is more difficult to interpret.

Denotation and Connotation: Lexical information is equally as important as acoustic and syntactic cues, especially when dealing with speech user interfaces. The first test of interpretation is whether or not a word (morpheme) is meaningful or meaningless. If it is not within a shared lexicon, it is meaningless. If a word is within a shared lexicon, then it is said to have meaning. There are two properties to meaning: *denotation* and *connotation*. Denotation is a word's literal, or dictionary, definition. Although dictionaries can be incomplete and imperfect, they do provide us with a basic lexicon, or at least a common reference to debate the English lexicon. If you don't know the literal meaning, you will likely fail to understand the word.

Connotation is supplemental to denotation. Connotation is the suggestive meaning of a word. For example, consider the word *bug*. Its denotation is an insect. However, it can also have a connotation of a computer problem or defect. Connotations may be positive or negative. In some instances, a word may have both a positive and negative connotation.

Ambiguity: One problem faced in language comprehension is ambiguity. Consider the following sentence:

They are baking stones.

This sentence has two meanings depending on whether *baking* is interpreted as a verb or an adjective. If interpreted as a verb, then the sentence means "these people are cooking stones in an oven." However, if *baking* is taken as an adjective, then the sentence means "the stones are used for baking." Syntactically, this sentence has two possible deep structures, but only one surface structure.

A listener will select only one meaning for an ambiguous clause. If their meaning proves to be incorrect, they will reinterpret the clause later. Part of the listener's decision regarding meaning involves the pragmatics of language.

Pragmatics

Pragmatics is the linguistic subfield that studies language usage. *Usage* is the term employed for relating the intended and/or interpreted meaning of a message to the context in which it was spoken. The primary considerations of usage are social and behavioral.

Social relations and culture have a tremendous impact on language, particularly meaning and usage. If the social context of a conversation is informal, speakers use less literal intentions and less strict text structure. If the social context of a conversation is formal, then both speaker and listener have expectations of more literal word meanings and stricter text structure. A current television commercial illustrates the irony that occurs when that paradigm is violated. The commercial depicts an older businessman in an expensive suit walking up to a podium and clearing his throat at the microphone. The scene then pans to employees around the world sitting in front of video monitors preparing to hear what we are led to believe is an important speech in this teleconference. The businessman then begins to emphatically recite a rhyming and nonsensical lyric from a popular rock-and-roll song, prompting smiles and chuckles from the audience. The social context was formal, but the usage was informal, making for an incongruent experience. Therefore, when interpreting meaning, one pragmatic test listeners apply to a message is determining whether or not the language usage is proper in the social context of the dialogue.

Behavioral considerations refer to a speaker's intentions and a listener's interpretation regarding what the speaker wants the listener to do with the information contained in the message. In an imperative statement, the speaker intends for the listener to provide a direct response, typically an action. For example, when told to "Take out the trash," the intention is explicit. However, in a declarative statement the speaker's intention is, at a minimum, to relate new information to existing information. Therefore, the speaker has an assumption regarding what information in the message is new to the listener. The linguistic conventions that convey these assumptions are described in the theory of supposition and assertion.

> Social relations and culture have a tremendous impact on language, particularly meaning and usage.

Supposition and Assertion: *Supposition* refers to information that the speaker assumes is part of the listener's prior knowledge of the world. *Assertion* refers to information that the speaker assumes is new to the listener or justifies emphasis.

There are syntactic and acoustic cues used by speakers to connote supposed and asserted information. For example, one syntactic strategy is to include supposed information in the subject of a sentence and asserted information in the predicate. Another syntactic strategy is to use the definite article *the* preceding a noun phrase that includes supposed information. Conversely, speakers use the indefinite article *a* to indicate asserted information. Asserted information can also be indicated phonologically by suprasegmental phonemes, such as stress. Consider the following sentence:

Cheryl fired Joel.

What happened to Joel was that Cheryl fired him.

In the first sentence, *Joel* occurs in the predicate, thus it is likely that it is supposed information that Joel has been fired and the listeners want to know who fired him. However, in the second sentence, *Joel* occurs in the subject. So, the supposed information is that something happened to Joel and the listener wants to know exactly what happened. Therefore in the second sentence, the asserted information is that Joel was fired. The fact that he was fired by Cheryl is secondary.

In the following sentences, indefinite or definite articles indicate whether the given information is supposed or asserted:

Your son provoked a fight.

Your son provoked the fight.

In the first example, the indefinite article *a* indicates that the occurrence of the fight is asserted information. In the second example, the definite article *the* indicates that the information is supposed and the listener (probably the boy's parent) wants to know who started the fight.

Supposition and assertion also apply when using multiple sentences. Compare these two examples:

> Peter was given a watch for graduation. The watch was his favorite gift.

> Peter wanted a watch for graduation. The watch was his favorite gift.

The second sentence of each example is identical. In the first example, the initial sentence introduces a specific antecedent for *the watch*. Although the watch is mentioned in the second example, it is not an antecedent.

In negative sentences, a positive is supposed while the negative is asserted. For example, consider the sentence "Randy is not my friend." The sentence supposes that *Randy* is my friend, but asserts the opposite.

In speech user interface design, the theories of supposition and assertion have implications regarding response time in dialogues between computers and humans. Studies have shown that supposition and assertion affect the time it takes a listener to comprehend a sentence and therefore react to the information. Thus, the given strategies can be used to create more efficient and effective dialogue.

"By studying language we may discover abstract principles that govern its structure and use, principles that are universal by biological necessity and not mere historical accident, that derive from mental characteristics of a species. A human language is a system of remarkable complexity. To come to know a human language would be an extraordinary intellectual achievement for a creature not specifically designed to accomplish this task."

From Noam Chomsky's Reflections on Language

Summary

Most people who design GUIs have some level of training in visual design. However, the educational and professional development systems within our industry do not typically provide opportunities to learn about the building blocks of speech user interfaces. While the visual interface designer works with fonts, shapes, colors, and widgets, the building blocks for the speech interface designer are sounds, words, and sentences. A designer has only as much freedom as they have knowledge. The quality of a speech interface is partially determined by the designer's knowledge of the nature of language. However, quality is also impacted by the designer's knowledge of the speech technologies discussed in our next chapter.

Speech Technology

To design effective speech interfaces you need to know the technologies currently available. Part Two includes:

Chapter 5: Speech Technologies. Defines and describes the main terms in the field, including speech recognition, speech synthesis, continuous versus discrete speech, and natural language.

Chapter 6: Computer Software. Surveys the current state of speech software on the market, both applications and development tools.

Chapter 7: Hardware. Covers hardware such as sound cards, microphones, voice cards, and modems that affect the usability of speech applications.

Chapter 8: Application of Speech Technology. Describes how speech applications are being used today.

Chapter 5

Speech Technologies

"It only works if you ask
it a budget question."

"When speech recognition becomes genuinely reliable, this will cause another big change in operating systems."
Bill Gates, The Road Ahead (1995)

To create usable speech interfaces designers must first be familiar with the basic concepts and terminology relevant to the input and output of speech to a computer (or other electronic system). This chapter offers an introduction to specific technologies that affect interaction design using speech and audition.

Speech Recognition

"My grandkids are going to look back at the keyboard and giggle."

IBM product evangelist David Barnes, Home Office Computing *(September 1999)*

The term *speech recognition* refers to the technologies that enable computers or other electronic systems to identify the sound of a human voice, separate that sound from noise in the environment, and accept the messages from the voice as input for controlling the system.

Speech recognition has been a popular topic with technologists for decades. Although speech recognition has existed in research laboratories and as part of extremely sophisticated computer systems, only now has the technology become sufficiently advanced to be practical in typical household and business computer systems. The speech recognition software that is part of these typical systems can be divided into two categories: *continuous* and *discrete*.

Continuous versus Discrete Recognition

Continuous recognition allows a user to speak to a system in an everyday manner without using specific, learned commands. This technology is related to natural language, which will be discussed later. Although continuous recognition systems do exist, they are found mainly in niche markets, such as medical and defense systems, and in newer dictation systems. Continuous recognition systems are the technology promised by science fiction— several people interacting with a computer simultaneously and using normal language and speech patterns. Such systems go far beyond simply recognizing speech. They are able to actually understand the meaning of spoken language. These systems are currently error prone, and extremely expensive to develop. The phonology, grammar, and semantics of English require a lot of computational power to interpret the complexity and react to the subtleties of spoken language. The more pragmatic technology commercially available today is discrete recognition.

Discrete recognition software recognizes a limited vocabulary of individual words and phrases spoken by a person. The system can recognize a predetermined lexicon of commands which represent predictable tasks the system can perform. Discrete recognition software relies strictly on phonological input, not the grammatical or syntactic interpretation used by continuous recognition systems. Unlike continuous recognition, the speaker may only use specified words and phrases and must pause between utterances. To use a discrete recognition application, the user speaks one of the predetermined commands and the

Radio Rex

Believe it or not, the earliest research regarding speech input goes back to 1911. *Radio Rex* was a toy dog who would come out of his doghouse when called. He was even "programmed" to jump if he heard a loud noise!

computer carries out the prescribed action. These applications are often called command-and-control. For example, Table 5.1 contains spoken commands for editing text with IBM's ViaVoice software.

You say	You get
Undo this	Undoes your last typed character, word, or phrase.
Scratch that	Deletes the last dictated character, word, or phrase.
Cut this	Deletes the selected text and copies it to the clipboard.
Copy this	Copies the selected text to the clipboard.
Paste this	Pastes the copied text into your dictation.
Delete this	Deletes the selected text.
Select this	Selects the word the cursor is on.
Select <text>	The <text> is a word or phrase that will be selected.
Select right/left	<1 to 20> words/characters where <1 to 20> is the number of words (or characters) to select from the cursor location.
Try again	After selecting a word or phrase, by saying "Select <text>," say "Try again" to select the next occurrence of that word or phrase.

Table 5.1 Discrete Commands from IBM's ViaVoice

Discrete recognition software typically uses a range of several dozen to several hundred commands. Although it is not as natural or easy to use as continuous recognition, the discrete commands are easy to learn and provide a high rate of accuracy.

In addition to words that are part of the lexicon of commands, many discrete recognition applications can accept dictation. In dictation mode, the software will transcribe each word spoken by the user. This is viable technology because the software doesn't have to interpret meaning or decide upon an action based on the user's words. In dictation mode, the software simply acts as a recording device. It captures the user's words into a standard text file, wordprocessing, or proprietary document. Such applications are sometimes referred to as "listening typewriters" and are considered to be the most fundamental commercial application of speech recognition today.

Listening typewriters are not without their problems. Issues similar to those faced in continuous recognition also affect dictation. To be effective, dictation software needs to have a low error rate, as well as easy error recovery, or correction capability.

Dictation software must interpret a word accurately on a phonological level. This presents decision points where the application has to distinguish between similar sounds, such as a user saying "Barb" but the software interpreting it as "Bard." Current commercial software uses customized language models to supplement acoustic analysis. When a user installs their dictation software, they are required to perform a reading of text provided by the installation module. This process is sometimes called enrollment. Enrollment allows the software to analyze a speaker's

Type A for Albert

Tangora was the development code name for IBM's ViaVoice software. It was named after Albert Tangora who is on record as being the world's fastest typist. (Which is no small feat considering that he set his record in the early 1900s using a manual typewriter!)

phonological idiosyncrasies and create a custom language model that the system uses to make specific decisions about word interpretation.

In addition to potential phonological confusion, the use of homophones can easily cause errors in recognition. How can the computer distinguish between "to," "too," and "two," or "accept" and "except"? To address this issue, some software will have default spellings, while others will have remedial syntactic interpretation. Errors regarding similar phonology and homophones are common. Because of these errors, the correction capability of dictation software often determines whether it is efficient and usable.

> The correction capability of dictation software often determines whether it is efficient and usable.

Speaker Dependence versus Speaker Independence

Speech recognition applications can be classified as either speaker-dependent or speaker-independent. Speaker dependent applications require the user to complete an enrollment process. During enrollment, the user reads a predetermined text which the application optimizes for that person's voice and speech patterns. Speaker-dependent software lacks flexibility since it cannot be shared, but it makes for a more dependable tool. Recognition accuracy is substantially greater for speaker-dependent applications. For this reason, most of the commercially available recognition applications are speaker-dependent.

Speaker-independent systems are designed to work for multiple users, and do not use enrollment to personalize the application. Such systems are not reliable for tasks that require a large or specialized lexicon. Speaker-independent applications tend to be used for specialized, single-task systems, such as querying or inspection systems. A reasonable vocabulary for a speaker-independent application at the present is 40 command words or less, plus the digits zero through nine. However, some experts believe the industry will eventually overcome technology limitations and develop speaker-independent continuous recognition systems.

Word Spotting

Word spotting is a technique used by some discrete recognition applications to provide an illusion of continuous speech. This makes interaction with the system seem more natural. In typical discrete recognition applications the user must say an isolated command, and include silence before and after the spoken command. In word spotting applications, a user can say a complete sentence or phrase that includes the command. The software simply filters out everything except the accepted command. For example, a user might say "Computer, I would like to surf the Web" or "Hey, I want to surf the Web." The computer, using word spotting, will filter the antecedent and respond to the discrete command "surf the Web" which launches a Web browser. This technique is also referred to as *parsing* and allows the user to perceive interaction as more intuitive and natural.

Speech Synthesis

The term *speech synthesis* refers to the technologies that enable computers or other electronic systems to output simulated human speech. They provide acoustic information that is phonologically acceptable yet has meaning to human listeners. Speech synthesis has an even longer history than speech recognition but is still an evolving technology used for reading computer screens and providing verbal instruction, feedback, or assistance.

Speech synthesis technology can be divided into two categories: *concatenated synthesis* and *formant synthesis*.

Concatenated Synthesis

Concatenated synthesis uses computer assembly of recorded voice sounds to create meaningful speech output. Because concatenated synthesis uses recorded human voice sounds, it tends to sound more natural than formant synthesis, which uses machine-generated speech. The basic process for developing concatenated synthesizers is to have a human reader read units of speech and store the recorded units of speech. These units are then assembled on demand according to given business rules. This is cost-prohibitive for many applications because of the necessary storage space, computational power required for assembly, and myriad of speech units required for natural sounding speech. Concatenated synthesis works best for systems requiring a small vocabulary.

Concatenated synthesis works best for systems requiring a small vocabulary.

One might assume that the requisite voice sounds typically recorded for assembly are whole words, syllables, or phonemes. However, because of the effect of coarticulation, these units are impractical to use as building blocks for natural sounding synthesized speech. Instead, concatenated synthesizers draw upon an inventory of either diphones or demi-syllables.

A *diphone* represents the transition between two phonemes. It is a unit of acoustic data comprised of two phonemes recorded from the center point of one phoneme to the center point of the next phoneme. They are recorded in this manner to capture the coarticulatory effects on neighboring sounds. When the units are assembled as part of concatenated synthesis, they are perceived as naturally spoken. A natural sounding inventory of diphones would require about 1000 recorded units.

A *demi-syllable* is half of a syllable and is recorded either from the beginning of the sound to its center point, or from the center point to the end of the sound. Using demi-syllables in concatenated synthesis allows for even more coarticulation and provides even more natural sounding speech than diphones. This is because diphones are inaccurate when coarticulation occurs over several phonemes, such as in some utterances of /r/. A natural sounding inventory of demi-syllables would require approximately the same number of recorded units as a diphone inventory.

Once the speech unit inventory is recorded, it is *coded* using one of several voice coding techniques. Coding provides for changes in frequency, pitch, and prosodic effects. (Prosodic effects are the nuances of speech that involve the suprasegmental phonemes.) The coding process allows the inventory of speech units to be as small as possible for the required lexicon. This minimizes the need for vast amounts of storage space and for the time necessary to record a human voice.

Some interactive voice response (IVR) and voice mail systems use a concatenated stored speech technique that is more primitive than concatenated synthesis. These systems typically store recordings of whole words. For example, a credit card company might have a voice response system that provides customers with their current balance and recent payment information. So, to give a customer their account balance of $344.44, it would store and concatenate a string of words, for example: "your+balance+is+three+hundred+forty+four+dollars+and+forty+four+cents." This technique can sound erratic and unnatural, making the system's voice hard to understand. This, in turn, makes it difficult for users to remember the data provided and degrades the overall usability of the system.

Formant Synthesis

Formant synthesis uses a set of phonological rules to control an audio waveform that simulates human speech. In contrast to concatenated synthesis, which uses recorded human voice, formant synthesis creates true machine-generated speech. Formant synthesis is also called synthesis-by-rule because of the rule-based process used to generate the synthesized voice. Currently, this is the dominant technology in the marketplace and the focus of most speech synthesis research. Current formant synthesis technology produces highly intelligible speech but it still sounds unnatural. The "computer accent" that one hears in commercial speech applications is the result of formant synthesis.

> Current formant synthesis technology produces highly intelligible speech but it still sounds unnatural.

The benefit of formant synthesis is its ability to produce nearly unlimited speech. And unlike concatenated synthesis, mass storage is not an issue. The major obstacle in producing quality speech with formant synthesis is the complexity of the required linguistic rules.

Formant synthesis is most widely applied to text-to-speech (TTS) applications, where text data is output as speech. TTS technology may be applied to a "screen reader" for users to hear text they have typed or received, or it may be applied from behind-the-scenes of an application to produce verbal messages that the system conveys to the user.

For example, The American Heritage Talking Dictionary is a "screen reader" where TTS technology is used to speak the appropriate pronunciation to the user. (See Figure 5.1)

In some programs users view text as it is read by the system. In other programs, all feedback from the system is auditory, even though there is a text-based script behind-the-scenes. Both represent applications of TTS technology.

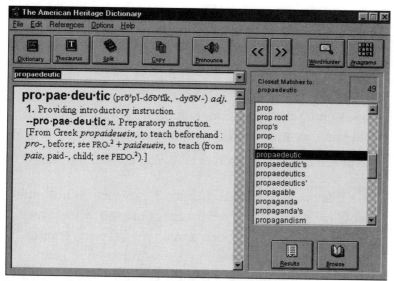

Figure 5.1 The American Heritage Talking Dictionary.

Producing TTS output involves the following six steps:

1. **Text input.** The text is derived from a source, such as entry by a user, from a database, or imported from another file.

2. **Normalization.** The text is normalized. *Normalization* is the editing procedure that converts abbreviations into full alphabetic forms. For example, "Dr." would be converted to "doctor" and "2nd" converted to "second."

3. **Conversion to phonemes.** Strings of words and punctuation are analyzed for syntax and converted to phonemic data by referencing a dictionary. At this point, linguistic rules are accessed and used to make decisions where there are potential multiple pronunciations. For example, consider the word *close*. It could be read as either a verb or an adjective. Its part of speech determines its pronunciation. Phonemic data may be parsed into either diphones or demi-syllables to account for coarticulation.

4. **Exception processing.** Exceptions are processed for instances where the pronunciation dictionary fails. Pronunciation decisions are made using rules for converting letters to sounds.

5. **Prosodic analysis.** Prosodic information, such as intonation and duration, is computed and applied to the final pronunciation specifications.

6. **Speech output.** Speech is synthesized and output.

Using this process, a synthesizer can produce an unlimited vocabulary without any recording of human voice. The resulting speech has smooth transitions between sound units and reasonable mass storage requirements. This makes formant synthesis a flexible and promising speech technology. However, it is constrained by the complexity of rules and computing power needed to create natural sounding speech. Such constraints require expertise in linguistics and acoustics among the development team and can often lead to extended development cycles.

Evaluating Synthesis

Two factors determine the success of synthesized speech in an interface: intelligibility and naturalness. Users will not know or care what method was used to create the speech they hear. Nor will they care what difficulties were overcome to create a synthesized voice. They will primarily judge quality on a morphological basis. Users are concerned, consciously or subconsciously, with correctly recognizing meaningful sounds. If they can correctly recognize words and phrases, they will judge the application as having a high level of intelligibility and will be fundamentally satisfied with their auditory experience. Even given technological constraints, it is possible at this time to achieve levels of intelligibility for synthesized speech that are comparable to human-to-human speech.

Intelligibility can be measured objectively by comparing the number of phonemes produced by an application and assessing the number of phonemes correctly interpreted by users. Naturalness is a subjective measure and can be equally important to users in judging the quality of a speech interface.

...on of how ...uman speech. ...d in every ...naturalness that ...task, and ...not desire a ...al feedback from ...est suited for ...uman-sounding ...Synthesized ...sychological ...serve to establish ...em's interaction. ...ory application ...eech. Users may ...aling with ...want the system ...n.

> The degree of naturalness that is desired and optimal depends on the user, task, and context.

...echnology that has ...t may eventually have a profound impact on both speech recognition and synthesis. This technology can be used for both input and output. Because of the multi-disciplinary community involved in speech user interface development, the term *natural language* has several connotations.

From a linguistic standpoint, a natural language is the language spoken and written by a given culture. Therefore, English, French, Italian, Spanish, German, Japanese, and Chinese are all natural languages. All facets of linguistic analysis apply to a natural language. It can be discussed in terms of its phonological, grammatical, semantic, and pragmatic characteristics. From an interaction standpoint, the speech user interface designer is particularly interested in a pragmatic analysis. We are concerned with how people use language in an everyday manner and how that usage can be applied to controlling a computer. We also seek to build a computer that responds consistently under a variety of circumstances.

It is common to use special, or artificial, languages to facilitate communication in specific fields and aid problem solving. For example, notational languages are used for mathematics, music, and chemistry. Computer programming languages follow a similar model. They are specialized languages developed with their own lexicons and syntactic structures. To control a computer and help users perform automated tasks, there are specialized languages, including command languages. A command language is a specialized language that allows a user to type a brief command and have the computer perform the anticipated action. For example, MS-DOS is a command language. Users type brief commands, such as "del notebook.txt" and the computer responds by performing the desired action. This application of a command language is antithetical to natural language in human-computer interaction. To perform the same action using natural language, a user would type a statement such as "Delete my file named 'notebook.'"

In the computing community, natural language implies an alternative to other modes of interaction, such as command

In the computing community, natural language implies an alternative to other modes of interaction, such as command languages.

languages. This applies to natural language technology used as typed and spoken input and output. Natural language can be applied to programming, scripting, database querying, and general interaction. Interface designers look at natural language as a form of interaction. For example, we compare natural language to command languages. In speech user interface design, natural language is often closely associated with continuous recognition technology and has a specific connotation that is the opposite of discrete recognition. In speech synthesis, the application of natural language takes on a more linguistic definition, where the objective of the synthesized voice is to have it sound more natural, or human.

For many proponents of speech technology the goal is for continuous natural language human-computer interaction. At the present, however, it is more practical to apply natural language technology to specialized uses such as querying data and to general interaction only in a modified format.

Specialized Usage

One current and effective application of natural language technology is information retrieval from computer databases, both in the form of natural-language queries and text-database searching.

Natural-language queries (NLQ) are an alternative to structured query language (SQL). Both allow users to construct database queries and format results sets. NLQ is a limited use of natural language technology that allows users to construct queries using conversational requests. Structured query language often results in faster performance, but users must be trained in complex syntax. Comparatively, NLQ allows users to simply ask questions and state desired formatting parameters.

Structured query language often results in faster performance, but users must be trained in complex syntax.

Text-database searches are increasingly popular and commercially available. These systems analyze natural language requests grammatically and apply additional linguistic analysis and business rules to create a request and return results. A remedial application of such technology is *parsing*, which is similar to word spotting techniques used in voice recognition. This is where the system strips extraneous words from the message and uses the remainder as key words. In an advanced implementation, users can make complex requests for substantial research in specialized markets such as the medical and legal professions. These systems will not only parse queries for key words, but search for and apply synonyms, accommodate incorrect usage such as singular versus plural nouns, and apply additional natural language techniques to retrieve related information and rank the results set.

Let's look at a simple example that illustrates the ease of use of natural language requests. We will compare the interface for two Web sites, AltaVista (www.altavista.com) (see Figure 5.2) and Yahoo (www.yahoo.com) (see Figure 5.3). On AltaVista, which is a search engine, a user may ask a question using everyday language. Yahoo is a directory, not a search engine, and uses a key word search. So, if you were visiting Minneapolis and wanted to find a seafood restaurant, on Yahoo you would type "seafood AND restaurant AND minneapolis." Therefore, you would have to know in advance how to concatenate the three keywords with the logical operator *AND*. Alternatively, you could use "seafood+restaurant+minneapolis" but again you would have to know that specialized syntax. By contrast, on AltaVista, you ask the simple question, "What seafood restaurants are in Minneapolis?" The system parses your natural language query, assumes logical operators, and returns the desired results.

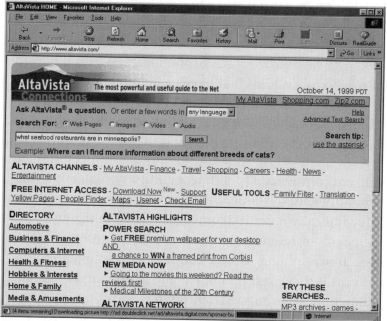

Figure 5.2 An AltaVista query.

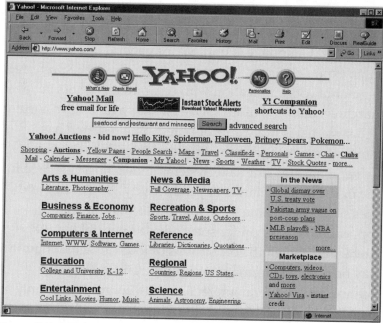

Figure 5.3 A Yahoo query.

Ask Jeeves

For another example of natural language requests, go to www.ask.com and ask Jeeves a question!

In addition to natural language usage for input, natural language text generation is used to create output for some speech synthesis applications. There are many such systems available for medical and legal reporting, as well as successful systems that have been implemented for generation of weather reports. Currently, the National Weather Service uses natural language synthesizers to read weather reports for radio broadcasts.

Current commercial speech recognition applications are primarily speaker-dependent discrete recognition systems. They typically have 100 commands that a user must memorize or reference to interact with the computer. The benefit of applying natural language technology to these systems is that users do not have to memorize or reference commands, or even search through menus.

There has been much debate in the area of using natural language systems for general interaction with computers. Byron Long explores these competing ideas in a review of the literature (1994). It has not yet been conclusively proven that natural language is optimal for general interaction. Some experts believe that natural language is the preferred manner of communication with computers. Others believe that direct manipulation (such as what's available in current GUI systems) is more appropriate. Some research has shown that a comparison of general interaction between GUI and natural language systems shows no advantage to one or the other in terms of productivity. However, there does seem to be some truth to the idea that for some applications, users prefer speech-based natural language interaction. Given the constraints of today's technology, it may be most appropriate to employ natural language technology to general interaction with computers in only a modified format. This modified format may include using a limited vocabulary. Users will still need to learn the

For some applications, users prefer speech-based natural language interaction.

parameters of acceptable language to control the interface, but that acceptable language can be designed to be more conversational. A multi-modal approach is likely to be the best solution in many settings. The user will interact with speech when appropriate, and use direct manipulation—for example, pointing and clicking—when appropriate.

An adequate user and task analysis is mandatory before making design decisions. Natural language may not always be optimal. Discrete recognition or other modalities may provide a better design solution.

Usability testing is vital to the success of the interface, especially if natural language has been used.

Interview with Candace Kamm

Division Manager

Speech Processing Software & Technology

AT&T Labs—Research

Candace Kamm is Division Manager at AT&T Labs of Speech Processing Software and Technology. She has a Ph.D. in Cognitive Psychology from UCLA, a Masters in Audiology from California State University in LA, and a B.A. in Psychology from UC Santa Barbara. She spoke with us about the current state of speech technology and her ideas of the future.

Tell me how you would describe your particular area of expertise.

I've been working in speech technology research organizations since 1984. The area that I am most specifically working on now, and seem to be known for, is user interface for speech systems. I've worked a little bit with speech recognition algorithms and I have worked some with text-to-speech systems, so I know the technologies. I focus on trying to make systems work given the imperfect technologies. This requires that you craft the interface carefully. That's where I have been focusing on. In the research that goes on in my department right now, we are looking at more advanced dialog systems. We have been pushing the envelope, so in this interview I'll probably be going back and forth between what I would do in today's systems versus getting to the ultimate goal of more natural conversational interactions, more goal-directed interactions between machines and people.

> I focus on trying to make systems work given the imperfect technologies. This requires that you craft the interface carefully.

So the work you are doing right now is really focused on what we out here would consider the future.

Yes, but you get glimpses of it now and then. Now we have the robust people-proof applications that you tend to see if you go to Web pages for small companies that are putting out applications. They have speech engines that are much more highly structured so that you can get tasks accomplished even if you have to put more limits on the user. That's where we are now. Where everyone would like to go is to something more open-ended where there is not so much burden placed on the human to know what the system is expecting.

Can you give me your impression of the time line of interface design issues? What were you dealing with back when you started in 1984, and what are the interface design issues and challenges for the products that are out there now versus the ones in your lab that you are working on for the future?

Back in the early '80s we saw systems that were just trying to deal with the ability to recognize the words "yes" and "no." Those turned out to have some interesting challenges in and of themselves. Yes/no seemed liked a simple recognition problem, but when you started putting these into an application you found out that people didn't really say just "yes" or "no"; they said things like "sure," "OK," "no way," or "nope." This immediately taught us that we had to expand the vocabularies that these things would work with.

The other thing that became obvious is that people don't wait their turn in an interaction. If they know the answer to a question they are likely to barge in on top of the system's prompt. The system says, "I have a collect call from Susan. Will you accept the charges?" But as soon as that information about Susan comes out people tend to say, "Yes." In the olden days we didn't have "barge-in" on our system. I actually recorded and played an interaction at a workshop a number of years ago where the person says "No, no, no", and finally when the prompt was over the person says, "I said, 'no!'" Of course that was not in the Yes/No vocabulary so the person never got recognized. The machine was not listening to the first three, and couldn't deal with the last thing they said. It became apparent that what you had to do is craft the interface to handle the limitations of the technology and basic system architecture. Those were some of the earliest lessons, and some of the things you are always trying to deal with.

People don't wait their turn in an interaction.

Craft the interface to handle the limitations of the technology.

Another unchanging aspect is that we are always trying to make speech recognition technology more robust for different kinds of background conditions. That gets more challenging as we start using wireless telephones.

Are you talking about background noise in the different kinds of environments people are in?

Wireless phones in airports, the speaker phone, hands-free environments. Where does the microphone sit in the GUI or Web-based interfaces that have speech in them? You need the interface to overcome problems.

So just as you're making progress on the technology, the environments degrade on you?

People want to use it in more places. As soon as it starts to work in one environment, all of a sudden you want to use it in a lot of other situations that are more challenging. One of the dimensions by which speech recognition is typically described is vocabulary size. We've been able to make great strides in what size of vocabularies we can deal with at one time. Another dimension is this environment dimension. If you have a close talking microphone and quiet background you do a whole lot better with recognition than if you are in the middle of a train station trying to talk through a microphone that isn't protected from environmental noise, or isn't directional enough to be focusing on your voice.

Then there is the output side. What you see in a lot of applications dealing with the general public, if you can get away with it, are pre-recorded prompts. The reason is that text to speech hasn't sounded natural enough. There has been work here at AT&T on some new text-to-speech that sounds more natural. We are moving with text to speech in the right direction, getting it to the point where it sounds natural enough that quality isn't something that people are having bad reactions to. That's an improvement.

It sounds like some of these issues don't really change over time—the bar moves.

If you look at the government projects that have gone on in the past 20 years, they started with a 1000-word vocabulary, for example, resource management for ships. When performance got pretty good on that, they switched to a harder task, like dictation. And when performance got pretty good on that, they switched to an even harder task— conversational dialog over a telephone. It is raising the bar of what you want to do. In my opinion the goal of most speech applications is successful task completion, so you usually end up backing off from the state of the art to some more confined task. You back off to more confined or constrained grammars where the users are supposed to use the words that the system knows.

Then the burden is on the interface builder to teach the people what words the system knows, and the domain that the system knows. In some cases, it can be as simple as listing the words, and in some cases it's more difficult.

> The burden is on the interface builder to teach the people what words the system knows, and the domain that the system knows.

Give me an example of a more difficult case.

One of the systems that we are working on here is a system for routing calls that come into the operator who asks, "How may I help you?" When people have been disconnected, in the language of the company, we would say those people are asking for "billing credit." The actual customers, though, will say "I got disconnected" or sometimes they call and say "I dialed the wrong number." There are a number of salient phrases they may say that all refer to what we would call billing credit. But no one who is calling in with these problems is going to say, "I want a billing credit," or rarely. Newer systems will be able to handle this, compared to older systems where you actually had to craft what the system could recognize, word by word or phrase by phrase.

If you think about the processes of building a usable interface, whether it is for speech or GUI, assuming that people are doing good analysis (probably a dangerous assumption), do you think that analysis and design work is different for speech interfaces? Would the steps be different for following best practice for GUI interface design and speech? Where would they be going astray?

Collecting data on the exact utterances that people are going to say is very important.

A lot of the speech work is now based on statistical analyses. Collecting data on the exact utterances that people are going to say is very important, and that is the one thing that people used to GUIs might not do. If you look at the current "best in class" algorithms in speech recognition, they are all based on statistical models. For example, individual speech sounds and how they go into words, the language models that represent the statistics of expected word orders, and even mapping of expected words and salient phrases to the action that you want to do with the task. To create that entire chain it's useful to know what words people are actually using so that the performance of the recognizer can be maximized.

Another difference that is new, and not completely well understood, is how you are going to synchronize speech with GUIs. How do you keep track of when the system is listening and when it's not listening and convey that information to the user? You can storyboard what the sunny day scenario is for a particular application, but things can go wrong because of relative timing of some of the resources, such as the recognizer and some of the databases you are accessing. Until you get the whole system together, you don't see that there is a two-second delay here and a five-second delay here and that makes the whole system unusable. It may be hard to predict without actually mocking it up and trying it.

You have to have more heavy-duty error correction than you see in most GUI applications. If the system mis-recognizes and acts on that, you have to have some way of recovering or some way of detecting that your dialog isn't on the path for the task.

In our work we've been emphasizing the role of interface designer. Instead of having programmers and developers designing the interface, there are people who are dedicated to worrying about the interface and working closely with the developers. Do you think that model works with speech applications?

It will work to a certain extent. There is always going to be a communication mismatch. The more the interface designer knows about how the system is put together and what it can and can't do, the better off things are. It certainly won't work to make a design and throw it over the wall to the developer. I've seen that fail again and again. The best thing is to have the interface designer and the developer sit down together and go through scenarios of how things are supposed to work.

A few years ago, you could draw a call flow and hand it off to someone who could then go program it. But with object-oriented programming, the complexity of the dialogs, the content of the prompts, and even the distributed architecture of most of our systems, it's difficult to put things down in the order of a call flow. A lot is asynchronous and that makes it difficult to draw the old kinds of call flows to cover these types of applications. There can be many ways to get to a particular point, especially if the system is multi-modal. Someone could touch, or someone could talk, or someone could hang up, and any of these things can happen at any particular time. You have to be looking for all of them and if one thing happens, then you have to close off some of the others.

> You have to have more heavy-duty error correction than you see in most GUI applications.

It is still important to have more than one person doing the design and development of a system. The interface designer is pushing for usability and the application developer is pushing for convenience of programming. It takes a lot of compromise on both sides to come up with a really good interface. They have to work side by side and each has to know something about and appreciate the limitations and interests of the other person.

I was thinking about your comments about specifying the type of action and whether it is spoken or mouse click, or viewing something on a screen. Are there particular tools or documents that you use to specify those and document that in your design?

I don't know of any multi-modal design tools that are out there yet, especially for combining actions.

In the work we do on GUIs, we analyze task structure. We also look at it from the point of view of interface objects that the user is dealing with. Then we marry those two views, which shouldn't be at odds, but are not necessarily the same thing. Is task-based the dominant mode in speech applications, or do you need to take both tasks and objects into account?

You need to take both into account. Traditionally, it's been task-based and that gives you these serial call flows. That doesn't work for a lot of the complex dialogs that we want to. A strictly serial mode doesn't work very well, so you immediately get the application programmer thinking in a different way. The issue is how do you break the task into user interface objects, but still have the information elements you need to accomplish the task efficiently? In my experience, the weight given to one or the other depends on the symbiotic relationship between the interface designer and the developer.

The interface designer is pushing for usability and the application developer is pushing for convenience of programming.

How do you break the task into user interface objects, but still have the information elements you need to accomplish the task efficiently?

What's the state of prototyping tools for speech applications?

There are a number. *Speech Technology* magazine discusses these. Many of them are attached to a particular speech recognition engine. A couple of them are not. A lot of speech recognition engines will have toolkits for grammar; a few of them will have extensive toolkits for mixed initiative dialogs. There are tools out there, but you may have to buy into a particular recognition engine.

Do you have a sense of where either the most growth will be, or where the most interesting work will be? What are you most excited about? Is it the multi-modal work with speech and GUIs? The speech added onto handheld devices?

Where I think it is going to pay off the most is speech added to handheld devices, if the handheld territory is too small for a keyboard. It will be hard to achieve good performance there because the microphone is usually too far from the mouth, so we are going to have to work on robustness. Speech applications work where there's a clear value added for voice input, and handhelds are a place where I see a clear value added.

I'm also pretty excited about speech at the desktop, but that's more from a research point of view, because I don't think we know the answers about when speech would be used. It's partly preference and partly the task and what other tasks you are doing at the time. I'm interested in multi-modal interfaces at the desktop. How do people partition different tasks? What will they use speech for and what will they find easier to do with a mouse click or a keyboard?

In the long run, speech will offer us more natural language interfaces for information retrieval, where it will be easier

> Where I think it is going to pay off the most is speech added on to hand-held devices.

> Speech applications work where there's a clear value-added for voice input, and handhelds are a place where I see a clear value added.

to say a sentence about what you are looking for than type a long sentence.

Do you have a prediction about when we will be able to talk to this all-knowing computer?

We can already do it for a limited domain, and for the situation where the microphone is in a reasonable setting. What you are going to see is more graceful error correction and more intelligence built into the system. Then there will be a gradual expansion in the amount of different subjects that a particular interface can handle. I still think it is going to be a while, especially at the desktop. If speech doesn't have value added, people will stop using it for a particular task. For example, it's pretty easy for me to dial a ten-digit number. I'd rather do that than say the ten-digit number. But I'd rather say someone's name than having to remember the ten-digit number. That's when speech becomes valuable.

> I'd rather say someone's name than having to remember the ten-digit number. That's when speech becomes valuable.

Why do you like speech so much?

It's fun and interesting, and fun to use the systems when they actually work. I've always been interested in speech. When things go wrong, I like to try to find out why. Speech gives me lots of opportunities for that. Everything from the acoustics of the speech to how the recognizer works. It's a great opportunity for experimentation and improving ease of use.

Do you have any advice for the interface designer who is new to all this, who has just been told they are going to work on a project that involves speech? What would you tell them to do, how to prepare, or what to pay attention to? What are your words of wisdom?

The first word of wisdom is to understand the task they are trying to accomplish.

Did you mean that from a user task point of view or the system?

I meant it from a user task point of view. The system is important, but keeping the user task all the way through with your design is more important.

The second thing I would do is point them to places where they could see examples of systems and let them try them out and let them see how they work. Go to Web pages of speech engine vendors and try out demos. You can see how restricted some of the applications are.

If you want an application to work today, focus it as narrowly as you can and try to guide the user through it. This is different from the research I am doing now, which is developing a system where you don't have to guide the user so much.

> If you want an application to work today, focus it as narrowly as you can and try to guide the user through it.

I'd like to build systems that know more about users and their preferences and build a system that is more intelligent by having it make use of that information. For example, when you are starting a dialog and things seem to be going wrong, you'd detect that more easily because you have that path knowledge of how things typically work with this person. This is improving. We get little pieces in with little pieces of task domains. The question is: how do we ultimately get the system that people can talk to about any topic?

Summary

Designers must deal with the current state of technology, which presents issues of misrecognition and misunderstanding in speech recognition. They must also deal with the "robotic" tone to synthesized natural language voices that needs refinement in syntax and prosody. For both input and output, technologists have yet to get the pace of speech to truly match natural human tempo. These issues can be mitigated through usability testing, iterative design, and thoughtful use of natural language.

As the state-of-the-art in natural language improves, as well as the quality of speech recognition and synthesis, these technologies will become more prevalent and effective. However, even today speech technology is commercially available and useful for both niche and general markets. The current state of computer software is a litmus test for the status of speech technology and is discussed in the next chapter.

Chapter 6

Computer Software

"Sorry. I was calling 'Robots-Take-
Over-The-World Headquarters."

"I think there is a world market for maybe five computers."
Thomas (T.J.) Watson (1874-1956), chairman of IBM, 1943

This chapter provides an introduction to commercially available applications that use speech technology. As of 2000 the speech software market is dominated by speech recognition suites—collections of software that apply speech to more than one function, for example, dictation, command-and-control, and text-to-speech. In addition, many applications have been developed for vertical markets, such as the medical and legal professions. These vertical market packages are discussed in Chapter 8: Application of Speech Technology, along with proprietary systems that illustrate the various applications of speech recognition, synthesis, and telephony.

Speech Recognition Suites

As recently as 1999, most speech applications had dedicated functions. Some were command-and-control systems that allowed users to control an operating system, some were dedicated dictation packages, and some were screen readers that provided text-to-speech output. If you wanted to integrate speech control into your computer system productively, you had to purchase several programs which were not always guaranteed to be compatible. However, the field is rapidly changing and the leading commercial speech programs are now sold as suites that combine all of these functions. Now a user can purchase a single package that is a command-and-control and dictation program that also provides text-to-speech output. Interestingly, they are primarily marketed and sold under the category of speech recognition or voice recognition.

Four packages currently dominate the Microsoft Windows-based home and small business marketplace: IBM's ViaVoice, Dragon Systems' NaturallySpeaking, L&H's Voice Xpress, and Philips' Free Speech. They are similar in that they are multi-modal applications that provide nearly identical functionality.

Suite Web sites

ViaVoice (www-4.ibm.com/software/speech/)

NaturallySpeaking (www.naturalspeech.com)

Voice Xpress (www.lhs.com/)

Philips (www.speech.be.Philips.com)

Dictation

For the majority of users the most profound impact of speech technology is the ability to use speech input rather than a keyboard to enter text into a computer. ViaVoice, NaturallySpeaking, Voice Xpress and Free Speech are designed primarily for text entry. It is particularly useful technology for people who suffer from repetitive stress injuries, such as carpal tunnel syndrome, or who need to create long documents, such as articles, books, or reports.

"I am attracted by the machine's fluidity, its ability (or so it seems) to understand. That's the lure of voice-recognition software, and using it, I feel as if I'm living in science fiction, like I've become a character in a film."

David Ulin from his article "I Hear America Dictating" in Minneapolis' City Pages newspaper

> "There is no reason anyone would want a computer in their home."
>
> *Ken Olson, president, chairman and founder, Digital Equipment Corp., 1977*

According to the most recent marketing materials, today's software has the ability to support up to two million words. The most recent published tests, which are approximately a year old, show an active vocabulary of about 22,000 words with the ability to augment the lexicon with an additional 40,000 words. You can also add specific multiple-word phrases, including desired capitalization and punctuation.

Another recent development with these applications is that you can now import words into the speech software's dictionary by using any number of file types, such as word processing documents, HTML, RTF, or standard text files. In addition, there are industry-specific dictionaries available for the medical, legal, and other professions.

These packages require about 45 minutes for setup and training before users are ready to dictate. The marketing materials promise data entry capability of 150 words per minute, which is faster than most typists. Realistic use shows that 75 to 100 words per minute dictation is typical. Also, the faster you speak, the more errors occur. The most recent tests available show about a 90 percent accuracy rate (although marketing claims are made of up to 98 percent). For acceptable performance, a 95 percent accuracy rate is needed. Anything less than that is considered "frustrating" for users.

One study showed that it took 13 to 18 minutes to dictate a 350-word document. A 90 percent accuracy rate means that users had approximately 35 word errors in a 350-word document. These errors are always in need of correction, since a speech recognition program will enter actual words even if they aren't the intended words. Therefore, a spell checker is not an automatic solution. Users have to manually correct word errors, which produces frustration. A review from the March 10, 1998, *PC Magazine* stated that the programs "frustrated all five of our testers" (but it also offered the promise that "over time these products should become more accurate").

One advantage to recent improvements in dictation technology is that these applications are no longer modal. In the previous generation of dictation software, users were forced into either dictate or edit mode. Now you can edit "on the fly" including adding formatting attributes. However, because accuracy rates are still not optimal, it seems that editing is best performed at the keyboard for long documents.

Editing is best performed at the keyboard for long documents.

Interesting Dictation Errors

Speech recognition may have its faults…but at least sometimes they're humorous. The following are examples of interesting dictation errors as they were spoken and interpreted:

- "Mayor Rudy Giuliani" became "Mayor Rudy Julia I need."

- "WWW" became "Debbie Adobe debut."

- "Let's take a memo" became "Let's take a camel."

- "Subjects performed two tasks" became "Some checks performed at two tasks."

- "Performance was best with auditory input and spoken output" became "Performance was bass to with auditory input and Spokane output."

- "Performance was worse with auditory input" became "Performance was worse with auditorium plucked"

- "It's working fine" became "It's working vine."

Speech Output from Dictation Software

Most of the functionality in the leading suites is geared to speech input used in dictation and command-and-control. However, they all provide text-to-speech (TTS) functionality. The TTS functionality is implemented as a screen reader that will read documents a user has created, Web pages, and help topics. Combined with the voice input functionality, this TTS feature is especially useful for visually impaired users. (See Figure 6.1 for Woodrow, the speech synthesizer agent in IBM's ViaVoice.)

Command-and-Control

Current speech suites have greater utility than prior generations of speech software because they are more than just recognition programs. One of the most disappointing aspects of earlier software was attempting to work between applications. One program was used as a command-and-control program to navigate through the operating system, but another program was used for dictation. This created opportunities for technical conflicts and it required users to learn multiple command sets. Now these fully-integrated programs assist in controlling home and office applications, including wordprocessing, spreadsheets, organizers, and Web browsers, as well as the operating system.

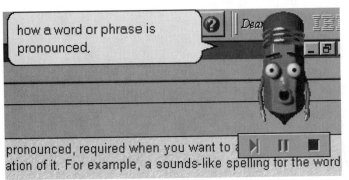

Figure 6.1 Woodrow, the speech synthesizer agent in IBM's ViaVoice.

The command-and-control aspect of such programs uses discrete speech recognition. The commands do take time to learn, but at least users are learning only one command set. Word spotting is also used to make interaction seem more natural. For example, in ViaVoice a user checks to see if they have any new e-mail messages by using one of two commands, either "Check my messages" or "Do I have any messages?"

ConversaWeb is a command-and-control application that lets you surf the Web by voice. It accepts your commands to move backwards and forwards through pages, allows you to speak the link you want to go to, and will even read you the links on a page.

For More Information

www.conversa.com

Buying Speech Software

When purchasing commercial speech software, beware of price comparisons. Many of the commercial applications have multiple versions, ranging from a "light" version to a full "suite." So, it can be unclear from catalogs and sales literature exactly what you're getting for your money. Look closely at the features and ask questions about integration. Also, take the system requirements seriously. Speech software tends to perform poorly if it doesn't have enough RAM available. Some experts recommend nearly twice the RAM listed as minimum system requirements!

Dedicated Software

Although suites have greater market share, there are still dedicated speech applications available. In some cases, the dedicated software is more robust than the suites are, especially regarding TTS technology. IBM has a version of ViaVoice that offers strictly dictation and another application that provides Web-based navigation and dictation for chat rooms and e-mail. Dragon Systems has numerous products with different features. L&H has focused on their consumer suite, but they also have many professional modules available for various industries and languages. In addition, other manufacturers offer reasonable text-to-speech solutions, such as First Byte's Monologue and Conversa's Messenger.

PlainTalk

Although the computer software examples in this book are Windows-based, user interface designers should be familiar with multiple platforms. Often, looking at a design solution from one platform will help solve a problem in another. The Macintosh operating system offers built-in support for voice recognition (in American English and Mexican Spanish) and text-to-speech. It has other features, as well, including speaker independence, a cadre of TTS voices with adjustable voice rate, and "push to talk" capability (www.apple.com/macos/speech/).

If you are designing speech user interfaces, you should purchase one or more of the commercial applications to analyze their strengths and weaknesses. By becoming a user of speech technology you will be able to better understand the tasks and appreciate the constraints involved with speech user interface development so that you can create improved design solutions.

Useful Web Links

http://dir.yahoo.com/Business_and_Economy/
Companies/Computers/Software/
Voice_Recognition/

www.tiac.net/users/rwilcox/speech.html

www.links2go.com/topic/Speech_Technology

www.zdnet.com/pcmag/features/speech/
index.html

Development Tools

Many companies offer development tools. The industry leaders in commercial software, such as Microsoft and Apple, provide speech-enabling development tools for their platforms. Both computer and telephony tools are offered by many of the telecommunications companies, for example, AT&T, Lucent, and Bell Labs. Naturally, IBM, L&H, Philips, and Dragon all offer speech software development tools to provide third-party development that complements their product lines. In addition, there are hundreds of development companies that often work with their own proprietary tools. This section gives an introduction to some of the currently available tools and provides resources for further information.

"#3 pencils and quadrille pads."

Seymour Cray (1925-1996), when asked what CAD tools he used to design the Cray I

Microsoft

Microsoft Research (MSR) is a computer science research organization founded by Microsoft Corporation in 1991.

They conduct basic and applied research in four areas: interactivity and intelligence, mathematical sciences, programming tools and techniques, and systems and architecture. Their projects include research in user interface design, spoken technology, and natural language.

The Speech Technology Group at Microsoft has three current projects that contribute to their speech development tools. These projects are Whisper, Whistler, and Leap. Whisper is a scalable, continuous, speaker-independent speech recognition engine. Recent tests have benchmarked Whisper at 92.3 percent accuracy for recognition. Whistler is a text-to-speech system that allows a user to record their own voice and "train" the system to use their speech patterns. The system then can use a synthesized version of the user's voice for converting text to speech. Leap is a project that works on natural language understanding to apply to the other technologies.

Currently, the Microsoft Speech SDK 4.0 enables the Microsoft Speech Application Programming Interface (SAPI), which allows developers to add speech capabilities to their applications. It will incorporate Whisper, Whistler, and Leap shortly after the release of Microsoft Windows 2000.

For More Information

http://research.microsoft.com/srg

http://research.microsoft.com/nlp

http://microsoft.com/iit

IBM

IBM offers software development kits for Windows, Java, and Linux platforms. In addition, IBM provides development tools for telephony. An interesting component to their offering is the ViaVoice Topic Factory. The Topic Factory allows developers to add specialized vocabularies that improve recognition accuracy. Each topic includes a set of words, desired pronunciation of the words, and a language model for usage. Topics are supported in American English and German.

The ViaVoice SDK for Windows supports SAPI 4.0 and ActiveX controls. With the ViaVoice SDK, developers can create speech applications in French, German, Italian, Japanese, Spanish, British English, and American English.

For More Information

www-4.ibm.com/software/speech/dev/

L&H

L&H offers speech recognition and speech synthesis development tools to create speech interfaces for devices such as cellular phones, navigation systems, set-top boxes, and smart phones. They also offer a word-based speech recognition development tool for Microsoft Windows CE. Their engines create speaker-independent or -dependent interfaces. In addition, they offer speech compression development tools for use with devices such as digital answering machines, personal digital assistants, voice recorders, and voice pagers. Compression allows speech technology to work with devices that have limited memory or low bandwidth.

For More Information

www.lhs.com/speechtech/embdprod.asp

Dragon

Dragon offers the NaturallySpeaking Developer Suite that allows developers to create continuous-speech applications using the functionality provided in Dragon's consumer products. Their suite provides ActiveX and COM support for SAPI. It also includes a tool for custom vocabulary development similar to IBM's product. Dragon supports American English, British English, French, Spanish, German, and Italian. However, their packaged suite only includes American English; other languages must be purchased separately.

For More Information

www.naturalspeech.com

Philips Speech Processing

Philips Speech Processing has speech development technologies as well as applications software. They offer recognition, synthesis, and telephony development tools. They also have their own dictation, telephony, and command-and-control products. Many products are available not only in English, but in several European languages.

For More Information

www.speech.be.philips.com/

Sun Microsystems

At their Web site, Sun offers speech specifications for Java to be used with other companies' technologies, for example, Apple, AT&T, Dragon, IBM, Novell, Philips, and Texas Instruments.

The Java Speech API specifies a cross-platform interface for command-and-control, dictation, and speech synthesis. The Java Speech Grammar Format (JSGF) provides control of speech recognizers, and the Java Speech Markup Language (JSML) provides control of speech synthesizers.

For More Information

java.sun.com/products/java-media/speech/

Other Companies

Several other companies provide development tools. AT&T offers Network Watson, a software product that supports client/server automatic speech recognition, speaker verification, and text-to-speech synthesis. Lucent Technologies offers multilingual speech recognition and TTS development environments. They also offer speech processing boards and an integrated speech server. Bell Labs offers multilingual text-to-speech solutions. Other companies offer everything from speech plug-ins for multimedia tools to thin-client speech development tools.

For More Information

www.att.com/aspg/

www.lucent.com/speech/

www.bell-labs.com/project/tts/

www.tiac.net/users/rwilcox/speech.html

Developing Speech Output for the Web

The World Wide Web Consortium conducted a Voice Browser workshop in October 1998, bringing together people involved in developing voice browsers for accessing Web-based services. Participants agreed to collaborate on an effort to bring speech to the World Wide Web. Aural Cascading Style Sheets and other extensions of HTML came out of that effort. The group has continued its work and is moving toward specifying even more speech capabilities for the Web.

Another exciting development in Web technology is in the emerging area of XML. IBM, AT&T, Lucent, Motorola, and approximately 40 other industry leaders have given support to the Voice eXtensible Markup Language (VoiceXML or VXML) standard which has released its preliminary specifications. VoiceXML is a new markup language that will provide voice access to Web content on the Internet.

The VoiceXML specification is expected to facilitate development of Web-based, personalized interactive voice-response services. It will enable phone and voice access to integrated call center databases, information on Web sites, and company intranets. It will also be useful for developing speech user interfaces for electronic devices.

"Often it was impossible for a developer to make a designer understand even the simplest elements of a programming problem. Just as often, designers would work for weeks on some aspect of a product only to be rudely told, when they finally showed it to a developer, that it was impossible to implement."

I Sing the Body Electronic: A Year with Microsoft on the Multimedia Frontier *by Fred Moody*

For More Information

www.lucent.com/speech

www.voicexml.org

www.w3.org/

A Comparison of Speech Recognition Suites

This review by Roland Racko is reprinted with permission from the November 1999 issue of *Software Development Magazine* Online (www.sdmagazine.com).

NaturallySpeaking Professional 3.52

Dragon Systems Inc., 320 Nevada St., Newton, MA 02160
Tel: (800) 437-2466
Online: www.dragonsys.com
Price: NaturallySpeaking Professional Version 3.52: $695; Mobile Recorder option: $199; Developer Suite: $695
Software Requirements: Windows 95 or Windows 98
Hardware Requirements: 200MHz CPU, 64MB RAM

RATING: ***

Pros:	Cons:
Most evolved macro facility.	Onerous training requirements.
Best dictation engine.	Mediocre integration of mobile recorder.
Best dictated English syntax interpretation.	Unfinished correction facilities.

ViaVoice 98 Executive

IBM Corp., 1133 Westchester Ave., White Plains, NY 10604
Tel: (800) 426-3333
Online: www.software.ibm.com/speech/
Price: ViaVoice Executive Version plus Online Companion: $169.90; Olympus D1000 Mobile Recorder option: $299; IBM ViaVoice Developer Kit: $995
Software Requirements: Windows 95 or Windows 98
Hardware Requirements: 166MHz with MMX and 256K L2 cache, 48MB RAM

RATING: ***

continues

continued

ViaVoice 98 Executive	
Pros: Most flexible command structure. Very good undo capabilities. Clear manuals, professional mobile device.	Cons: Very weak macro capability. Poor engine feedback. Lacks recorded voice playback.

Voice Xpress Professional Mobile 4.0	
Lernout & Hauspie, 52 Third Ave., Burlington, MA 01803 Tel: (781) 203-5000 Online: www.lhsl.com Price: Voice Xpress Professional Mobile 4.0: $229.95 (less $30.00 rebate); Voice Xpress SDK: $595 Software Requirements: Windows 95 or Windows 98 Hardware Requirements: Pentium II, 48MB RAM	
RATING: ***	
Pros: Best integration with chat software. Linux offerings. Professional mobile device.	Cons: Counterintuitive and occasionally incorrect syntax handling. Frail keystroke and command integration with other desktop applications. Weak macro facility.

Software Development's Rating System	
No Stars	Dismal
The product is buggy and could suffer from poor performance and an inadequate feature set. Using this tool will set your productivity back.	
*	Below Average
The product's performance, feature set, or stability could be weak. This product is barely functional, and you'd be wise to try before you buy.	

Software Development's Rating System	
* *	Fair
The product does what it claims to do, is generally stable, but could use improvement in the areas of performance or feature set. In general, it could use some more work.	
* * *	Good
This product is satisfactory and meets expectations. Its performance and feature set are adequate. Although it's not the best in its class, it's still worth looking at.	
* * * *	Great
This product exhibits exceptional performance and features. It's near the top of its class of development tools and probably belongs in your shop.	
* * * * *	Incredible
Best in class, even if you don't think you need it, you need it. Great performance and functionality—a "must have."	

Summary

An essential book for user interface designers is Jakob Nielsen's *Usability Engineering*. In this book, Nielsen describes the notion of *double experts*. Double experts are usability professionals with expertise in the type of interface being developed. They have been found to be more effective usability engineers than "single experts." As a designer of speech user interfaces, a certain amount of expertise as a user of speech interfaces is required. The current cadre of speech recognition suites is affordable and offers the consumer and interface designer a marvelous introduction to speech technology. Becoming a frequent user of even one of these suites will allow you to have first-hand experience of the usability issues your users will face.

In addition, gaining familiarity with the capabilities and limitations of the commercial development tools for speech software will assist you in becoming a more effective interface designer. Familiarity with such tools requires an understanding of speech-related computer hardware, which is the subject of Chapter 7.

Hardware

"Say -- you must be Harris. I've read
every program you've ever written.
I'm one of your biggest fans!"

The first fully automatic, sequence-controlled, large-scale calculator was called the Harvard Mark I and was completed in 1944 by Howard Aiken of Harvard University working with engineers from IBM. The completed Mark I was 51 feet long x 8 feet high x 2 feet wide; it weighed 50 tons and had more than 750,000 parts.
Adapted from www.webillustrated.com

Some designers relish opportunities to learn about, work with, and play with computer and electronic hardware. Others deal with hardware as little as possible. Regardless, to create usable software we need to have at least a rudimentary understanding of the hardware that facilitates and constrains our designs.

Computer Hardware

Computer hardware has come a long way since the Harvard Mark I. Howard Aiken and others may not have even dreamed of the level of computing power that personal computers have achieved today. As computer users, we take for granted on a daily basis the complexity of the systems we use. We can also be oblivious to the level of integration we have achieved. Our desktop and laptop boxes are the sum of many parts, all of which are needed to produce computing systems capable of speech input and output. We require sound cards, microphones, speakers, modems, and more to accomplish our speech computing tasks.

Sound Cards

The Altair, released in 1975 by a small company called MITS, was the first personal computer. It had no display and no keyboard. Input was accomplished by setting switches on a panel while output was a series of flashes in a row of lights. As personal computers progressed, the first sounds were made by the Apple II in 1977 using an alphaSyntauri sound card for creating simple crashes and battle noises in fantasy games. Meanwhile, MS-DOS-based PCs could only produce system beeps for a few more years. However, in the 1980s Stanford University developed a synthesis technique called Frequency Modulation, or FM synthesis. Yamaha Corporation purchased and promoted this technology, and the era of digital synthesis began. Previously, analog synthesizers existed, but they were cumbersome, inaccurate, and inefficient.

FM synthesis created new possibilities for employing audio in personal computing. AdLib offered an inexpensive sound card for PCs in 1987. It became the industry standard once PC video game programmers realized the possibilities of using sounds for gaming. A few years later CreativeLabs released the Sound Blaster which quickly became and remains the standard for PC sound cards. One of the major reasons that Sound Blaster became an industry standard is that it was the first sound card that was not only a synthesizer, but had the capability to record and play digital audio. Now, contemporary PC sound cards use FM synthesis or a newer technology called wavetable synthesis to create sound. They also include digital audio recorders, digital audio players, as well as filters, equalizers, and mixers that combine sound from CD, DVD, digital audio, and other sources.

Because of the demands placed on computer processors, a sound card is a necessary addition to personal computer hardware. Although a typical CPU could theoretically handle all the calculations required for synthesis, it would have to give precedence to the audio because of the precision timing required to produce accurate sound in real time. This would put a tremendous strain on system resources otherwise needed for performing calculations and manipulating the graphical display. The sound card is dedicated to those functions and can, therefore, improve overall system performance.

Microsoft released specifications for the Multimedia PC, or MPC, in 1990. This means that an MPC must have a minimum processor speed, a CD-ROM drive, a sound card, and speakers. With MPC, Microsoft also released an Application Program Interface, or API, to give programmers license and tools to create third-party applications that use the multimedia resources. With this, developers don't have to program for a specific sound card. They can simply make calls to a Windows driver that mediates commands.

Resolution

One measurement of the quality of a sound card's output is its resolution. Sound cards are typically capable of producing 16-bit sound, although some 32-bit cards are now being sold. The number of bits reflects the quality, or depth, of sound. 16-bit sound is considered "CD quality" and is high-quality sound by all standards.

Sound cards are typically capable of producing 16-bit sound, although some 32-bit cards are now being sold.

Frequency Response

The range of frequencies that a sound card can manage is called its frequency response. In Chapter 3, *The Nature of Sound*, we stated that humans are able to hear frequencies between about 20 and 22,000 Hz. A perfect sound-producing device would generate sound with equal amplitude for each frequency, so that frequency wouldn't

Bits and Bytes

Computers process all information in bits. Bits, which represent numbers, are the most atomic unit of measurement for data. A bit has one of two values, either 0 or 1. Bits are combined into large number strings that are interpreted using the binary numbering system (as opposed to our traditional decimal numbering system). This system, based on bits (also called binary digits), is used to measure sound as well as all computer data.

Each group of 8 bits is a byte. Bytes can represent numbers from –128 to 127, for a total of 256 digits. The previous audio standard had been 8-bit sound for many years, which would measure sound by dividing a sound wave into bytes, or 256 parts. 16-bit sound divides a sound wave into many more parts, which reproduces the sound more accurately.

affect the perception of sound. However, this isn't possible with current technology. Therefore, when sound cards are described in terms of frequency response, it is typical to include a figure after the response range that represents the deviation from a perfectly flat signal. This deviation is sometimes referred to as a tolerance limit and is measured in decibels. Most sound cards are between 0.1dB and 3dB, which is considered "perfect enough."

Dynamic Range

The difference between the lowest and highest amplitude that a sound card can manage is its dynamic range, measured in decibels. The resolution of a sound card affects its potential dynamic range. Typically, the higher resolution cards have greater dynamic range. 80dB dynamic range is considered acceptable. Most 16-bit sound cards have a dynamic range of 90dB or greater.

Signal-to-Noise Ratio

The signal-to-noise ratio of a sound card is the ratio of the desired sound to the undesired sounds. It describes how quiet a signal is. Signal-to-noise ratio varies depending on the frequency of the signal and the environment. Unfortunately, computers are fertile ground for undesired sounds. The casing prevents us from hearing most of these sounds, but if you put a microphone inside a computer and listened to the level of electromagnetic activity you might be surprised. Inexpensive and medium-priced sound cards are typically not considered quiet enough for professional sound quality. While they are acceptable for consumers using speech synthesis programs, they would not be quiet enough for high quality voice recordings.

Inexpensive and medium-priced sound cards are typically not considered quiet enough for professional sound quality. While they are acceptable for consumers using speech synthesis programs, they would not be quiet enough for high quality voice recordings.

Sampling Rates

If you are going to create a speech interface that uses concatenated synthesis, you may be recording a human voice. The quality of your recording, or sampling, will therefore affect the quality of the user interface. In our earlier discussion of the nature of sound we described a sound wave, or sine wave, and stated that it was measured in Hz or kHz. The goal of sampling is to reproduce the original sound wave as accurately as possible. To that end, we are indebted to Harry Nyquist. Nyquist was a mathematician who figured out that to digitize a sound accurately, it must be sampled at twice its frequency. Since we said that human hearing has an upper limit of about 22 kHz, the sampling rate needed to give us the highest quality sound is about 44 kHz.

It's a Blast

The CreativeLabs Sound Blaster is the common denominator for PC sound cards. It has the following specifications:
Resolution: 16-bit
Frequency response: 20Hz to 20 kHz
Signal-to-noise ratio: 80 dB
Sampling rate: 5 kHz to 44.1 kHz

Most sound cards can sample at 44.1 kHz or greater. Anything more than 44.1 kHz is considered "oversampling" and isn't necessary unless you are producing music. Most sound cards can also sample at rates lower than 44.1 kHz. The human voice can be adequately reproduced at a sampling rate of 11 kHz. However, even if your desired output is going to be a lower rate you should still record at 44.1 kHz then "downsample" the audio for final output. Many other factors impact the ultimate signal quality. Since your objective is to produce the best sound you can and sampling rate is under your control, this is an opportunity to achieve the highest quality sound.

Microphones

Microphones play a role both in controlling speech user interfaces and in recording the human voice. Individual models of microphones have many differences and the attributes that make one desirable for recording may be different from the attributes needed to control speech software. The best microphone for controlling speech software will be different for different user groups. Factors such as noise in the environment will affect your purchasing decision. In addition, telephony plays a role in making a purchasing decision for controlling speech software, as many users will want to have the ability to make telephone calls through their PC along with the ability for command-and-control interaction.

Technical Categories

Transducers: These are devices that change one form of energy into another form of energy. A microphone is a transducer that changes an acoustic signal into an electrical signal. There are three classifications of microphones: dynamic, ribbon, and condenser. They are distinguished by how they change sound into electricity.

- A dynamic microphone uses a wire coil and diaphragm suspended inside a magnetic field. The coil vibrates in

DSP on the WWW

Computer processing of speech is based on theories of digital signal processing (DSP). For information on digital signal processing techniques, go to the DSP home page on the World Wide Web: http://tjev.tel.etf.hr/josip/DSP/sigproc.html

the magnetic field when sound waves move the diaphragm. This creates an electrical signal that mirrors the sound wave.

- A ribbon microphone uses a metal ribbon suspended inside the magnetic field. When sound moves the ribbon, it creates the electrical signal.

- In a condenser microphone, sometimes called a capacitor microphone, a conductive diaphragm and metal plate are used together and charged with static electricity. When sound moves the diaphragm it changes the electrical wave so that it mirrors the shape of the sound wave. Because it is charged with electricity, it needs power to operate, either a battery or phantom power supply of DC electricity.

Each transducer type has certain attributes. For example, condenser microphones have very quick response times. Dynamic microphones can manage high amplitudes. However, each model has individual traits that are more of a factor than just the transducer type.

Polarity: Another distinguishing characteristic of a microphone is its *polarity.* The polarity of a microphone is the description of how it was designed to sense sound coming from different directions, as shown in Figure 7.1. There are three categories of polarity: omnidirectional, bidirectional, and unidirectional.

- An omnidirectional microphone responds to sound from all directions. It has the best general sensitivity to sound of all polarities. It has a low sensitivity to explosive voice sounds but will sense much ambient noise. This type of microphone is a good choice for use with a desktop computer where the user may be "roaming" the room and isn't guaranteed to be sitting directly in front of the microphone.

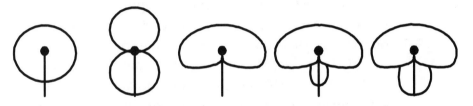

Omndirectional   Bidirectional   Cardioid   Supercardioid   Hypercardioid

Figure 7.1 Polar patterns of microphones.

- A bidirectional microphone responds to sounds from two directions, in front of and behind the microphone. It is rarely used in controlling speech-based software, but may be a candidate for recording human voice, depending on the situation.

- A unidirectional microphone responds primarily to sound from a single direction, directly in front of the microphone. There are three kinds of unidirectional microphones: cardioid, supercardioid, and hypercardioid. They differ in the pattern of polarity of their sensitivity. Some are intended to pick up more sound information from the back or sides. Unidirectional microphones are most commonly purchased by users with heavy dictation needs and headset style microphones.

Condenser and dynamic microphones are typically found in omnidirectional or unidirectional polarity. Some condenser microphones even have selectable polarity. Ribbon microphones are usually found in either bidirectional or hypercardioid polarity.

Stylistic Categories

The different technical types of microphones can be found in various styles that determine the placement of the microphone. A well-placed microphone can have a major impact on recognition accuracy.

A well-placed microphone can have a major impact on recognition accuracy.

Microphones that are built into a computer or monitor work well for commands, but not particularly well for dictation because they are far from the speaker and sensitive to noise. Microphones built into a computer keyboard are particularly poor for interacting with speech software and do not work well for either commands or dictation.

A clip-on microphone attaches to the user's shirt or jacket. They work better for dictation than microphones built into computer hardware, but are not as effective as desktop microphones. Sometimes the cords for these microphones can be a nuisance.

Headset microphones are worn on the head and typically have a swivel, called a boom, that allows the user to adjust the position of the microphone. They are ideal for speech recognition tasks because the boom is close to the user's mouth. They are also not very sensitive to background noise. They can be particularly usable for call center applications or other scenarios where combining the headset microphone with an earpiece eliminates the need for external speakers. However, like a clip-on microphone, the cord can be a nuisance.

Desktop microphones are a good compromise for general purpose computing. Although they can pick up ambient noise, they do not interfere with a user's body movement because the cord sits on the desktop.

There are additional factors that should be considered when purchasing a microphone. Like sound cards, microphones have specifications for frequency response and signal-to-noise ratio. Also, there are now several options for connectivity, including connecting to the soundcard microphone jack, USB port, or even a wireless connection.

> **I Like Mike**
>
> For information on the World Wide Web about microphones, start with these Web sites:
>
> http://microsoft.com/iit/documentation/mikes.htm
>
> www.microphones.com/

Manufacturers

There are many microphone manufacturers; however, not all are acceptable for use with personal computers. The microphones listed in Table 7.1 are recommend by IBM for use with ViaVoice and should be acceptable for almost any speech software interface. Consider usage conditions before making a purchasing decision or recommendation.

Manufacturer	Web Address	Microphone Model
Andrea Electronics	www.andreaelectronics.com	ANC-100
		ANC-200
		ANC-300
		ANC-500
		ANC-600
		ANC-700
		NC-8
		NC-12
		NC-50
		NC50u
		NC-60

continues

continued

Manufacturer	Web Address	Microphone Model
		NC-61
		NC-80u
Knowles Electronics	www.knowlesinc.com www.emkayproducts.com/	VR-3264
		VR-3185
		VR-3310
Labtec	www.labtec.com	LVA 8420L
Philips	www.speechmike.philips.com/	SpeechMike
Plantronics, Inc.	www.plantronics.com	CAT51VR
Telex Communications	www.telex.com	Nomad 300270
		Verba Pro – Dictate
		Verba Pro – Voice
VXI Corporation	www.vxicorp.com/	Parrott4TR

Table 7.1 Recommended Microphones for Speech Interaction

Speakers

Unless you are using a headphone to listen to the audio output from your computer, you will need speakers. Audio speakers for PCs are different than audio speakers for your home stereo. While they are smaller, that doesn't mean the sound quality is necessarily less. Some of today's PC-based sound systems produce the equivalent quality of sophisticated home stereo systems. Many PC vendors include a subwoofer as part of their standard computer package. From a technical standpoint, there are several differences. First, computer speakers necessarily contain their own amplifier. Therefore, they are generally known as "powered speakers." This eliminates the need for them to draw power from the computer. Second, they are shielded. This is important because otherwise they could interfere with your computer by disrupting performance or harming data. This is because speakers include magnets in their casing. Magnets and computers are a bad combination. A well-placed magnet can quickly destroy data. Generally, the larger the speakers, the better the sound response. Most computer speakers are comparable in terms of the quality of treble, or high pitched, sounds. However, for bass sounds the size of the speaker is important. The larger the speaker, the more clear and powerful the bass. This is why subwoofers are included. However, this is necessary only for gaming and music. Speech will sound fine from standard speakers as small as three inches in diameter.

Speaker design is an important issue in making a purchasing decision. Aesthetics are a subjective and individual choice, but from a human factors standpoint the size and shape of speakers can affect their placement. This is an issue that affects usability. If a user has badly-placed speakers, that will interfere with the auditory channel. Look for ergonomically acceptable designs that will fit well in your particular workspace.

From a human factors standpoint the size and shape of speakers can affect their placement.

Voice Cards and Modems

Using a computer for telephony requires either a modem or a voice card. In most consumer systems, a standard modem will allow for telephony integration. This allows a user to send and receive voice messages via telephone lines through the computer. A duplexing modem allows a user to send and receive simultaneously. Without this, each party must "wait their turn" to communicate. See Figure 7.2 for a computer telephony application.

Figure 7.2 An example of a computer telephony application.

Many speech development tools can integrate with voice modems. For example, Microsoft's device drivers support the following telephonic functionality:

- Wave playback and record to/from the phone line
- Wave playback and record to/from the handset
- Speakerphone capability
- Caller ID
- Distinctive ringing
- Call forwarding
- Operator application, which assists in determining the media mode of an incoming call (for example, voice or fax)

(Source: www.microsoft.com/DDK/DDKdocs/win98ddk/)

Such functionality in multi-modal applications presents interesting design challenges. There are many usability issues to address when user tasks include balancing keyboard/mouse input with voice input while responding to voice and visual output (for example, Microsoft NetMeeting, shown in Figure 7.3). A thorough task analysis is required to create effective design solutions in these instances. Such design (and technical) issues can be particularly challenging when integrating command-and-control with telephony functions.

A voice card is an expansion card that processes telephone calls, typically up to four lines. Computers with one or more voice cards are sometimes called voice response units, or VRUs, because they can respond to phone calls with prerecorded voice messages. These types of systems are usually found in call center environments where robust computer telephony integration (CTI) is important.

Figure 7.3 Microsoft NetMeeting.

Computer Telephony Integration

For more information about CTI, refer to the following sources:

- *PC Telephony,* by Bob Edgar, published by Flatiron Publishing, New York.
- *Voice and Data Communications Handbook,* by Regis Bates and Donald Gregory, published by McGraw-Hill, New York.
- *Computer Telephony Magazine* (www.computertelephony.com)

Free Long Distance

The age of Internet telephony is here. You can now use the Internet to make long distance phone calls with your PC for free. There's one catch: be prepared to watch a lot of advertisements while you talk. Selling advertising is how companies can offer the free service and the software.

Information Devices

"Nowadays, a computer screen can be anything, from a drive-in screen to a wrist watch."

Tim Berners-Lee, credited as inventor of the World Wide Web

In addition to using speech synthesis, speech recognition, and telephony with PCs, these technologies are being used in other information devices and appliances such as personal digital assistants, auto navigation systems, telephone answering machines, and other consumer and industrial electronics products. The following are examples of "cutting edge" information devices that employ speech technology:

- NeoPoint is a wireless digital mobile phone and personal digital assistant. In addition to the digital phone features, it has an address book, calendar, Web browser, alarm clock, and pager. It can dock with a PC and interacts with speech commands.

- The Speech Interface Group at MIT Media Laboratory has developed *Nomadic Radio*, a "wearable" audio messaging system. While that may sound like an ordinary pager, its actually more than that. The system uses a neckset casing by Nortel to house a Libretto 100 mini-portable PC driven by a pure auditory interface. Using wireless telephony, users can check e-mail, voicemail, and news broadcasts, and interact with their address book and to-do lists.

- A Florida company called Computer Voice Technology, Inc. sells a speaker-independent, natural language system called Hal2000 that lets users control most home electronic systems via speech commands through a telephone or microphone connected to a PC. Controllable systems include lights, security, heating and cooling, telephone, home theater, and appliances.

- The Microsoft Speech Research Group has a demonstration project called MiPad, which is a handheld PC partially commanded by speech. It includes functionality such as Web browsing, e-mail, and cellular telephone. It also acts as a control panel for other electronic appliances in an "Easy Living" environment.

- Olympus, Norcom, and others are marketing digital voice recorders that integrate with PCs. Users speak into a handheld recorder and later import their correspondence into a speech-commanded word processor for automatic dictation. Some of these devices even come bundled with the premiere speech recognition suites.

● Philips is working on applications of speech technology beyond their personal computing software and telephony solutions. Such applications include programming your VCR, selecting television channels, and brewing a pot of coffee via voice command!

Summary

Effective interface designers have many considerations when creating a new design. The considerations include stylistic, social, and technical issues that place constraints on and afford opportunities for design solutions. By understanding the limitations and capabilities of speech-related computer hardware, an interface designer can develop an appropriate design as well as work more efficiently with developers who are more intimate with hardware issues. As a design team, you then have the ability to create elegant design solutions for real-world problems. The types of business problems currently being addressed by speech interface design teams is the topic of our next chapter.

Application of Speech Technology

Tool: Something regarded as necessary to the carrying out of one's occupation or profession.
The American Heritage Talking Dictionary

At their best, computers and electronic devices can enhance our lives by providing a mechanism for entertainment, education, and communication. Fundamentally, though, computer technology and speech technology are simply tools. Most user interface designers are engaged in building tools to make our businesses more productive and efficient. This chapter provides descriptions of current and near-future applications of speech technology.

Interactive Voice Response

The earliest uses of speech technology in business were *interactive voice response systems* (IVRs). We have all been talking to computers via the telephone. In some cases we have gotten used to it (requests for our credit card number when we call to check our balance owed), and in other cases, such as directory assistance, we may not even yet realize that we are speaking with a computer. Although many IVR systems are still recorded messages, more and more use speech technology to interpret what you are saying as well as synthesizing speech back to you. A lot of the research on speech technology, menus, and prompting comes from this work on IVRs. As the synthesized voices become more human-like, the acceptance of IVR increases.

Medical

One of the vertical markets targeted for speech technology is the medical market. Doctors have been using traditional dictation devices for years. Doctors are highly paid, and their time is at a premium. They are on the move physically from room to room, floor to floor, ward to ward, or building to building. Their work often requires hands-free use. For all of these reasons, doctors have been using dictation. Speech technology is just a new device to meet their dictation needs.

Speech technology has advantages over regular tape dictation because tape dictation has to be transcribed from tape to a computer. Speech recognition technology eliminates that transcription step, saving time and reducing errors. Other health care practitioners, such as nurses, specialists, or the primary care physician, can receive information faster to act on treatment plans.

Speech recognition technology eliminates that transcription step, saving time and reducing errors.

Besides dictation, speech technology allows doctors to listen to patient records rather than having to read them. Often doctors need an eyes-free environment as well as hands-free. Speech synthesis allows the doctors to listen and look at the same time.

Legal

Lawyers are another niche market for speech applications. They are also pressed for time. Their work is language-intensive, writing long documents, reports, and briefs. By dictating these materials rather than typing them, they are able to speed their work. Or, if they have been using traditional dictation systems, they, like the doctors, can eliminate the transcription step.

Business

Unlike doctors or lawyers, many business executives do not have as specialized a vocabulary. This means that speech technology systems for this group must be able to handle a wide vocabulary. The applications for this group have been less successful so far than the specialized markets. As the technology improves, the general business market should grow. By using speech technology rather than typing at a keyboard, the business executive does not have to be an expert touch typist and can eliminate transcribing through dictation. In an office environment, dictation systems allow the executive to wander around the room, search for information in files, and shuffle papers, all while dictating reports or memos.

Commercial/Warehouse

Much of the press that speech technology receives these days is for continuous recognition dictation systems, like those described so far. But an even older use of speech technology is command-and-control systems used in factories and warehouses.

Interview with S. Ahmed Reza

Vice President

Speech Recognition-based Systems

Speech Interface Design, Inc.

S. Ahmed Reza is vice president at Speech Interface Design, Inc., in Pittsburgh, Pennsylvania. Mr. Reza has been involved with industrial data collection for the past 15 years, and speech recognition-based systems for the past 10 years. In the following interview he talks about his successes and challenges.

Tell me about your work and your company.

Speech Interface Design has been around since 1993. We're a provider of complete speech solutions for industrial, commercial, warehousing, and other business applications.

I categorize the speech market in four categories:

- dictation, which includes medical and legal
- command-and-control, where you command your cursor to go up, down, or backward, and read back to you

- telephony, where you call AT&T universal card services, for example, and they ask you to speak your 16-digit card number

- our market: industrial/commercial/warehousing

Our market is by far the least recognized or obvious market for speech. One of the parameters of speech is speaker-dependence—how dependent the system is on who the speaker is. The holy grail is, of course, speaker independence and a large vocabulary. Speaker-dependence is one parameter; vocabulary size is another parameter. The third parameter is ambient noise. In those three parameters, our applications are almost universally speaker-dependent, small vocabulary, and high ambient noise.

So in some ways you're the opposite of what the research groups are doing.

Exactly. This technology has been in place and working for almost 20 years. It's not anything new. Market acceptance has been slow to come, but this technology is stable, tried and true technology that has been in place for years.

Some of our applications might resemble command-and-control, but the rest of them are pure data collection, or data communication with the computer: data collection and speaking back to the person.

Can you give me a concrete example?

A good example is warehouse picking. A picker is standing in a warehouse for a large department chain. He's in a distribution center (DC), out in the warehouse, and, usually in a non-automated fashion, is given a list to pick from. His job is to pick products off the shelf for a particular store—a case of fabric softener, a case of this, a case of that, until a pallet-sized cube is filled. Then the picker takes that pallet to be wrapped and stamped in the doorway and it's sent off to that store. Picking works in waves. You have waves of pickers that all have assignments that all relate to one store or a set of stores. Before technology, someone would be handed a list and they would go pick one of these, seven of these, two of those. They would cross them off the list. That is obviously slower than an automated process and it's also error prone—your hands and eyes aren't free.

Our applications enable hands-free and eyes-free. They apply well to what were hands-busy, eyes-busy tasks. They are best suited to applications where someone is doing a task a significant part of the day. Because of the speaker dependence, they are not effective for a kiosk application or a telephony application where someone calls to enter a credit card number and they might never call again, but instead, tasks in which someone does the same thing for six to eight hours a day.

> Our applications enable hands-free and eyes-free

In the picking example, instead of a list, now the person is given instructions in the ear, go to aisle 6, shelf 5, bin 2, pick 4. He picks 4 and says, "4 picked" to confirm back to the unit. The unit directs him onto the next pick. He has nothing to carry and no device to look at. There are other process benefits. For example, he can read off a check digit on the shelf and the unit confirms in his ear—yes, you are in the right spot.

You can accrue great productivity benefits combining process improvement, enabled by the technology, and the technology itself, which allows the picker in a hands-free, eyes-free mode to perform his or her job. Distribution centers have seen productivity benefits of 15 percent to 30 percent doing this kind of picking over paper systems.

> Distribution centers have seen productivity benefits of 15% to 30%

The efficiency is coming from fewer errors and also greater speed?

That's right, over 30 percent compared to paper-based systems. Distribution centers are also using voice terminals to enhance productivity over handheld current radio frequency terminals. Traditional data collection terminals have buttons on them and laser scanners built in. There can be up to 15 percent improvements over even those. Voice can provide significant benefits in that application.

Another application is quality inspection. That's one of the big ones we address. Ceramics manufacturers, for example, have fire ware products like toilets and sinks coming down the line, and ceramics need to be individually inspected— every single one. Metal stamping can be statistically evaluated. You can measure two of out 100 and have pretty high assurance that the other 98 are good. But in ceramics, every single piece needs to be inspected.

Defects that are found in ceramics need to be logged because the casters who actually cast the ceramics are often paid based on yield. Now add that bar codes and other types of identification tags don't survive going through an 1800-degree kiln for 24 hours.

An inspector at the end of the line needs to inspect the product after it has come out of kiln, and then enter data from the product. The data has been stamped into the wet clay before it was fired, or painted on. Examples of data are a cast date, a caster number, a sprayer number, and a finisher number. Other automatic identification technologies such as bar codes aren't very useful in this process because they get obliterated going through the kiln.

The inspector has to inspect pieces as fast as one every 15 seconds or faster, and enter all the salient data about that piece in the cycle time that he or she has: model number, caster number, date it was cast, and some kind of evaluation. If there's a defect, they have to enter the defect and location of the defect.

So now we come to another driver for our technology, and that's qualitative data entry.

Quantitative is fairly simple. If you want to enter a weight, you can put a scale on the conveyer, but qualitative is tough to do:

"Clay crack, right side, bottom half."

With our systems you can speak it in. And the system asks,

"Any more defects?"

"No."

"Grade refire or scrap."

You have one person evaluating and entering data. Or one person reads it off to a tally person whose job it is to pick marks on a sheet, which then have to get entered.

Another good application is log processing—called log scaling. The profession is monitored and you have to be a certified log scaler. When logs go to a lumberyard, they have to be evaluated. The best way to do this with voice is to strap on a portable device and a headset, put a piece of chalk in one hand, and a scale stick in the other hand. They measure four parameters on every log. They give it a grade, a length which they eyeball, a diameter that they use their stick for, and any deduct information, for instance, the log is not perfectly straight, might have rot, or an unusually large number of knots. They go through every log and give it grade, length, diameter, and deduct. Grade, length, diameter, and deduct. That kind of thing is cumbersome manually. The piece of chalk is used to mark the log so they don't scale it again.

At the end you have 50 logs with chalk marks on them and the person says, "Done with this load." With radio frequency, the information is sent to the computer. By the time the person walks to the computer at the truck, there is a slip ready which has categorized grade, length, and diameter of every single log, and calculations on board footage, so the trucker instantly has a slip which has qualitative as well as quantitative data on what he delivered. This is perfect for voice because your hand is busy and your eyes are busy—for safety purposes you want to keep your eyes on the logs as they come off the truck. The process is natural to voice—you're looking at something, evaluating, speaking.

> This is perfect for voice because your hand is busy and your eyes are busy—for safety purposes you want to keep your eyes on the logs as they come off the truck.

A lot of these are custom systems?

Almost all of them are.

What are some of the special challenges because it's speech, and what are the challenges with acceptance in the organization?

Acceptance is one of the biggest challenges. People oftentimes are averse to taking the risk, even if they know that other people are using it. Speech is just starting to hit the mainstream market. It's past the early adopters for some industries. But one of the obstacles is convincing customers that it will work.

> Acceptance is one of the biggest challenges.

The second obstacle I have termed "voice overhead." I always evaluate applications based on whether they meet the criterion that they overcome voice overhead.

Explain voice overhead.

You can pick up a handheld bar code terminal and pretty much use it right away. There are some issues with training users in what to do when the screens come up, but you can build some of the training into the screens themselves. "Go to this location. Say 'yes' when you're there." There is less you need to do to teach someone how to push a button than there is teaching them to speak to the system. But in a non-visual application there is voice overhead. In our applications, everything is spoken through a headset—people walk around with portable terminals and headsets on, they're not in front of screens and there is no heads up display. Voice overhead involves understanding where you are in the program. It involves knowing how to speak so the computer recognizes you, knowing what options are available to you, and knowing how to control your device, start it, stop it, and turn it on. It's a different paradigm than a handheld terminal.

Number one in voice overhead is the voice training. All of our systems are speaker-dependent. That means anyone using our system has to spend 15 to 30 minutes training on the system one time. That's part of the overhead.

The second thing they have to do is understand how to speak so the system recognizes them—in a relatively consistent tone, and consistent with the training. Every word that they would say is trained in our applications. Our applications are typically 1000 words in vocabulary and well-designed ones are under 100 words. When you have things like defects you have ten digits, 26 alphas, a few dozen defects, plus asking for help.

> Our applications are typically 1000 words in vocabulary and well-designed ones are under 100 words.

But you must be getting a reduction in errors.

Yes, first-time recognition accuracy is above 99 percent. And that's really required, because if you have someone doing this all day long they're not going to put up with errors on a regular basis. The dictation engines have accuracy rates of 95 to 98 percent. Is that what you've found?

First-time recognition accuracy is above 99 percent.

They don't seem to do that well with me, although they're supposed to.

Those applications are not robust enough for what we do.

Are there other challenges with voice overhead?

User training. There is an intimidation factor. People are not looking at anything, so they don't know what to do. When you give them commands like Terminal Help, Terminal Backup, Terminal Where Am I, sometimes they're still intimidated about what to do.

They don't have a context.

Right. They don't have a context about why they're saying, "Terminal Help" rather than just "Help."

The way we've solved that is heavy training and heavy onsite presence during start-up. That makes up for these issues if you're there to help train.

What other challenges? What about technology?

When people think of voice-activated or speech recognition, they think of HAL from *2001: A Space Odyssey*. So the expectation versus the state of current technology is very different.

Technology is sometimes a challenge. Sometimes the recognition performance is not as good as it needs to be. We often don't accept projects because of this. A challenge is reality versus user expectation. When people think of voice-activated or speech recognition, they think of HAL from *2001: A Space Odyssey*. So the expectation versus the state of current technology is very different.

Another challenge is price/performance. Almost all of these systems are cost justified based on labor savings, accuracy, and a better process. Because the technology is still relatively expensive—$5000 to $7000 a seat—it's sometimes hard to put voice systems in.

More expensive than what?

More expensive than doing it another way. And that's just for the system. The initial programming can run up to $25,000 for the site. This is compared to having that person sit there and tally what the other person is saying. Luckily this is a tight labor market now, so freeing up that one person to do something else in the organization is a much more urgent need. You have a two-person task that can be turned into a one-person task.

How are the programming tools for what you are trying to do?

You have to understand the recognizers' capabilities and limitations. We develop our own software tools. Working with the client's software tools can be more difficult.

Are you fitting in with software they already have?

Most of the time we fit in with what they have.

So it depends on how good that is.

Right. We interface to their database. Sometimes we write a completely new application, but most of the time we interface to something they have already.

How did you get into this? What were you doing before, and what got you excited about speech?

Before, I was in the bar code field. Around 1990 I joined a manufacturer of industrial voice terminals as a field engineer and I designed and implemented systems for five years there.

What is the future for your industrial/commercial/ warehouse applications?

I think the future will be relatively aggressive growth over the next few years. Now companies are starting to realize the benefits of enabling their workers with speech recognition technology. You've probably heard Peter Foster speak of it as "the ever-receding impending boom." It's constantly in the future. There are probably 10 million PCs out there that have been factory preloaded with some form of speech recognition technology. Very little is used. There are very few killer apps that you would want to use voice for. In general, there's very little that isn't easier to do with a mouse. Our applications, on the other hand, actually pay dividends, you actually get a return on investment, typically 12 months or less. You can take that to the bank. The price points are coming down slowly. That's why I say moderately aggressive growth.

So you've seen some changes in the last year.

Yes, in the last year I've seen a lot more people get excited about applications, specifically warehouse picking. That market is definitely growing. But that is a specialized niche market.

Do you get frustrated by all the press and excitement that gets generated by the other types of speech applications?

I get frustrated when the attention is negative. Most people assume that speech is not ready yet. That has nothing to do with the industrial markets we work that have been working for 20 years. I get frustrated by the lack of market distinction. The telephony applications work relatively well, too. You can't make blanket statements about the industry. There are definite differences and we have

There are very few killer apps that you would want to use voice for.

We have applications that work extremely well that have worked well for years.

applications that work extremely well that have worked well for years.

If you could give some words of wisdom or advice to programmers or interface designers or project managers who are just starting to get into the field of speech technology, what would you say?

Work from an experience base. Learn about speech applications fully and test and test and test before you implement. Because speech applications are such a paradigm shift compared to keyboards, people will be very willing to can it and say, "It didn't work," and they don't really care what the issues are. If a word was not available, the programmer would say, "We'll throw the word in," but the user says, "It didn't understand me saying 'enter.'" You can't explain to the user why the system doesn't understand.

> Test and test and test before you implement.

It's critical that a speech application works right the first time. If there is something about it that is not intuitive or people don't understand what they are supposed to say, people are very quick to say, "It doesn't work. I want to go back to the old way." It's critical that a speech application work right the first time.

> It's critical that a speech application work right the first time.

Universal Access

Speech technology provides many people access to information or use of computers who may otherwise have little or no access. Using text-to-speech software, people who are visually impaired or have reading problems can have their computer screen or Web page read to them. People who cannot effectively use a keyboard and/or pointing device, such as a mouse, can use commands to

> Using text-to-speech software, people who are visually impaired or have reading problems can have their computer screen or Web page read to them.

control the computer. For example, a woman working for a corporate information services department developed carpal tunnel syndrome that left her hands irreparably damaged. Not wanting to accept disability status, she convinced her employer to allow her to use voice recognition software to perform her work. She has continued working in her position, spending several hours a day at the computer creating training materials and wordprocessing. Universal access is covered in more detail in Chapter 12.

Handheld Devices

Opinions vary on whether speech technology for handheld devices is the next market with a killer app or just a temporary fad. Those who think it's the next big market point to the increasing popularity of small devices, such as personal digital assistants, cell phones, and pagers. Although many of these devices have some sort of display, it's limited. If you want to communicate with the handheld device or the device is displaying information for you, the size of the screen imposes limitations. In addition, these devices are often used in a hands-busy, eyes-busy environment. People use these handheld devices while walking or driving. For these reasons, many believe that voice integrated into the handheld device is the wave of the future.

The opposing camp says this is a fad example. They cite unlikable scenarios (such as 50 people in a room all talking to their handheld devices), the lack of privacy, and the problems with environmental noise.

Toys and Education

Texas Instruments developed a children's toy called the Speak & Spell in the late 1970s. This toy would present spelling words to children by "sounding out" the word and waiting for the child to properly spell the word using keyboard input. It was an early and successful use of speech synthesis. The toy enjoyed high sales for over a decade without modification of the original design.

Toy manufacturers are researching numerous toys that have both speech recognition and speech synthesis capabilities. One factor inhibiting these applications is that most speech recognizers are calibrated for adult speakers. There is significant work ahead on recognition engines before these recognizers can handle children's speech sounds and patterns.

Most speech recognizers are calibrated for adult speakers.

In an education example, Swift Jewel publishes software called *Talking Typing Tutor*. The software is a CD-ROM-based tutorial that presents a series of keyboarding lessons. It uses speech synthesis to give users "real time" mentoring, such as telling them when to speed up or slow down during a lesson.

Automobile Applications

There seems to be no end to the activities we would like to conduct in our cars. We already talk on the phone, and now we can check our satellite position or even surf the Internet. Many of these automobile applications are similar to handheld devices in that they have limited screen space. But safety is an even greater issue. Whenever we take our eyes off the road or our hands off the steering wheel, we increase the likelihood of an accident. Speech technology will help in this eyes-busy, hands-busy environment by allowing us to listen and talk rather than use hands or eyes to operate devices.

"Voice-recognition technology will develop to the point where, if you're driving to an island you can just say, 'What's the ferry schedule?' to get oral answers from an in-car Web link."

Tim Berners-Lee, credited as the inventor of the World Wide Web

For example, years ago J.R. Davis at the Massachusetts Institute of Technology developed two applications—Direction Assistance and Backseat Driving—that used synthetic speech to give driving directions. Using the first application, drivers would enter an origin and a destination. The application would use synthesized speech to provide directions. The second application was the successor to the first and could automatically determine an origination location so that drivers would receive directions based on wherever they were at the time. Several commercial programs now provide even more robust functionality. They use global positioning technology combined with speech synthesis and speech recognition to allow drivers to interact with their automobiles.

Summary

Speech technology applications are coming into their own. With the exception of interactive voice response, most speech applications still are not in the mainstream, but advances in technology have made many of these applications almost ready for prime time.

Laws and Guidelines for Speech Interface Design

Part Three provides specific advice on how to improve the usability of speech applications, including:

Chapter 9: Laws of Interface Design. Describes 20 laws of human factors that apply to speech interfaces. The discussion of each law includes the human factors research behind it.

Chapter 10: Speech Guidelines. Provides specific guidelines for designing speech interfaces. These guidelines are based on the laws from Chapter 9, and contain the dos and don'ts to follow when designing speech applications.

Laws of Interface Design

"Welcome to another voice-mail adventure! To begin your journey, just press 1."

> **"The beginning of wisdom is to call things by their right names."**
> *Chinese proverb*

The study of human-computer interaction has been ongoing for the last half of the twentieth century. It has its roots in human factors and man-machine studies from the 1940s. In the last 20 years of the twentieth century, several practitioners and academics have postulated principles or laws to help organize the field of information. We compared the work done by Ben Shneiderman (1998) and Jakob Nielsen (1994), and added our contributions and that of Julie Nowicki from Optavia Corporation. From these sources we distilled the 20 Laws of Interface Design that are defined and discussed in this chapter. These laws form the basis of the specific guidelines we recommend in the next chapter. By understanding these basic laws about people and their interaction with computers, you will be better able to understand the reasoning behind the dos and don'ts of the next chapter. The laws are:

1. User Control
2. Human Limitations
3. Modal Integrity
4. Accommodation
5. Linguistic Clarity
6. Aesthetic Integrity

7. Simplicity

8. Predictability

9. Interpretation

10. Accuracy

11. Technical Clarity

12. Flexibility

13. Fulfillment

14. Cultural Propriety

15. Suitable Tempo

16. Consistency

17. User Support

18. Precision

19. Forgiveness

20. Responsiveness

Each law is defined and some background information on the human factors issues behind the law is presented. We discuss technology considerations as well as implications that the law has for interface design and usability engineering work on speech interfaces. At the end of the chapter we present an interview with Kate Dobroth from the American Institutes for Research who discusses the philosophies behind interface design laws and their implementation.

User Control

The first law of interface design is User Control: The interface will allow the user to perceive that they are in control and will allow appropriate control.

Human Factors

To be comfortable using a computer, users need to feel they are in control of the computer, and not the other way around. If users feel they are not in control, they may react emotionally. How this reaction plays out depends on the individual, but some common manifestations of a user feeling not in control can include anger, apathy, resentment, and confusion.

At the very least this will result in more errors, and at its worst, users may stop using the interface/application altogether if they feel they are not in control.

There is a difference, however, between *feeling* in control and *being* in control. For some actions, users actually need to be in control, but there are other times when the user may feel in control but not necessarily be in control. Users who feel in control can do the following:

● Predict what the computer will do next

● Take the next action they decide is appropriate

● Go back and fix problems they discover

● Do their work the way they want to, instead of changing their work to fit the way the computer wants them to do it

Technology Considerations and Implications

In a GUI application the computer is "only" a screen, and it is easier for the person to feel they are in control. But in a speech application where the computer is speaking, it is easier for the person to feel that the computer has as much control, or even more control than the user does. This feeling of loss of control is exacerbated when there are a lot of recognition errors by the computer. The computer may start directing the flow of the conversation to try and fix the recognition problem. This, however, results in the person feeling less and less in control.

It is important that the interface of speech applications give the user as much perceived control as possible. Features such as barge-in, where the user can interrupt the computer's speech, are critical. The area of error handling, especially during speech recognition, is also critical if the user is to feel in control.

Human Limitations

The second law is Human Limitations: The interface will not overload the user's cognitive, visual, auditory, tactile, or motor limits.

Human Factors

Humans have cognitive, visual, auditory, tactile, and motor limits on the quantity and quality of information that they can process. For an interface to be easy to use, it cannot overload any of these limits.

Memory

People can remember between five to nine things for about 20 seconds in their working or short-term memory. To remember more than that, the information must be chunked in some way, so that they are required to remember less, or the information must be semantically coded or given a meaning. For example, this string

eibjwlfikqqk

is seen as 12 separate letters because it has no meaning. But this string

dogcatcowpig

is read as four chunks or four separate words. The latter is easier to remember than the first because there are only four items to remember or memorize. It is also easier to remember because it is semantically coded—the letters create meaning by being the names of animals (Sanders and McCormick, 1993, 67).

The easiest information to remember has three to four chunks with three to four items per chunk.

The easiest information to remember has three to four chunks with three to four items per chunk. Sanders and McCormick (1993, 67) discuss the research of G. Miller. His article, originally published in 1956, is "The Magical Number Seven, Plus or Minus Two" (Miller, 1956). Miller found that people can only handle seven plus or minus two pieces of information at a time, or five to nine items. This seems to be a fairly universal phenomenon that holds true for visual, auditory, cognitive, decision making, and memory processes.

Decision Making

Human decision making is not a perfect art. Sanders and McCormick (1993, 68-69) discuss research by Wickens (Wickens, 1984) on decision making. According to Wickens' research, decision making is flawed in the following ways:

- People give early evidence too much weight. If they receive one piece of information early, they believe it over what they hear later.

- People do not extract as much information out of the data they have.

- People are more sure of their decision as they get more information. Just having a lot of information makes people feel they are making the right decision, regardless of the quality of the information.

- People seek more information than they can actually handle or extract data from. They will continue to seek more, even when they have enough information to make a decision.

- People treat all the information they have as equally reliable, even when common sense would normally cause them to question data from some sources as not reliable.

- People can only deal with three or four hypotheses at a time. If they have more alternatives, they will discard some of them and only consider three to four.

- People focus only on a few attributes. Rather than consider all the relevant material, people focus on only a few aspects they deem critical. Complicated issues are therefore reduced to overly simplified ones.

- People seek information that confirms a decision they have already made. People tend to make up their minds and then try to find data that matches what they have decided.

Visual

If the interface has a visual component, then you must consider limitations on human visual processing. For example:

- People do not read everything on a screen, page, or window.

- People will not be able to find information if it is on a screen that is too full and cluttered.

- People get distracted easily with visual stimuli such as graphics, animations, or too much information.

- People have trouble reading fonts that are too small, or of too many different styles or sizes.

Motor

If the interface has a motor component, then you must consider limitations on human motor processing. For example:

- People cannot hit targets that are too small on the screen (such as a very small arrow for a drop down list box). Fitts Law ($MT = a + b \log_2 (2D/W)$ defines a formula for computing how large a target must be for a user to hit it reliably. D represents the distance of movement from the start to the target center; W is the width of the target; and a and b are constants based on the type of movement (arm, wrist, finger) (Sanders and McCormick, 1993, 291-292).
- People may have difficulty double clicking.
- People do not always realize they can or should drag and drop.
- People do not like to be constantly switching between a mouse and a keyboard.
- People must have time to get used to pointing devices such as trackballs and mice.

Depending on the task, some pointing devices are better than others. Touch screens and light pens are fastest. Mouse, trackball, and tablet come next. A mouse is a little faster than a trackball, but trackballs are a little more accurate.

People have more trouble remembering messages spoken in synthesized speech than in natural speech.

Speech

People have more trouble remembering messages spoken in synthesized speech than in natural speech (Sanders and McCormick, 1993, 216). Listening to synthesized speech requires more processing capacity than listening to natural speech. Synthesized speech is harder for humans to encode. This extra difficulty disrupts working memory and the transfer of information to long-term memory. However, once encoded, synthesized speech is stored as efficiently as natural speech.

Technology Considerations and Implications

Interfaces make constant demands on human capabilities. GUIs require users to view information on the computer screen, interpret and decide on the information, make judgments, remember material, and take motor actions. Physical devices, such as telephones or voice recorders, require users to view information on buttons, possibly listen to messages and sounds, make judgments and remember material, and take motor actions. Speech interfaces require users to listen, make decisions and judgments, remember information, and respond. In addition, if the interface is multi-modal, it also requires users to view and interpret information on the screen and perhaps take motor actions.

If the interface has a visual component, you must minimize the number of unique margins on the screen so it is uncluttered. Keep only critical information on the screen, and minimize the amount of eye movement.

If the interface has a motor component, you must be sure you are using an appropriate device. Do not force users to switch back and forth from keyboard to mouse.

For the speech part of the interface, use natural speech as much as possible. Slow down the speed of synthesized speech to help the encoding process.

Use natural speech as much as possible. Slow down the speed of synthesized speech to help the encoding process.

In this book we will assume that users are trying to complete a task that involves work, and that the goal is to reduce the demands.

We assume we should minimize the demands we make of users. But this is not always the case. For instance, a game played on the computer is an interface in which one or more of the limitations has been challenged. Simulation games purposely raise the cognitive demands. Action computer games purposely raise several demands, such as visual, cognitive, and motor. For our purposes in this book, however, we will assume that users are trying to complete a task that involves work, and that the goal is to reduce the demands. This means that we must break decision making into small steps, pick the best modality or modalities for the task at hand, and minimize the memory demands of the interface. We must provide only the information that is needed, not overwhelm the user with too much information. Specifically, for speech interfaces this means making sure we use speech where it is appropriate, and watch out specifically for memory issues. In a speech-only interface, the memory limits are fairly inflexible and must be adhered to.

People do not remember long complex auditory messages.

The memory issues surrounding auditory interfaces are critical. Interface designers need to keep in mind that people do not remember long complex auditory messages. Although the ability to replay or hear a message again may be somewhat useful, it is a feature that in practice is not used very often. If long or complex information needs to be remembered, you may need to use multiple modes.

Modal Integrity

The third law, Modal Integrity, states: The interface will fit individual tasks within whatever modality is being used: auditory, visual, or motor/kinesthetic.

Human Factors

Some tasks are best performed using speech, others using vision, or others with motor/kinesthetic or tactile modes. Still others are best performed using multiple modes (multi-modal).

In research done by Wickens (1984), subjects performed one of two tasks, verbal or spatial. The type of input and output was varied: input for some subjects was auditory and for others was visual. Output was either spoken or manual. For verbal tasks, performance was best with auditory input and spoken output. Performance was worse with visual input and manual output. For spatial tasks, performance was best with visual input and manual output. It was worse with auditory input and spoken output.

Robert Bailey (1982, 44) notes that people can perform multiple tasks in multiple modes *if* they have a high skill level in both activities. Sanders and McCormick (1993, 169) provide information on the advantages and disadvantages of presenting information in a visual mode versus an auditory mode. The auditory mode is especially effective when

People can perform multiple tasks in multiple modes *if* they have a high skill level in both activities.

- information is short and simple.

- information is needed immediately, but not later on (does not have to be remembered).

- information is temporal in nature (refers to events over time).

- the message is a critical warning.

- a verbal response is required.

- the visual system of the person is already overextended.

- the environment is not conducive to a visual display (for example, the lighting is insufficient).

- the person needs to stay "dark adapted" (that is, it is important that light levels stay low).

- the person needs to be moving continually.

The visual modality is especially effective when

- information is complex and long.

- information needs to be remembered.

- the information deals with spatial relationships; for instance, maps.

- the person's audition is overextended.

- the environment is noisy, or creating noise in the environment is not acceptable.

The average time it takes a person to hear a signal and make a simple response is 150 milliseconds.

Bailey (1982, 41) notes that the average time it takes a person to hear a signal and make a simple response is 150 milliseconds. The average time it takes a person to see a signal and make a simple response is 200 milliseconds. The auditory mode can therefore be faster.

Technology Considerations and Implications

Many tasks are best suited to a multi-modal interface. Some tasks are especially suited to a motor modality; for example, scrolling, clicking, or choosing from a list. In a multi-modal interface, users can specify actions and objects that are visible by saying them. They can use a pointing device, such as a mouse, while speaking or viewing information online.

It is important to use the best mode for the task at hand. Where possible, use multiple modes to decrease any inherent disadvantages of one mode, and increase the overall strength of the interface. In a multi-modal interface, for example, users could view a map, use a pointing device to draw an area on the map, and then issue a spoken command.

If a multi-modal interface is not possible, then accommodations must be made for deficiencies in the match between the task and modality. For example, a hand-held device without a screen or monitor that requires users to speak commands will be hard to use in a noisy environment. Interface designers must pay attention to which areas of the interface are not a good match, and ameliorate the problems as much as possible.

If you use multiple modes and multi-tasking, be sure the users are proficient in each mode before asking them to combine modes. For example, do not expect users who have never used a speech interface before *and* have never used a pointing device, such as a mouse, to be able to use a multi-modal interface that uses speech recognition and pointing simultaneously.

Accommodation

Accommodation, the fourth law, states: The interface will fit the way each user group works and thinks.

Human Factors

The assumption behind this law is that the system should accommodate itself to the user, not the other way around. To accommodate specific user groups, design the interface so that it matches the way users want to do their work.

Design the interface so that it matches the way users want to do their work.

Technology Considerations and Implications

Documenting how users currently do their work (current workflow) and then deciding on and documenting what tasks the user will do with the new system and how they will do them (future workflow) are critical to accommodating the interface to the users.

Linguistic Clarity

The fifth law of interface design is Linguistic Clarity: The interface will communicate as efficiently as possible.

Human Factors

Users must understand an interface before they can use it. And in order for them to understand the interface, it must be clear. In this law we are concerned with the clarity of the language itself (as opposed to clarity on a monitor, or clarity in the sense of no errors).

For the interface to be linguistically clear, it must provide context and speak in the user's terminology.

Context

Information without context cannot easily be assimilated and stored in long-term memory.

People need context to process information. Information without context cannot easily be assimilated and stored in long-term memory. Take for example, this paragraph:

Equipment Instructions:

First, sort the items into like categories. Sorting by color is common, but you can also use other characteristics, such as texture or type of handling needed. Once you have sorted the items, you are ready to use the equipment. You want to process each category from the sorting separately.

It is hard to understand what these instructions are about, because you have no context. Now read this paragraph.

Using Your New Washing Machine:

First, sort the items into like categories. Sorting by color is common, but you can also use other characteristics, such as texture or type of handling needed. Once you have sorted the items, you are ready to use the equipment. You want to process each category from the sorting separately.

The text is the same, but by adding a clear title we have added context and made the information easier to understand.

People need context when they are presented with information in any modality. In speech applications, context is often lost if users only hear information without also viewing it. It may be hard to "place" the information relative to other information received.

> In speech applications, context is often lost if users only hear information without also viewing it.

Terminology

Using terms and labels that users will understand is not just a "nicety" that you build in—it is a necessity. It takes time to analyze what the terms are that a particular user group uses in a certain domain. It is necessary if you are to be linguistically clear.

Technology Considerations and Implications

Speech interfaces often suffer from the lack of context. Spoken words presented temporally have less context than labels, terms, or words on a screen. If users lack this kind of terminology match and context, they will feel lost and confused while using the interface.

In any interface it is important to use understandable terms and to provide context. This is especially true for speech interfaces. Careful work will need to be done during analysis to ensure that the correct terms are being used, and careful work will need to be done during detailed design to make sure that enough context is built in.

Aesthetic Integrity

Aesthetic Integrity is the sixth law and it reads: The interface will have an attractive and appropriate design.

Human Factors

In usability engineering work, we often focus on the performance aspects of an interface. Will it be easy to learn and use? Will people be able to get their work done efficiently? There is another aspect that can affect acceptability: preference. You can measure how well humans perform a set of tasks using an interface, but this does not mean that you have measured how well they liked performing the task with that interface.

It is not possible to totally separate human performance from preference.

Humans have emotional responses to most events. It is not possible to totally separate human performance from preference. To complicate matters, people often have preferences that go directly against performance data. In our experience, users often "prefer" poor interface designs that actually slow down their work, but are familiar.

The goal in interface design and usability engineering is to design an interface that maximizes both performance and preference, although this is not always possible.

Aesthetic Integrity refers to the issue of preference. For example, when users have completed their work, would they say they preferred using the interface over their previous method? Would they say that the experience was pleasant?

Aesthetic integrity is often tied to visual interfaces, GUIs, for example. Aesthetic integrity is important for all aspects of a multi-modal speech interface, but especially so with regard to the speech component. For example, Susan Boyce (1999) describes her research in which users expressed greatest satisfaction with a voice that was casual and used the first person ("I") compared to other combinations of casual/formal and "I" and "Not I". When asked to rate how satisfied they were with the speed of the system, their ratings reflected their overall satisfaction, and were less a reflection of how quickly they performed their tasks.

User preferences depend on the task. Research by Philip Cohen and Sharon Oviatt (1994) shows that pilots preferred to hear warnings with synthesized speech because it sounded different from other voices in the immediate environment. Normally people prefer natural voices, but in the special instances, such as a warning, they prefer the synthesized voice because it is different.

Pilots preferred to hear warnings with synthesized speech because it sounded different from other voices in the immediate environment.

Technology Considerations and Implications

If there is a visual component to the interface, then format and layout issues are important. You must also be aware of the general preferences for speech, such as pitch, pacing, and natural versus synthesized voice. If there is no visual component, then the sound of the system's voice will be the basis for the user's assessment of the aesthetics of the interface.

Chapter 10, Speech Guidelines, provides guidance on pacing, pitch, volume, and natural speech.

Simplicity

Simplicity, the seventh law, states: The interface will present elements simply.

Human Factors

The best tool is simple and transparent.

People use their computer as a tool to perform a task. The best tool is simple and transparent. Users should not have to figure out what the tool is and how to use it.

Technology Considerations and Implications

A simple interface takes more time to create than a complicated interface.

The essence of a simple interface is good design. The better the design, the simpler the interface will seem. A simple interface takes more time to create than a complicated interface. Beware of equating lots of features with complexity, or simplicity with too few. An interface that employs simplicity will do just what the user needs it to do and will do it easily. A simple interface is not "interface lite," but "interface right."

Predictability

The eighth law is Predictability: The interface will behave in a manner such that users can accurately predict what will happen next.

Human Factors

For users to predict how an interface will work, it must mesh well with the user's mental model.

When using an interface for the first time, people either have, or quickly create, a mental model of how the interface will work. This mental model may even exist before they start to use the interface. If they have heard or read that the new interface will be like using a tape recorder, for example, then they have the mental model of a tape recorder in place before even trying out the new interface.

People always have a mental model operating. The mental model they have may not match the conceptual model of the actual interface. If the interface is well designed, then the designers will have consciously chosen a conceptual model for the interface, after analyzing likely users and their mental models. When an interface is not consciously designed in this way, the conceptual model will not mesh well with the user's mental model.

People always have a mental model operating.

Users can and do change their mental model of a particular interface. Training can help them adjust their mental model. Their experiences with the product itself also helps to adjust their mental model.

Technology Considerations and Implications

Speech interfaces are particularly difficult to create a conceptual model for because they are usually temporal. If the interface is not multi-modal, then the information you present (for example, a menu of choices) "exists" for a short time—only long enough for it to be spoken by the computer. This adds to the challenge to convey enough information about the conceptual model.

If a user's mental model does not mesh well with the interface's conceptual model, the interface will be hard to use and learn.

Mental models are an important concept in interface design and usability engineering. If a user's mental model does not mesh well with the interface's conceptual model, the interface will be hard to use and learn. Designing and communicating a conceptual model that works well with the user's mental model are two important tasks of the interface designer and usability engineer.

Interpretation

The ninth law of interface design is Interpretation: The interface will make reasonable guesses about what the user is trying to do.

Human Factors

Users should not have to guess how a system works or how it will react to their input. The computer should be able to monitor user behavior and make a reasonable guess as to the action or speech the user is trying to apply.

Technology Considerations and Implications

One of the biggest challenges still confronting speech interfaces is that of accuracy. Even though technology has advanced, there are still significant errors in what the computer can recognize. In continuous speech recognition, a common error is computer misinterpretation of what the user says. The more closely the computer can interpret, the more usable the interface. In a discrete speech application, the types of errors are different. But there is still room for the interface to attempt an interpretation of the user's speech or actions based on context.

The more progress that is made in accuracy of speech interfaces, the easier the job will be on the interface. For now, however, the interface must take up the slack by being even more vigilant in interpreting user actions and speech.

Accuracy

Accuracy is the tenth law, which states: The interface will be free from errors.

Human Factors

Out of all the laws in this book, this one is the furthest from reality. There is no speech application on the market that can claim it is free from errors.

Technology Considerations and Implications

Errors in speech technology are rampant. That does not mean, however, that interface designers and usability engineers should either give up or refuse to work on speech applications because there will be errors. Until errors are significantly reduced through improved technology, it is the interface designer's job to minimize the impact of errors and make it as easy as possible for users to detect and correct errors.

Until errors are significantly reduced through improved technology, it is the interface designer's job to minimize the impact of errors and make it as easy as possible for users to detect and correct errors.

Technical Clarity

Law #11 is Technical Clarity: The interface will have the highest possible fidelity.

Human Factors

To use an interface effectively, users must be able to perceive the attributes of the interface clearly, whether that is a visual display, sound through speech, or buttons on a keypad.

Technology Considerations and Implications

Technical clarity refers to the level of quality or fidelity that portions of the interface carry. For example, a visual display with high clarity or fidelity will have a high resolution that allows users to read the text and view the graphics. Buttons on a device with technical clarity will be discernible and easily pressed. For a speech interface, technical clarity means that the sounds and the speech of the machine are of a high enough fidelity to be understood.

Flexibility

The twelfth law of Flexibility states: The interface will allow the user to adjust the design for custom use.

The goal of accommodation is to account for what 80 percent of the users need to do 80 percent of the time. Beyond this is flexibility so that you can take care of the other 20 percent.

Human Factors

In the law of accommodation we covered adjusting the interface to match the way users work. Flexibility involves letting users customize the interface for their own work. The goal of accommodation is to account for what 80 percent of the users need to do 80 percent of the time. Beyond this is flexibility so that you can take care of the other 20 percent.

Technology Considerations and Implications

Even if you design for what most people need most of the time, there are people and situations that have not been taken care of. Building in enough flexibility to take care of these situations means that you have built in ways to go beyond the 80 percent towards 90 or even 95 percent. It is unrealistic to assume you will be able to build in enough flexibility so that all people have all needs met, but you try to stretch that limit as far as it can go.

Examples of flexibility in speech interfaces include allowing barge-in so users can interrupt the system and take over the interaction, the ability to speak to a human at any time, and allowing users to customize menus.

Fulfillment

Fulfillment is law #13 and it states: The interface will provide a satisfying user experience.

Human Factors

Part of usability is user acceptance, and part of user acceptance is the experience of satisfaction. When users believe and feel that the system allows them to do their work in a productive, useful way, with a minimum of work and hassle, then users feel fulfilled and will rate the experience as satisfying. Candace Kamm of AT&T Labs, interviewed in Chapter 5, says that when speech interfaces have value added and when they are both useful and fun, that is when the technology is working best.

Technology Considerations and Implications

For an interface to provide fulfillment and add value, it must do three things. It must offer a better way to do a task than the current alternatives; it must match the way users do their work; and it must perform basic tasks efficiently and simply.

Cultural Propriety

The fourteenth law, Cultural Propriety, states: The interface will match the user's social customs and expectations.

Human Factors

Humans interact with their environment within broad contexts. As a person talks to another person, their conversations are within the context of the room, the building, the organization, the city, and the country they are in. In addition, there are social roles they may be playing; for example the role of boss, worker, expert, parent, or child. Human beings are social animals, and these larger contexts affect their behavior.

Users now expect that their computers will interact with them the way humans do.

Users now expect that their computers will interact with them the way humans do. Initially users did not expect computers to interact like humans. If the computer crunched the numbers correctly, people were happy. Improved technology and more sophisticated interfaces have led users to expect their computers to interact with them and converse with them as though they were people, not computers. Speech applications are at the heart of these expectations. Users may understand they are speaking with a computer and not a person, but that does not mean that they expect any less. They still expect to have a human-like conversation with the computer. This will only increase as speech applications become more sophisticated and more common. This "ups the ante" for interface designers and requires them to understand and know human conversation at a deeper level, and when and how to simulate that human quality in speech applications.

Users may understand they are speaking with a computer and not a person, but that does not mean that they expect any less.

Technology Considerations and Implications

Social issues affect user interaction with a computer on several levels. On one level, how users perceive the role of the computer affects how they behave with the computer. If they see the system as an intelligent assistant, their conversation will be less formal and more-open ended. If they see the system as a simple machine, their conversation with the machine will be more formal and terse.

On another level, you must be concerned about how a speech application may affect the relationship and conversation between people. For example, if an insurance salesperson is making a presentation to a client, what will happen when the salesperson starts talking or listening to a computer or a handheld device in the middle of the presentation? Will that seem like a rude interruption, as if another person has entered the conversation?

Beyond these individual issues, cultural and global issues must be taken into account. Terms or actions that are acceptable in one culture or language may not be acceptable in another. For example, certain hand gestures in interfaces, such as an icon with a thumbs-up sign, are common and acceptable in some cultures and offensive in others (Fernandes, 1995).

Suitable Tempo

Suitable Tempo, law #15, states: The interface will operate at a tempo suitable to the user.

Human Factors

If the pace of the conversation with the computer or the speed with which text is spoken is too slow, users become frustrated and try to speed up the interaction, which may result in more errors.

Because speech interfaces are temporal, with events occurring one after another, the issue of suitable tempo or pacing is important. If the pace of the conversation with the computer or the speed with which text is spoken is too slow, users become frustrated and try to speed up theinteraction, which may result in more errors. If, on the other hand, the pace of the interaction is too fast, then users may not understand what is being spoken or what they are supposed to act on.

Technology Considerations and Implications

Speech interfaces must be prototyped, iterated, and tested with real users to assure if the tempo or pacing is appropriate. It is hard to simulate small pieces of this. Since a particular user's path can differ from another's, it is necessary to test real people trying to do real tasks with the real system, not a low-fidelity prototype.

Consistency

The sixteenth law is Consistency: The interface will be consistent.

Human Factors

When an interface is inconsistent, users cannot predict
what will happen next or what their next action should be.
People need consistency in order to perceive the
underlying conceptual model, and to adjust their mental
model to better fit the conceptual model. If the interface is
consistent, this adjustment is more easily made.

People need consistency.

Technology Considerations and Implications

Consistency includes not only terminology, but the feel,
behaviors, and actions of the system itself, and the actions
required of the user.

For example, if the user has learned that "Go Forward" is a
valid command, the mental model would suggest that "Go
Back" is a corollary command. If, instead, you use
"Previous," you are being inconsistent and making it
harder for the user to create a mental model that allows
them to predict what to do next.

User Support

User Support is the seventeenth law of interface design:
The interface will provide additional assistance as needed
or requested.

Human Factors

Users expect some kind of support or assistance. In a
traditional human factors approach, this support—training,

help systems, or help desks—is part of the interface. Although people like to have support available when it is needed, they do not like to get help when they haven't asked for any.

Technology Considerations and Implications

Many speech applications are used on machines and in settings that are different from the usual desktop setting. This means that some of the traditional ways of providing support (help messages on a screen, user documentation, or calling a help desk) are unavailable or inappropriate. Most assistance must be built into the application, both in terms of increased design and usability, as well as prompts, cues, and error correction.

Precision

The eighteenth law is Precision, which states: The interface will allow the users to perform a task exactly.

Human Factors

Users want to know that when they perform a task, it will be done accurately and the results will be correct.

Technology Considerations and Implications

Precision will go awry for three reasons:

- There are errors in the underlying code.
- The user and the computer have different expectations of the definition of a task or its outcome.

- There are errors during the interaction, such as speech recognition errors that lessen precision.

The first item—errors in the underlying code—is not directly related to the interface; however, the second and third issues are related. They must be addressed during the design process to minimize their occurrence and the negative effect on precision.

Forgiveness

Forgiveness, the nineteenth law, is: The interface will make actions recoverable.

Human Factors

Examining forgiveness in a system means examining errors. Humans make mistakes as they are using machines. They make mistakes when they use any interface, and speech interfaces are no exception. In fact, speech interfaces have some of the highest error rates compared to other interfaces, such as GUIs, because of the characteristics and limitations of the technologies.

Sometimes mistakes happen because users do not understand what they are supposed to do. This may stem from actual user error. Often, however, errors happen because the interface is at fault—one or several of the other laws have been violated, making the interface hard to learn, understand, or use.

Sometimes mistakes happen because the user pushes a wrong button, or chooses something other than what they meant to choose. For example, the user may say "two" to a menu, when they really meant to say "three." The user

Speech interfaces have some of the highest error rates compared to other interfaces, such as GUIs, because of the characteristics and limitations of the technologies.

intended to say or do one thing, but actually said or did something else.

Technology Considerations and Implications

Although speech recognition technology and interfaces have improved greatly in the last 15 years, it is still common for users to experience insertion and substitution errors. We must assume that errors will occur, and therefore build mechanisms into the interface to handle the errors in as forgiving a way as possible. For some system errors (for example, the common speech recognition errors inherent in today's technology), the error is clearly the fault of the system. These errors we should try to correct with technology, and mitigate potential errors by designing an improved interface.

Sometimes it is hard to determine who caused an error. For example, if we know that users continually choose the wrong menu item, does this mean the users have not learned the menu structure, or is the interface at fault for not having a better menu structure? From a usability engineering point of view, we first assume it is an interface problem, until it is proven otherwise.

Assuming then that people are going to make mistakes, it is the interface designer's job to design the system to minimize the number of these mistakes.

Assumption #1

People will always make mistakes. If you need to design a fail-safe system—for instance, an interface for nuclear power plant operators—you must increase the design time and the training time. Requiring no errors doubles design time and doubles training time. Assume you will need to at

---

We must assume that errors will occur, and therefore build mechanisms into the interface to handle the errors in as forgiving a way as possible.

Requiring no errors doubles design time and doubles training time.

least double the design time, since you must do a thorough interface analysis, conceptual model, and design. Then you will need to iterate and re-iterate and test and re-test. In addition, you will need to train and test the users thoroughly to be sure the information has been learned. Even with additional design time and training time, you can assume that someone, some day, will make a mistake.

Assumption #2

It is the interface designer's job to minimize the number of errors users make. Even assuming that users will make mistakes, you should operate under the assumption that it is possible to reduce the number or errors. It is your job as an interface designer and usability engineer to minimize the number and severity of errors.

> It is your job as an interface designer and usability engineer to minimize the number and severity of errors.

Responsiveness

The final law, Responsiveness, is #20 and it says: The interface will inform users about the results of their actions and the interface's status.

Human Factors

Users need feedback on their actions and feedback on the system's actions. Feedback is especially important when users expect that they are having a "conversation" with the machine.

Technology Considerations and Implications

To be responsive, you need to assist users who make errors and provide feedback on what the system is doing.

Assisting with Errors

Most errors are self-detected and self-corrected.

Most user errors are self-detected and self-corrected. This means that most users recognize their error before the system discovers it. Although editing routines are important in the programming code, it is even more important to permit the user to detect and correct an error before the system intervenes.

For example, a user says, "Two," and realizes right away that they should have said "Three." The user has "self-detected" an error. The critical question is, can the user easily self-correct the error? Do they know how? Is it easy to fix? If the system has "barge-in" capability, then the user can interrupt the system and change course. Many users, however, will be unaware of the barge-in features, and therefore will not use them. Responsiveness means letting the user know what the error is and what they can do to correct it.

Providing Feedback

The system does not need to let the user know what it is doing in order for the system to function correctly, but users need to know what the system is doing. A common problem in speech applications is that users do not know when the system is ready to hear from them, that is, when it is "their turn to speak." This leads to errors if the user talks when the system cannot accept input. Providing feedback to the user about the status of the system, for instance, "System Listening," is a way to be responsive.

Interview with Kate Dobroth

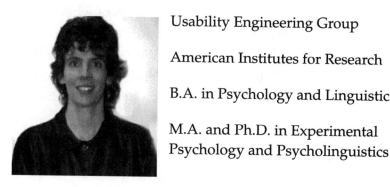

Usability Engineering Group

American Institutes for Research

B.A. in Psychology and Linguistics

M.A. and Ph.D. in Experimental Psychology and Psycholinguistics

Kate Dobroth is with AIR, the American Institutes for Research. Kate works out of the New England office, with the Usability Engineering Group. She has a B.A. from Wesleyan, in Psychology and Linguistics, and an M.A. and Ph.D. from Northeastern in Experimental Psychology and Psycholinguistics. Her studies have concentrated on how people comprehend spoken sentences.

Tell me about your current work.

Right now I'm working on the electronic assistant applications that all the big telephone companies are putting out. Something that will let you do voice dialing and will let you access information.

Tell me about what you think are some of the challenges for GUI interface designers. What are some of the things in the process or challenges in the interface that are different? What might throw them?

The thing that throws everybody, regardless of whether you are working on a handheld, a speech-only, or integrating a speech into a GUI, is that people have really high expectations of how speech recognition ought to work.

People have really high expectations of how speech recognition ought to work.

Too high?

Yes, definitely. They think it ought to work better and they think it ought to be conversational. What you hear all the time is people saying, "I can't wait until this is speech-enabled. I'm going to be able to go right up to it and just start talking to it like it is a person." And that's never the case. The design challenge is really to figure out some way to constrain what people say. You don't want to give people the impression that they can say absolutely anything, because they can't. It actually turns out that people are more comfortable if you give them an idea of what they are supposed to say. This issue is something that I've done a full circle on in the ten-plus years that I've been thinking about these issues.

The design challenge is really to figure out some way to constrain what people say.

What do you mean a full circle?

I started out thinking that speech interfaces should be very conversational. As user interface designers, we are trained to think about metaphors. What is the right metaphor for the interaction? For a long time I thought that conversation was the right metaphor. Then some colleagues I was working with convinced me that it shouldn't be conversational, but now I've decided it needs to be a little bit human-like to add appeal to the application. Sort of like how we've gone from having ugly gray windows applications to having screens that are more pleasing and appealing, and give the overall impression that this is something that is well-designed and works.

Take, for example, the prompts that are read back in a speech-only application. I used to make them very plain and efficient and non-obtrusive. But now I feel more comfortable in working in an anthropomorphic way, having a person or a character who says, "Can I do something for you?" You do that to make it more appealing, but at the same time you can't have the person say, "Well, hey, how's it going? What do you want to do?" That's too open ended.

It sounds like you'd have to be very careful in the design of the prompting to get that balance. It has the aesthetic appeal of sounding like a person, but it also gives clues as to how you should respond.

Yes. This is the general approach as you talk to more people, especially people who do speech-only interfaces. More than anything, people want spoken interactions to be fast. The general approach is to start with a prompt that is short and give them a chance to respond. If they don't say anything, you give a prompt that is more explicit. If they still don't say anything, you say something that is even more explicit. This works well for experts as well as novices because the experts get a chance to go fast, and the novices get a chance to get all their options spelled out for them automatically. And that's the approach that I tend to take.

> More than anything people want spoken interactions to be fast.

What about the design process? What must a usability engineer or interface designer do because they are using speech?

If it is speech-only and you're designing prompts that the system is going to say, you absolutely have to read them out loud to yourself while you're saying them. The process of reading something on a page is really different from the process of listening to something. If you are listening to me

> The process of reading something on a page is really different from the process of listening to something.

talk, you have no control over how fast or slowly I'm going. If you want to go back and listen to something I said, there's no natural way of doing it. If you're on a page, on the other hand, your eyes can go anywhere you want. You can look at something a second time, you can go fast, slow, you can skip. This is not possible with speech. What I always tell people is that something that looks good on a page might not necessarily sound good. It's important to read things out loud.

So writing a script can be really dangerous.

Yes, definitely. So, during testing you can get a lot out of just reading prompts to people.

> During testing you can get a lot out of just reading prompts to people.

I get even fancier with prompts and my old work with prosody kicks in. Say you have the prompt: "You want to use VISA or MasterCard?" If you say it in one pitch until the end and then you raise it, the implied answer is "yes" or "no." If, however, you say it so that the pitch goes up on the word VISA and down on the word MasterCard, then the implied answer is "VISA" or "MasterCard." So when I read prompts out loud I make notes to myself using this transcription for prosody called ToBI: tones and break indices (Silverman, 1992).

So there's actually a notation to do that?

Yes. It can be kind of subjective, but people who are in the speech and prosody communities are all converging on this system. It was first introduced at the 1994 International Conference on Spoken Language.

How do you tell a synthesizer what kind of pitch contours it ought to have? Some synthetic speech systems will use these symbols, such as a pitch accent that is a star. There are six different kinds of pitch accents: there's a low and there's a high and there are bi-tonal ones.

When I'm reading out loud to myself, I'll make notes on how I want the prosody to be. Very often prompts get written out on paper, and they don't get read out loud, and when they go into the recording booth the person is reading them and has no idea about the context they appear in. One of the things that you need to keep track of is what information in this discourse is new and what information is given. We use prosody to keep track of that. If you take a sentence completely out of context and record it, that prosodic information is going to get disrupted and it will make it hard for people to keep track of all of that.

That's kind of my special pet rock area.

This is important and people who are new to this might miss it. They might think about the wording, but they would miss some of these other elements that are critical.

I think it is possible, and this is what my research is all about—whether you can be a lot more efficient in your wording if you are able to take advantage of prosody. This is something we want to actually prove in the lab.

> You can be a lot more efficient in your wording if you are able to take advantage of prosody.

Are there other issues?

Here's something for the hand-held crowd. How do you get someone to remember what the command language is? The comparison between a command language and a prompted interaction is like the comparison between UNIX and a GUI. If it's hand-held and you have to know what to say when you come up to it, there are no affordances there. With a GUI there's a button and it looks like you are supposed to click on it. With UNIX you have no idea what you are supposed to do with it. Same thing with a prompted interaction. It asks you a question and you have some idea of what you are supposed to say. With a hand-held there is nothing that tells you what you are supposed to do. Unless there is some kind of visual environment, some kind of LCD or instruction on it, how are people supposed to know or remember what they're supposed to say? You have to think about how much benefit it's going to give. If someone is going to use an application all the time and it really is going to save them time, it might be worth it to get them to learn commands because it's going to be a time saver and they're going to have enough practice to learn it.

Another area is using non-speech sounds. Instead of saying, "Please wait," Speechworks (previously AL Tech) used to have a nice popcorn popping sound that is unobtrusive, doesn't get in your face, but it does communicate. It tells you that the system is doing something. It doesn't make demands on your cognitive load to listen to it, but it still comes through. It's another way to add appeal.

Tell me why you got into speech in the first place. Why are you excited about it, and why does it continue to capture your interest?

I've always been interested in languages. That is the root of it. When I was a kid I didn't say I want to grow up designing for speech recognition. But when I was a kid I thought it would be fun to speak about 100 languages. That's what turned me into a linguistics major when I was an undergraduate. I went to work at GTE Labs where they were looking for someone who had a psychology background and also knew about language. Back then speech recognition was incredibly frustrating. The technology was not there at all.

One of the projects I worked on there was studying transactions between customer service reps at GTE and customers. We were trying to identify transactions that could be automated. When I left GTE in 1991 to go to grad school, I thought I would want to get out of this field because the technology was so frustrating. By the time I got out of grad school in 1995 I was amazed at how the technology had improved. All of these things that had been in the distant future were suddenly there. There was competition, and there were different approaches to speech recognition. There was more than one game in town. Being able to make comparisons among different recognizers and being able to select which recognizer was the best given the application you had—that was exciting.

A lot of the challenge in user interface design for speech systems is in error recovery. What everybody always says about speech systems is they work really well if you don't make any mistakes. It's not the person making the mistakes, it's the recognizer. A lot of interface design is error recovery. One of the things that has come up in the past decade that is really exciting is designing for error recovery, for example, *end best*. If the system says "Where would you like to travel to?" The user says "Boston." The system then says, "Was that Austin?" If the user says "no," you take Austin out of the running and you have the next best candidate and that might be Boston. Then the system says, "Was that Boston?" and they say "Yes." End best is just starting to work well.

Going back to one of your earlier questions about what you would say to someone just starting out: When speech recognizers make mistakes, they don't make mistakes the same way that people make mistakes. The system says, "Where are you traveling to." The user answers "I'm traveling to Boston." If the system says "Was that Orlando?," that can give people the impression that the thing just doesn't work.

When speech recognizers make mistakes, they don't make mistakes the same way that people make mistakes.

Imagine that you are designing for a GUI and your input method is a mouse and keyboard where one out of every ten mouse and key presses is interpreted incorrectly. That makes it a lot harder. You take a speech recognition system that's at 90 percent accuracy, and that's what you've got. The easy stuff is designing when there are no errors, but 80 percent of design is what happens when something goes wrong.

What do you think the growth areas will be in speech applications? As a usability engineer, what kinds of applications that involve speech will people be asked to work on in the next three to five years?

We have to find applications where speech adds benefits. One of the bottom lines is that people want to go faster, and speech isn't always faster. Speech is often slower. So it can be very challenging to find an application where speech really does add benefit over other kinds of media. If it's a GUI application, you can do something faster using a keyboard and a mouse. If it's a telephone application, you can almost do it faster using a touch tone keypad. This is something that David Spay at GTE Labs did a lot of research in. If you have applications with both touch tone and speech recognition, he found that people preferred touch tone because it was faster.

Things that people seem to want to speech-enable a lot are handhelds. I think that this is one of the growth areas, and I think it's one of the hardest to do because of what we were talking about earlier with command languages. It's harder to learn and remember what you are supposed to do. I took a workshop at CHI on speech-enabling handheld devices. They had an exercise where they handed out all kinds of handheld devices and we had to talk about the benefits and challenges of speech-enabling this thing. It was hard to imagine that some of these devices would be better if they had a speech interface.

Speech isn't always faster. Speech is often slower.

Let me rephrase my question then. What should be a growth area? If you were a venture capitalist and wanted to put your money into a speech application, what would you put it in?

The handheld market is what people want to try out, and speech over the Internet is an intriguing possibility.

Summary

The 20 Laws of Interface apply to any human-computer interface. In Chapter 10 we provide specific guidelines that apply these laws to the design of speech and multi-modal interfaces.

Speech Guidelines

"We think in generalities, but we live in details."
Alfred North Whitehead

In the previous chapter on the laws of interface design, we covered the basic principles of interface design. This chapter applies those laws and provides specific guidelines to follow when designing the interface for a speech application. The guidelines are organized into the following categories:

Errors;

Feedback;

Confirmations;

User expectations;

Keypads and motor actions;

Social and environmental issues;

Command-and-control;

Continuous speech recognition;

Conversation and prompting;

Menus;

Non-speech audio/auditory icons.

Errors

Being error-prone, current speech technology is very much a matter of dealing with errors. One of the roles of the interface is to help reduce the number and severity of the errors the user can make, as well as to help mitigate the effects of the errors the computer can make.

Use Specific Error Messages

Error messages should be specific and tell the user exactly what to say or do. An inadequate error message either gives no information ("An error has occurred") or merely repeats a command. Consider the following exchange between a computer and a user:

> System: "Say the departure date."
>
> User: "Tomorrow."
>
> System: "Say the departure date."
>
> User: "I want to travel tomorrow."
>
> System: "Say the departure date."

The user does not know what response the system wants and the system is not providing helpful or new information. An adequate error message tells the user what is wrong, why, and how to correct it. An example of this is shown in the following improved exchange:

An adequate error message tells the user what is wrong and why, and how to correct it.

> System: "Say the departure date."
>
> User: "Tomorrow."

System: "I do not understand that date. Say the month, date, and year. For example, say October 13th, 1999."

User: "July 1st, 1999."

In this example the system indicated that it did not understand the user's initial response and provided a specific format for a reply.

Limit Background Noise

Background noise leads to an increase in insertion errors. The computer thinks the user has said something, when what it really heard was background noise. Minimize background noise as much as possible.

Allow the User to Turn Off the Input Device

Make sure it is easy for the user to turn off the input device, such as a microphone. Users may need to have a different conversation with another person or machine, need to think about their next step, or gather materials or information for the next step. Allowing the user to turn off the input device eliminates background noise and, thus, reduces insertion errors.

If the interface is multi-modal, provide an icon, such as a picture of a microphone, to allow the user to turn off the input device. Figures 10.1 and 10.2 show examples from IBM's ViaVoice. The icon toggles on and off when clicked.

Figure 10.1 Microphone icon turned on in IBM's ViaVoice.

Figure 10.2 Microphone turned off in IBM's ViaVoice.

If there is a physical device, such as a microphone, allow the user to mute it with a button press on the device itself. If there is no visual or physical device, then allow the user to issue a command that turns off the input mode. For instance, in some applications you can put the speech interface into "sleep mode" and then issue a "wake" command to re-activate input mode.

Provide an Undo Capability

Because limitations in the technology mean that there will be errors, make it easy for users to undo previous actions. Build in ways for users to cancel out, go back, and undo actions.

Build in ways for users to cancel out, go back, and undo actions.

Use an Auditory Icon

Play an auditory icon to signal when an error has been made or when an error message is about to be shown or spoken.

Use Multi-Modal Cues for Errors If Appropriate

If the interface is multi-modal, use more than one mode to signal an error. For example, use an auditory icon and an error message dialog box if there is a visual/GUI component to the interface. Then speak the error message feedback while the error message dialog displays on the visual interface.

Consider Offering Replay

Replay modes allow the user to replay a particular command, menu, or prompt. They can help, but are not used very often by users.

Don't Assume People Hear Everything

You can't assume that people heard something just because the system spoke it to them. Put important information first or last to improve the likelihood of its being heard and remembered.

Feedback

People need feedback from the computer to know what is going on during an interaction. When a user issues a command, they want the system to acknowledge that they have been heard. They also want feedback when the system is busy so they know when to wait.

Supply Alternative Guesses

Although technology continues to improve, there are still limitations that result in errors. For example, a user may say one word, but the computer hears a different word. One way to help with these corrections is for the computer to provide the user with alternative guesses. For example, if the user says "Boston" and the computer is unsure of what was said, it could respond, "Did you say Austin or Boston?"

Acknowledge the User's Speech

After users speak, they expect the computer to respond with appropriate feedback. They want to be sure that the computer has heard what they have said. If the user has requested that an action be taken, the best type of response is to carry out the action itself. For example, if the user has spoken "2" to go to menu option two, then the best form of feedback is for the system to go on to menu option two.

Show When It Is the User's Turn to Talk

People need feedback to know whether it is their turn to speak or the computer's, and to know what is going on. If the interface is multi-modal, use visual feedback to indicate status or whose turn it is. If the interface has no visual component, use auditory cues to signal when it is the user's turn. Figure 10.3 shows this feedback for ConversaWeb software.

Figure 10.3 ConversaWeb signaling it's the user's turn.

Allow for Verification

People tend to verify more when using a speech interface than a visual interface. Make it easy for users to verify and check the status of what is happening now and what has happened recently.

Use Visual Feedback

If you have a visual component to your interface, use visual feedback. This reduces the amount of verification the user will have to ask for. Since the visual feedback continues to display, the user does not have to remember what was said.

Use Non-Speech Audio

In a paper by Lisa Stifelman et al. (1993), researchers talked about the use of speech feedback and non-speech audio. For example, in an early design of a voice recording design, when the user wanted to move from one category to another, they would speak the category name. The system would repeat the category name as a cue that it had moved to that category:

> User: "Things to Do."
>
> System: "Things to Do."

This was not effective feedback, however, because it was not clear to the user whether the recorder had actually moved to the new category or was just repeating what was said for clarity and confirmation. In the next iteration, the researchers added the phrase "Moving into" to signal the move:

> User: "Things to Do."
>
> System: "Moving into Things to Do."

This feedback conveyed that the system had moved into the new category, but now the researchers found the feedback was too long and wordy. Their next tactic, therefore, was to try a non-speech feedback. They used a short sound effect (called an *auditory icon* or *earcon*) to signal that the move had been made.

> User: "Things to Do."
>
> System: Makes an earcon sound.

Users rated their satisfaction higher with the earcon than with the other feedback methods.

Avoid non-speech feedback that sounds like equipment noise. For example, don't use static as an auditory icon.

Avoid non-speech feedback that sounds like equipment noise.

Use In-Progress Messages

If there is more than a three second-delay between when the user issues a command and when the system responds, issue an in-progress message immediately and repeat it every seven to ten seconds until the system responds (Gardiner-Bonneau, 1999). A delay of two to three seconds is acceptable. An auditory icon during the delay (such as music or a tone) does not increase user acceptance of the delay. Here is a sample dialog between a user and a computer properly using an in-progress message:

> User: "List the categories."
>
> System after two seconds: "Retrieving the categories. Please wait."
>
> System after seven to ten seconds: "Your request for categories is still being processed. Please wait."

A delay of two to three seconds is acceptable.

Confirmations

Confirmations are questions you ask of the user to be sure that the user has been heard correctly. We discuss here guidelines for using effective confirmations.

Use Confirmations Appropriately

Since there are many errors associated with the computer recognizing human speech, you may have to use confirmation questions to assure that the computer has heard the right phrase or message. Here is an example:

> System: "What do you want to do next?"
>
> User: "I want to schedule an appointment with my manager."
>
> System: "Do you want to set up an appointment?"
>
> User: "Yes."

You have to balance the cost of making an error with the extra time and annoyance in requiring the user to confirm a lot of statements.

Ask for Clarifying Information

If the computer cannot figure out what the user wants to do, have it ask a clarifying question. For example, consider the dialog in the previous section. If the user's final response has more than one possible meaning, the computer could ask, "Do you want to set up an appointment or contact the person by phone?"

Use Confirmations for Destructive Actions

If the user's action is destructive or will delete large amounts of information, require a confirmation. However, you can minimize the use of confirmations with expert users.

If the user's action is destructive, require a confirmation.

Be Specific

If the system does not recognize what the user has spoken, be specific about what the system needs. Use "Please repeat the date again," rather than, "Please repeat." Do not use a confirmation such as, "Do you mean October 19?" unless you are fairly sure you know what the user said.

User Expectations

One of the biggest challenges in the design of speech interfaces is dealing with user expectations. Users expect talking computers to understand more than they are capable of, and to provide more information than they are capable of. Your interface design can help set appropriate expectations.

Identify the Computer

Users will adjust their speech and their expectations if they know they are interacting with a computer and not with a human. They will speak more briefly and exactly, and enunciate more clearly. Let the users know up front that they are speaking to a computer. For example, start an interaction with "Welcome to the XYZ Voice Response System. What directory to you want to search for?" rather than "What directory do you want to search for?"

Use enough words and a long enough greeting to convey this information. In a study by Susan Boyce (1999), she used different versions of a greeting. The first three were recorded human voices:

> "AT&T. How may I help you?" (Standard version)
>
> "AT&T Automated Customer Service. How may I help you?" (Short automated version)
>
> "AT&T Automated Customer Service. This service listens to your speech and sends your call to the appropriate operator. How may I help you?" (Long automated version)

In a fourth version, the long automated version was used but it was played with a computer-synthesized voice rather than a human voice. Both longer versions resulted in shorter utterances from the people calling in. The short automated version did not help shorten the utterances—people did not seem to catch the automated connotation. The shortest utterances resulted from the synthesized voice, but that version had the lowest satisfaction rating.

Let the users know up front that they are speaking to a computer.

In a follow-up study Boyce used an audio logo to signal an automated system, and then used a brief "How may I help you?" This proved as effective as the longer greetings. Guidelines on initial greetings, therefore, are the following:

- Use a longer greeting or an audio cue.
- Explicitly state that it is an automated system.
- If possible, use a recorded human voice rather than a synthesized voice.

Build in Training Time

Most people have not used speech interfaces, and will need time to get used to talking to the computer. Just as when GUIs first became available and people needed training on mice and windowing, first-time users of speech interfaces need to get used to this new way to interact.

Introduce the Voice

Provide an introduction or training message to familiarize the user with the system's voice.

Keypads and Motor Actions

If the interface includes a keypad or a motor component, such as a keyboard or mouse, here are some guidelines for these devices.

Avoid Key Combinations

If the interface includes keypads, avoid key combinations. For example, do not require the user to press the # key after each command or the * key before each command. These add time and keystrokes to the task.

Use ISO Standard Letter Mappings

If you are using a keypad, for instance with telephone interactive voice response systems, use the ISO standard letter mappings as shown in Table 10.1

Key	Letter Mapping
1	None
2	A, B, C
3	D, E, F
4	G, H, I
5	J, K, L
6	M, N, O
7	P, Q, R, S
8	T, U, V
9	W, X, Y, Z

Table 10.1 ISO Standard Letter Mappings

Q and Z are not printed on most telephone keypads. If you use these, you must remind the user where to find them.

Reserve 1 and 2 for Frequent Actions

Reserve the numbers 1 and 2 for frequent and critical actions. Do not use these numbers for destructive commands, such as *delete*.

Avoid numbers 5 and 8 for destructive commands. Since the numbers 5 and 8 on a keypad are usually surrounded on all sides with other numbers, they are the most likely to be pressed accidentally.

Use the Appropriate Word for Keypresses

Use the word *enter* when you want the user to press multiple keys on a keypad. Use *press* when you want the user to press one key.

Assign Command Labels Consistently

Be consistent with commands. Assign the same key or word to the same function across the entire application.

Social and Environmental Issues

Interfaces are used in the context of people's work and their physical environment. The guidelines here relate to these social and environmental issues.

Decide on Flexibility

You will need to decide on how flexible your interface is for different users and tasks. Maximum flexibility is not always best. If users are under stress and need to do some tasks quickly or infrequently, it may be best to lead them through step by step without a lot of flexibility. If, on the other hand, they need to complete simple tasks quickly and in an unpredictable order, you may want to build in flexibility. Flexibility is a continuum with no particular right or wrong point.

Flexibility is a continuum with no particular right or wrong point.

Consider Stress

People react to all stimuli differently when they are under stress. For example, an easy application can become difficult if the user is also dealing with a customer or co-worker who is upset. Analyze the amount of stress that will be in the environment when people are using your interface. Then analyze the amount of information and the type of activities your interface requires. For users under stress, you may need to make design decisions (such as reducing the amount of information or the amount of navigation) to compensate for the confusing effect of stress.

Consider Social Interaction

If people use software while they are interacting with another person, you must be aware of the impact your interface has on the social interaction between the individuals. For example, a salesperson speaking with a customer does not want to be distracted or have the customer distracted by the computer. If the interface becomes a distraction to the human interaction, its effect will be negative. Consider carefully how introducing a computer into a social interaction may affect the interaction as a whole.

> Be aware of the impact your interface has on the social interaction.

Match the User's Work

Make sure you know how the user is going to do the work when the new software is in place, and design for that order and process of work. Don't make users change an optimal work flow to fit your design.

> Don't make users change an optimal work flow to fit your design.

Command-and-Control

Command-and-control speech applications refer to a type of speech technology that recognizes a limited vocabulary of individual words and phrases spoken by a user. There are some special guidelines to follow when designing an interface for command-and-control applications.

Don't Use "I"

In a command-and-control interface, the system recognizes only certain commands and terms spoken by the human. If the computer uses the first person, "I," users tend to talk in longer phrases, make more vague requests, and are more polite. These tendencies lead to more errors in systems that require specific commands.

Use Modeling

In a GUI interface, users are constrained as to their behavior—they can press only certain buttons or controls. In a speech interface, however, users can say anything (although the system will not always respond well). To constrain user speech to a form that is better understood and minimizes errors, use modeling to convey to the user the terminology and structure they should use. For example, this first script does not model constrained speech and results in unconstrained speech by the user:

> System: "Welcome to ABC Travel Automated System. We look forward to servicing your travel needs. What are the dates of travel that you would like me to check for?"

> User: "We are interested in traveling the first week of July, say July 1st to July 5th."

If the speech engine can handle this type of continuous speech, then you will not have a problem. But in a command-and-control system, you require more exact and constrained speech. In this case the beginning statement by the system is too open—it implies the system can handle continuous, natural language.

If you need to constrain speech, give the user a role model:

> System: "Welcome to ABC Travel Automated System. Say the departure date of travel. For example, say October 1st, 1999."
>
> User: "July 1st, 1999.
>
> System: "Thank you. Say the return date of travel."

In this model, the user will follow the lead of the computer and speak in the same manner, resulting in fewer errors.

Be Brief and Terse

People model the length of system speech. If the computer speaks in short, terse sentences, the users will also.

People model the length of system speech.

Continuous Speech Recognition

Continuous speech recognition systems allow the user to talk to the system without stops and pauses. Continuous speech recognition systems can recognize more utterances than a command-and-control system. The guidelines for continuous speech recognition differ somewhat from those for command-and-control.

Use "I"

In a continuous speech system, humans can speak in a continuous stream. Susan Boyce's research (1999) shows that when the system speaks using the first person, "I," users report higher satisfaction with the system. The use of "I" in a continuous recognition system does not degrade user performance.

When the system speaks using the first person, "I," users report higher satisfaction with the system.

Simulate a Conversation

When two people converse, they take turns talking and listening. A speech interface should do the same. When the computer finishes speaking, it should pause and wait for the human to respond.

Avoid Modal Interference

If the user is speaking to another person, for instance, a customer, and is then required to also speak to the computer, this produces modal interference. Modal interference will cause the user to be distracted and confused.

Conversation and Prompting

What screen design is to graphical user interface design, conversation and prompting are to speech interface design. Taking care when designing the conversation and prompting will reduce errors and increase user satisfaction.

Choose the Appropriate Word

Use the word "say" when you want the user to speak, rather than "enter." Use "enter" for key presses. If you want the user to speak the words "yes" or "no," then use the phrase, "Say yes or no." Here is an example:

"Do you want to transfer funds now? Say yes or no."

rather than:

"Do you want to transfer funds? Enter yes or no."

Use as few words as possible between "say" and the command. This gives the user less to remember. Since speech interfaces place a heavy memory demand on users, it's important to be as brief as possible and still communicate clearly.

For example use: "Say yes or no."

rather than:

"Say the word yes or no."

Avoid Personal Pronouns when Asking for a Response

Avoid using a personal pronoun when asking the user to respond to a question. For example, use:

"Say your credit card number."

rather than:

"Tell me your credit card number."

Using a personal pronoun places an extra word between the command (say) and the information the user is supposed to respond with (credit card number). To decrease the memory demand, use as few words as possible between the two elements. In addition, use the command "say" as it is clearer and more imperative than "tell."

Change Voices Appropriately

Different voices can be used to signal a mode change, for instance, when the user is in one part of the application versus another. Different voices can also be used for different languages. If you do not want to signal a different mode or language, then use the same voice throughout. Warnings, however, should be presented in a voice that is qualitatively different from other voices used by the system so the user will be alerted to pay attention.

Decide on Alerting Tones

If synthesized speech is used exclusively for warnings, don't use alerting tones.

If synthesized speech is not used exclusively for warnings, then use an alerting tone to precede warnings.

Use Small Steps

In a visual interface, people can accomplish fairly large, complex tasks without specific instructions. Speech interfaces, however, strain the user's memory capabilities, so they need to work in smaller steps. Unlike GUIs, speech interfaces users prefer the computer to query them at each step.

Avoid Long Prompts or Menus

If there is no visual element to the interface, you should avoid using prompts or menus with many options. Human short-term memory quickly reaches its limit in speech interfaces. Users are able to remember about three or four menu or prompt options at a time.

Avoid Jargon and Technical Terms in Prompts

Make sure that the users will understand all the terminology used in your prompts. Avoid jargon and technical terms in prompts.

Use Progressive Prompting

When you need to prompt the user, start with short high-level prompts such as:

> System: "Welcome to the XYZ system. What would you like to do?"

If the user does not respond or gives an unrecognizable response, then go to:

> System: "You can check your account status, obtain current market quotes, or view a list of other actions."

If the user still does not respond or gives an unrecognizable response, then go to:

> System: "Say one of the following: Account Status, Quotes, or List."

Use Prompts to Signal Going Back

If there are no visual cues or actions to take the user back to a previous step, use a speech cue, such as "What Next?" This tells the user the dialog has stopped, and the system has returned to a previous node.

Make Prompts Directive and Exact

In a discrete system (as opposed to a continuous speech system) where a user must speak a specific phrase or word, using synonyms can result in an incorrect command by the user. For example:

> System: "Say Activate Recording to turn on the recording feature."
>
> User: "Turn on Recording."

The inexact and inconsistent wording of the prompt (*activate* versus *turn on*) influenced the speaker to use a synonym. Use this wording instead:

> System: "Say Activate Recording to activate recording."
>
> User: "Activate Recording."

Use an Appropriate Time-Out Period and Action

If the system has requested a response from the user and the user has not responded, use the time-out periods and actions shown in Table 10.2. In general, use ten seconds as the time-out period unless the user has to compose or look up information. The type of system action depends on the user task.

Allow Non-GUI Terms

Users recognize GUI terminology on a computer screen, but do not necessarily expect those words to be spoken. Nor do they expect they should have to speak them. For instance, *delete* is a common word on a button in a GUI interface, but users may say "remove" or "erase" instead. Spoken language is less formal than GUI terms on a window. Therefore, the computer should accept both GUI and non-GUI terms.

Spoken language is less formal than GUI terms on a window.

Allow Relative Dates

In a GUI interface, it is common to see dates such as 09/03/1999. In speech, however, users tend to refer to dates in a more relative way, such as "next Friday," or "the day after tomorrow." Although some of these may be hard to interpret, try to interpret them as best you can.

Users tend to refer to dates in a relative way.

User Task	Time-Out Period	System Action after Time-Out
Say a standard command	10 seconds	Repeat prompt. If no response, give message and connect to operator if available
Say continuous speech that may require composition or look-up	Unlimited time-out	None
Say a menu choice	10 seconds	Repeat menu. If no response, give message and connect to operator if available
Press a key or use a pointing device	10 seconds	Repeat prompt. If no response, give message and connect to operator if available

Table 10.2 Time-Outs and System Actions

Avoid Long Pauses

People are uncomfortable with long pauses in conversation. If you have long periods of silence, users will want to fill that space. They will, therefore, talk more, using less meaningful words and sounds, for instance, uhs or umms. This will result in more errors. Use an "in progress" message or a non-speech sound when a long pause is necessary.

Choose an Appropriate Speed

Users will mimic the
speed of the computer.

Users will mimic the speed of the computer. If the computer is reacting and speaking slowly, the user will tend to slow down. If the computer is reacting or speaking quickly, the user will speed up. Select an appropriate speed that keeps the interaction moving naturally, but minimizes errors. Use an appropriate speech rate: for natural speech, use a rate between 150 to 180 words per minute; for synthesized speech, use 150 to 170 words per minute.

Use "Barge-In" Techniques

Allow users to interrupt the computer. If there is a visual component to the interface, they can click on a button to interrupt what the computer is doing or saying. If there is no visual component, barging in refers to the user speaking to stop the computer.

Use Tapering

If you must provide the same message or information over and over, start with more detailed instructions and then taper the number of words used. For example:

> System: "Say the street address, city, and state of the business you are interested in."

The next time, use less detail.

> System: "Say the street, city, and state."

Eventually use the least amount of detail.

> System: "Say the business address."

This mimics the way people converse. If you do not use tapering, the conversation is slower and users will become impatient.

Be Consistent

Use the same terms in the documentation as you do in the interface.

Use Prosodic Features

Prosodic features are pitch, volume, speed, and pause. You can vary the pitch of spoken text to introduce new topics and emphasize important sections of work. Increasing pitch also makes the computer sound more lively. Varying speech too much can make the output hard to hear, so use caution. People are used to a human-like intonation of sounds and words which computers cannot easily simulate. Try to get the prosody as natural as possible.

Increasing pitch makes the computer sound more lively.

You can vary the volume in the same way as pitch, but not as much. Volume quickly becomes either too loud or too soft.

Slowing down speech makes it easier to understand, but can be annoying if it is too slow.

Pauses are important in human-to-human conversation, but they can be ambiguous in human-computer interaction. Use pauses to suggest that it is the user's turn to act.

Menus

Some speech-only systems, especially IVR (interactive voice response) systems, rely on menus as their main navigation tool. The design of these menus is therefore critical to the usability of the system.

Use Result-Action for Menus with More Than Two Options

In a menu with more than two options, describe the result first and then the specific action. For example:

> "For a list of categories, say 1. For a list of people, say 2. To access your account status, say 3. To open a new account, say 4."

rather than:

> "Say 1 for a list of categories. Say 2 for a list of people. Say 3 to access your account status. Say 4 to open a new account."

If you state the menu choice first, the user may forget which choice they want before hearing all the menu options.

Use Action-Result for Menus with Two Options

If there are only two options, place the action first, as in:

> "Press 1 for yes, or 2 for no."

Let the User Know When the Menu Is Complete

Cue the user that all the menu choices have been given. You can do this by telling them to select one—for example, "Make your selection now"—or by the inflection in the voice.

Order the Menu Appropriately

Place the most frequently-used options at the top of the menu hierarchy, both in terms of nesting as well as within a particular menu. If a menu item is temporarily unavailable or unavailable to that user, leave it off the menu.

Use Results as Feedback

The best feedback for a menu option is to present the results of the choice as shown in the dialog here:

System: "For a list of categories, say 1."

User: "1."

System: "The categories are…"

Do not use a confirmation message for menus. For example, do not use:

System: "For a list of categories, say 1."

User: "1."

System: "You chose 1. The categories are …"

Constantly telling users what they chose is redundant and takes time. Users will grow tired of the extra wait.

Use an Appropriate Amount of Nesting

If the user does not know what they want until they hear the options, then limit the number of menu options to four and use nesting (sub-menus). This way, users will choose a category first, and then go to the choices for that category. If, however, they know what item they want, then breaking up the choices into categories will waste time. Minimize nesting in this case, and allow more than four items per menu.

Non-Speech Audio/ Auditory Icons

An auditory icon is a non-speech audio signal based on a real-world sound. For example, the sound of a police siren signaling an emergency is an auditory icon. You can alter the character of the sound to imply a change in the characteristic of the object. For example, a cash register sound can get louder the more money is deposited.

Use Standard Sounds with Their Usual Meanings

Many auditory icons are already used in other applications. If you are going to use these, be sure to use them in an expected context. Table 10.3 lists some common auditory icons and their uses.

Auditory Icon	Usual Meaning
Busy signal	Action is not available because it's already being used by another
Beep	Error or attention
Siren	Emergency
Dial tone	Open line, ready

Table 10.3 Auditory Icons and Their Meanings

Stay within an Octave for a Sequence

If you are using a sequence of tones that must be distinguished from another sequence, keep each sequence within an octave so that you can use the octave change as a signal of a different sequence.

Use appropriate scale movements. For example, rising tones imply "up" and falling tones imply "down."

Use Volume to Signify Meaning

A tone that grows quieter indicates that something is going down. A tone that grows louder signifies that something is going up. Avoid very loud noises unless you purposely need to startle users.

Interview with Sharon Oviatt

Co-Director, Center for Human-Computer Communication

Department of Computer Science and Engineering

Oregon Graduate Institute of Science and Technology

Sharon Oviatt is co-director of the Center for Human-Computer Communication (CHCC) in the Department of Computer Science and Engineering at Oregon Graduate Institute of Science and Technology. Dr. Oviatt has a Ph.D. in Experimental Psychology from the University of Toronto (1979), an M.A. from the University of Toronto (1974), and a B.A. (with highest honors) from Oberlin College (1972).

Oviatt has researched many of the detail decisions we make on speech interfaces. Her discussion about these decisions, the guidelines, and their implications is presented in the following interview.

Tell me how you got into the speech area.

I've been doing speech and language-oriented work for the last 20 years, but my interest in it has shifted. I started out doing research on human memory and cognition, and infant speech perception. I did a degree at the University of Toronto in the Psychology Department developing a signal detection method for measuring infant language comprehension before they were actually speaking. It wasn't until the late '80s that I switched to the Artificial Intelligence Center at SRI and started working on computationally-oriented issues. After working at SRI for about seven years, I moved to the Computer Science Department at the Oregon Graduate Institute and have been here for almost six years.

You have an HCI (human-computer interaction) program there?

We're in a Computer Science department that is quite innovative and non-traditional. There is a speech group studying speech technology issues, and our group studies spoken language interfaces, human-computer interaction, multi-modal interaction, agent technology, and collaboration technology. We're interested in human use of speech in the context of multi-modal systems. We have both masters and Ph.D. programs, and an internship program that has been sponsored by the National Science Foundation for more than six years.

What are some of the issues there that you are grappling with that you see as problems for the practitioners?

From an interface perspective, for practitioners, researchers, or users, one problem is the topic of errors and error handling. This is not a problem unique to speech. It is an issue for any new recognition-based media, whether speech, pen, gaze tracking, and so forth. These all are recognition technologies that are inherently error prone, and a lot of effort has to go into analyzing the source and the cause of errors in such systems, and into building interfaces that do a better job of avoiding errors and recovering from errors gracefully.

That's the number one interface problem for speech technology right now, in my view.

Do you think that will always be the job of the interface, or do you think there are some underlying technologies in the future that will take the burden off the interface?

I think that interface design will always be a main ingredient in making recognition-based technologies succeed or fail. Technologists and engineers who have worked on speech technology have not realized this fully in the past. They have assumed that it was their burden alone to figure out how to build new algorithms that would give us 100 percent recognition rates. That's unfortunate, because there are whole teams of people around the world who have worked incredibly hard trying to process different types of spoken language, who have struggled considerably, and sometimes they have had difficulty making progress on a technical basis alone. They make changes to algorithms and may only reap a 1 to 2 percent improvement in recognition rates.

> Interface design will always be a main ingredient in making recognition-based technologies succeed or fail.

Here's an example of where interface design can make a difference to the success or failure of speech technology: One of the things we did was to look at one major source of failure for speech recognizers, which is disfluent and fragmented speech.

Can you give me an example of what you mean by disfluent speech?

If you had a recording of my speech now you could listen to it later and notice a lot of non-word fillers, like "uh" or "um." I may make content self-corrections, like "Give me the green, no, I mean the blue one." I may also make grammatical false starts, for example, where I start to cast a sentence one way but then break it off and start all over again. For example, I might say something like "I'd like to go, I want to go" in which I finish the sentence another way. Another type of disfluency is verbatim repetitions. I might say, "Give me the, the blue one," where I repeated the word *the*. A disfluency is an interruption to the smooth flow of an otherwise coherent utterance. There's lots of disfluency research and people have different definitions, but the kinds of examples I'm giving you are pretty common throughout the research.

A disfluency is an interruption to the smooth flow of an otherwise coherent utterance.

We started doing data analyses and quantitative modeling of when and why human disfluencies were occurring during spoken interaction with computers. We assumed they were not just messy nuisance variables, but that human disfluencies are a systematic phenomenon, characteristic of speech. We assumed there is regularity to when and why people are disfluent, and that analyses could identify what factors are associated with an increase or decrease in disfluent speech. We also assumed we might be able to guide users' speech to be less disfluent in a way that would support improved recognition rates.

Human disfluencies are a systematic phenomenon, characteristic of speech.

In this research, we were able to account for about 80 percent of the variance in human disfluencies to computers. We studied the same user completing the same task, but designed an interface one way versus another and showed that we could reduce the number of disfluencies in users' speech by as much as 80 percent. We did this in part by providing more interface structure. That is, we used a more constrained interface design that guided users' speech to be divided up into briefer utterances. When people need to plan and then articulate increasingly lengthy utterances, the density of disfluencies skyrockets, especially in

We could reduce the number of disfluencies in users' speech by as much as 80 percent.

constructions over about 12 to 13 words in utterance length. On the other hand, if you can structure a user's interaction such that her utterance length is briefer than 10 to 12 words in length, ideally even under seven to eight words in length, then you can substantially reduce the total percentage of disfluencies that a speech recognizer would have to process.

One thing that was interesting to us in this work was that the users weren't even aware that they were being disfluent. The fact that people are disfluent is not something they tend to pay attention to. So when we structured an interface to be more or less constrained, people weren't aware that the level of the disfluencies was changing at all. In fact, if you asked most people about disfluencies in their speech, they would probably deny that they spoke that way!

> If you asked most people about disfluencies in their speech, they would probably deny that they spoke that way!

There's this fantasy that we would be able to use this kind of disfluent speech and the computer would understand us. There are two ways of looking at it. One is that we should head toward technology that would be able to handle these disfluencies—we should figure out how to do it. Or the other point of view is that people do not need to talk to computers like people. They can learn to use constrained speech and that won't bother them. This is quite a philosophical difference.

From the point of view of processing disfluencies, there are a couple of different routes people can take, both of which are productive and can be helpful. One is what I've just described—I can manipulate the way I present information such that a person will be transparently guided by the interface to be less disfluent. Basically, we can eliminate up to about 80 percent of the disfluencies in users' speech through interface design, and this is our gift to the technologists. However, we are not magicians and we can't

> We can eliminate up to about 80 percent of the disfluencies in users' speech through interface design, and this is our gift to the technologists.

make speech disfluencies disappear completely. Someone is still going to have to process the other 20 percent of disfluencies in users' speech.

Another complementary approach is to model speech disfluencies, just as we model non-speech articulations. We can model coughing, laughing, silence, background noise, so why not model disfluencies? If we do this, the recognizer identifies and distinguishes disfluencies and doesn't choke on them. Instead it says, "Okay that was an 'uh' rather than a 'the,' " and it can perform more accurate natural language processing as a result.

These two approaches—either attempting to transparently manipulate users' disfluency level through interface design or attempting to model their speech disfluencies—can be used together. I can develop an interface design that will relieve a lot of the burden of having to process disfluent speech, but I can also clean up more by modeling the disfluencies that remain. Both approaches can improve recognition rates.

The other thing I should say is that sometimes developers have assumed that users prefer an unconstrained interface to a constrained interface. What we've learned from our research is that that isn't always the case. In some of our studies, two-thirds of users actually have reported a preference for a more constrained interface that guided them and gave them a sense of closure when they were done with a task. So developing a more constrained interface isn't always a bad thing from either a user's point of view or from a system processing point of view. However, sometimes there will be applications for which we don't want a constrained interface, for example, some entertainment or educational applications.

Two-thirds of users actually have reported a preference for a more constrained interface that guided them and gave them a sense of closure when they were done with a task.

Besides errors—which seem to be a very large issue in interface design for speech—what are some of the other interface design issues?

Another enormous one is handling the speech of diverse users.

In many respects, speech technologists have done an unbelievable job improving the technology and beginning to bring it to market. On the other hand, they've focused mainly on adult native speakers of English. Just within the last few years, people have become more interested in collecting data on children's speech. I have companies come to me and say, "We'd like to build an interactive toy that kids can talk to and we have speech recognition technology, right? Can't we use these recognizers now to build an interactive toy for kids?" And I have to point out that there is going to have to be a lot of data collected relevant to children's speech signal characteristics, spoken language modeling, and interface design specifically for children before speech-activated toys can be anything other than frustrating for a young child. The error rate for processing children's speech using an adult recognizer typically is two-to–four-fold higher than for an adult. Children's signal characteristics and language are different and more challenging than adults'. Children's disfluency levels are higher, their lexicons are developing, and these kinds of factors cause processing difficulties.

Children's speech is just one example of a challenging user group. Other user groups, such as the elderly or accented speakers, also have spoken language with different signal characteristics that need to be modeled. Non-native, heavily accented speech also can result in three- to four-fold higher error rates than a native speaker. Let's say you want to build a public information kiosk and handle the realistic

> There is going to have to be a lot of data collected relevant to children's speech signal characteristics, spoken language modeling, and interface design specifically for children before speech-activated toys can be anything other than frustrating.

population that exists in the United States, which is 10 to 20 percent accented speakers. There are going to be accents of every imaginable kind. You are not modeling a single particular accent, and this creates a processing challenge.

Speech technologists have not wanted to highlight the fact that the recognition rates they report typically are for adult native speakers of English. As soon as you have an accented speaker or a child, the recognition rate degrades considerably. So handling the realistic array of diverse speech that exists and building systems and commercial products for all of these constituencies will require collecting data, developing language models, and designing new interfaces. Some of these considerations are just beginning to be addressed.

Is there more of a recognition in the speech world of the criticality of interface design, or is there less, or is it about the same as the role of interface design in GUI applications or Web applications, where there is a visual and perhaps a motor part to the interface?

It's hard to compare. In some respects, the role of interface design might be more appreciated in connection with speech and new media. People have had to struggle more with the issue of recognition rates and the robustness of the technology. And each new medium is so different: gaze tracking or human speech. It's more important than ever that developers understand the cognitive science basis for these different human communication channels. In some respects, there may be more appreciation that input modes (like speech and gaze) are highly automatic systems and not necessarily so easily trainable. You can't easily get a speaker to talk the way a recognizer needs them to! People are not always consciously aware of their speech; they're not able to adapt everything about their speech, such as its timing and disfluency levels, in a way that is ideal for the technology.

Therefore, technologists are coming increasingly to the realization that they are going to have to understand what natural speech patterns and gaze behavior are like, and to try to build their technology to work for the reality of what people deliver. This means the role of interface design becomes more critical than ever. It also means that the interface designer is not a mechanical role; it's a more meaningful cognitive science role. It's the person in the middle who is trying to help the team understand what the systematic patterns are for a given input mode, and what the implications are for structuring the interface, as well as what is or isn't buildable in a robust way at the current time.

Tell me about the multi-modal work you are doing.

I became interested in multi-modal interfaces in the early '90s. I guess that means our group was one of the first to explore this topic. At the time I was at SRI, which was a rich environment for both speech and handwriting technology. There were groups working on both technologies there. SRI had people like Hugh Crane, who is one of the founders of CIC Corporation, which developed handwriting recognition software and dynamic signature verification. It also had Hy Myrveit, one of the main architects of SRI's speech technology, which has become the basis for Nuance Corporation. I was surrounded by interesting and innovative people who often argued with one another about which technology was better: speech or pen. As a cognitive scientist and interface designer, when I listened to them argue I was struck by the fact that each technology had its strengths and weaknesses, and that human beings use both, and sometimes they use both at the same time. I thought it might be interesting to consider building an interface for people in which they were free to use either input mode. That is, people could use one instead of the other at a given moment, or they could use them together if they wished.

> The role of interface design becomes more critical than ever. The interface designer is not a mechanical role; it's a more meaningful cognitive science role.

So I wrote my first NSF grant in the early 1990s and started doing exploratory work on multi-modal systems that combined speech and pen input. We mocked up a front end that looked like a real system. We would bring people in off the street who were not computer scientists, and tell them we had a multi-modal system that could process their speech and pen input. We had people do everything from real estate transactions to personal banking to car rentals: applications where they talked and wrote to the computer. We analyzed their language, the way they used these natural input modes, and their preferences. After several years of user modeling, we built our first fully functional QuickSet multi-modal system.

During this design and development process, we used what I would describe as a proactive HCI research method. First, we conceptualized what a multi-modal interface might be like, and we considered the functionality of different kinds of applications. We designed the layout of what the graphical output of the interface would look like for such a system, how people would engage the microphone and talk to the system, and so forth. We developed scenarios of what the user would input and how the system would respond, and we developed a new high-fidelity simulation infrastructure that we began using for data collection.

After that, we were able to build our first multi-modal system prototype fairly easily, because we already had data on the vocabulary and specific information about how people would talk and write to such a system. We had the whole interface designed, and really just had to swap in pen and speech recognizers and begin augmenting the architecture. We had our first prototype up and running within a few weeks, actually, because we had done so much proactive HCI work before we ever built our first multi-modal system.

This was quite a different progression from the way graphical user interfaces were developed, where engineers worked from intuition in designing and building their interfaces. We needed to know how human beings actually would use speech and pen together, for example, and how they would integrate and synchronize these input modes, and what kind of lexical information would be delivered in one mode versus the other before we could build a successful system. We had to research these topics before the first multi-modal technology was built, because we had no idea what kind of temporal thresholds would be needed to unify the input signals. And we needed to know when it was appropriate to integrate and synchronize two parallel signals into a single utterance. So we collected and analyzed a large amount of data from users to develop the fundamental prerequisites for the first multi-modal system prototype.

What did you find out?

We have written papers that summarize what we found out specifically about the way that people use speech and pen multi-modally. One of the main ones is a CHI '97 paper. For example, I might be working on a dynamic map and draw a line between two objects with my pen while at the same time I say, "How far from here to here?" What I'm doing is a simple request for a distance calculation–I want the system to tell me what the distance is between two points. I'm delivering a series of XY coordinates with the pen signal and speaking at the same time, and I expect the system to integrate these two signals to interpret the meaning of my utterance. In analyzing the way people use speech and pen in cases like this, we've discovered a lot. For example, in human multi-modal communication, what you typically get is a mixture of uni-modal and multi-modal constructions, so it's important that any multi-modal system be able to distinguish the two, and know

Pen input usually precedes or is overlapped with speech, but never by more than a three- or four-second lag.

when it's appropriate to integrate two signal pieces. We also discovered that pen input usually precedes or is overlapped with speech, but never by more than a three- or four-second lag. Of course, this has implications for the temporal thresholds established for time-sensitive multi-modal architectures.

Can that be figured out?

Yes, these issues can be figured out, but not without data. A programmer cannot sit down and simply guess how human beings organize their normal patterns of multi-modal communication to a computer. You actually have to collect data.

Is this really different than the way systems were built before, or is this just the way pre-multi-modal systems should have been built? In the evolution of graphical user interfaces, maybe we'd have been better off if empirical data had been collected on that as well. Some of it was.

My perception is that people were more easily able to build a GUI system and its interface based on the intuition of the primary system architect. Whether those systems would have been better if more proactive HCI work had been done, including empirical data collection, certainly is a good question!

Is your work going on and moving forward with systems being built on that data?

Yes, our primary development to date has been different versions of the Quickset multi-modal system. Now we're working on speech and multi-modal interfaces for diverse user groups. We're also doing a lot of work on speech and multi-modal interactions in mobile environments where noise levels are continually changing. We are discovering many performance advantages of building new multi-modal architectures.

Do you have corporate sponsors?

We've been fortunate to have excellent corporate support. We've had support from Intel, who is interested in diverse user speech, in multi-modal interfaces, and in error handling issues. We've had Microsoft and Boeing support, as well as support from many telecommunications and other computer companies. For example, Boeing has been interested in multi-modal simulation training for pilots and aircraft maintenance.

Do you have advice for interface designers and programmers just getting going in this field—things to watch out for?

It's hard at the present time for people to design good speech or multi-modal interfaces from simple guidelines. The process of building a speech interface is not easy in the sense that we don't have a lot of predictive information and simple formulas for developing specific applications capable of yielding a particular recognition rate. The advice I would have for interface designers is to take some courses specifically in speech technology and interface design or, better yet, do an internship at a good research center where such interfaces are actively being pioneered and built. And don't assume that the basic interface design ingredients and conventions suitable for speech are the same as those used for traditional GUI interfaces.

Summary

Designing a usable interface means making dozens of decisions during design that all together create a usable interface. The guidelines in this chapter are a starting point for these design decisions. In the next chapter, we discuss a process for ensuring that design takes usability into account.

PART

Four

Best Practices

Part Four covers best practices in interface design and usability engineering, including:

Chapter 11: Usability Processes and Techniques. Describes a comprehensive method for designing applications to ensure they are usable, and the basic usability engineering techniques used in the process.

Chapter 12: Universal Design. Discusses designing for universal design and accessibility.

Usability Processes and Techniques

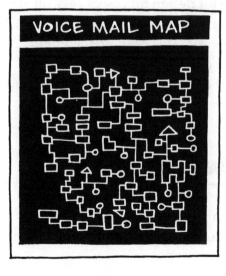

VOICE MAIL MAP

GOFF

> **"If you can't describe what you are doing as a process, you don't know what you're doing."**
> **_W. Edwards Deming_**

A good user interface doesn't just happen. It requires a proven process for success. The process needs to be efficient and produce specific deliverables that will be used as input when creating the interface. These deliverables include simple minimalist pieces of documentation, which are created at each step in the process.

Although best practice for design processes vary for speech versus graphical versus Web interfaces, there are more similarities than differences. This chapter, therefore, describes how to apply our standard design process, InterPhase 5, originally designed for GUIs, to the design of speech interfaces.

Process Description

InterPhase 5 is a design methodology that divides the process of user interface design into five phases:

1. Investigation
2. Analysis
3. Conceptual Model Design
4. Detail Design
5. Implementation and Evaluation

Phases. Each phase is discussed in detail in this chapter. For each phase, we provide a table that describes the steps, sub-steps, tools, and techniques for that phase.

Steps and sub-steps. Each phase is broken into steps. Some steps have sub-steps. For example, in the second phase—analysis—the fourth step is Develop current task analysis. Its sub-steps are Document the task list and Analyze the current workflow.

Tools. Most steps and sub-steps have one or more tools that are produced during that step or sub-step. For example, the fourth step mentioned in the preceding paragraph (Develop current task analysis), results in the production of two tools: the Current task list and the Current workflow diagram. Tools are listed in the table for each phase, and described in the text for each phase.

Techniques. Techniques refer to possible ways that you can create the tools. For example, to document the task list, possible techniques include conducting a contextual study, collecting artifacts or conducting interviews. These techniques are also discussed in this chapter. You may want to use other techniques not discussed. We do not recommended specific techniques for all steps and sub-steps.

Deliverables. Each phase results in a deliverable that summarizes the work done for that phase and compiles the tools that will be needed in a later phase.

Investigation

During the first phase, investigation, you determine what work has already been done, and how that work can be used or modified. During the investigation, you review project goals and timeframes, and decide which tools and deliverables will need the most work. Table 11.1 summarizes the steps and sub-steps of the investigation phase. All the work involved in this first phase is documented in the interface design and usability engineering project plan.

Step	Sub-Steps	Tool	Recommended Technique or Comments
1. Identify current state and scope	a. Evaluate the project documents	None	
	b. Develop an interface design and a usability project plan	Interface design and usability engineering project plan	

Table 11.1 Phase One: Investigation

The first and only step involved in the investigation phase is identifying the current state and scope of the project whose interface you are designing.

Identify Current State and Scope

Usability engineering takes place within the context of software projects. Often you come into the project after the technical work has begun. There is often, therefore, some technical work that has already been done. For example, the software project team may already have some user profile descriptions. This means you may not need as much time during the analysis phase to gather user information. A review of existing profiles and their modification for interface design purposes may be all that's needed. The two sub-steps of this step are: evaluate the project documents, and develop an interface design and a usability project plan.

Evaluate Project Documents

What documents you should evaluate depends on what documents have already been produced. Many of the items on the following list may not yet be developed by the time you join the project. Hopefully, you have joined the interface design team early in the design phase. Some of these items might never be produced for your project. Here is a list of possible system documentation that may be available or helpful to you during the investigation phase:

- system proposal
- system feasibility reports
- system requirements
- use cases
- database entity relationship diagram
- business process analysis
- project plan
- application architecture
- QA test plan
- marketing materials
- data flow diagrams
- data dictionary

Review the materials and compare them against what is needed for all the phases, steps, and sub-steps. This comparison forms the basis for planning the tools and deliverables necessary for the rest of the phases.

Use a Checklist

Create a checklist of the documents you have reviewed and their implication for your interface work. For example, there are use cases, but they are very detailed. For the interface design, you can use the use cases as a starting point, but you will need to create some high-level user scenarios. Include on the checklist the document name, the date it was reviewed, and the consequences it has on your interface work. Here's a sample checklist:

Document	Reviewed On	Comments
System proposal		
System feasibility reports		
System requirements		
Use cases		
Database entity relationship diagram		
Business process analysis		
Project plan		
Application architecture		
QA test plan		
Marketing materials		
Data flow diagrams		
Data dictionary		

Investigation Checklist

Develop Interface Design and Usability Project Plan

After you investigate the current documents, the next step is to develop a project plan. This plan describes the work remaining to be done in phases two through five, based on the results of the investigation. The Interface Design and Usability Engineering Project Plan evaluates the information gathered so far, identifies what is missing from an interface design and usability point of view, and recommends a plan for the remaining interface design phases.

Analysis

In the analysis phase, the second phase, you determine who your users are, how they work, and how you expect them to work in the future when they have the software whose interface you are designing. When analysis is complete, you have a description of the requirements of the interface from the user's point of view. The analysis is critical work that feeds directly into design. The deliverable for this second phase is the analysis document and the steps included in this phase are outlined in Table 11.2.

Historically, analysis for interface design has either not been done at all or has not been given enough time and attention to be truly effective. If you don't have this critical information, how can you possibly design an interface that will be easy to learn and use? Without proper analysis, you may spend as much as 10 times the amount of money later, to rework the design.

> Historically, analysis for interface design has either not been done at all or has not been given enough time and attention to be truly effective.

Steps	Sub-Steps	Tools	Recommended Techniques or Comments
1. Define usability vision	None	Usability vision	Brainstorm
2. Describe design considerations	None	Technical, style, environmental, and social considerations list	
3. Identify user groups and characteristics	None	User descriptions (matrix, profiles, or narratives)	Use contextual studies Conduct interviews
4. Develop current task analysis	a. Document the task list	Current task list	Use contextual studies and collect artifacts Conduct interviews Categorize task list, if appropriate
	b. Analyze the current workflow	Current workflow diagram	Use an appropriate level of detail
5. Develop future task analysis	a. Describe the problems and opportunities	Problems and opportunities list and map	Use brainstorming Use a fishbone chart Use an affinity diagram
	b. Create a future task list	Future task list	
	c. Analyze the future workflow	Future workflow diagram	

Steps	Sub-Steps	Tools	Recommended Techniques or Comments
6. Develop usability objectives	None	Usability objectives	
7. Revise tools and develop analysis document	None	Analysis document	

Table 11.2 Phase Two: Analysis

Define Usability Vision

The vision statement answers the question: What are the goals and priorities? The vision statement concentrates on usability, not technology. Later in the analysis, you will get more specific with usability objectives; here you are setting high-level usability goals. Figure 11.1 is an example of a usability vision for the Speech Now user interface. Speech Now is a fictitious case study that we will use here to show examples of tools and deliverables.

Usability Vision

The primary goal for the Speech Now user interface is ease of learning. Speech Now must allow users to dictate and proofread documents without attending a training class. Speech Now should be a seamless add-on to their current document tools.

Figure 11.1 Usability vision example.

Brainstorming

Loosely, the term *brainstorming* is often used to mean any type of creative thinking. We are using it here in a slightly more formal sense. Brainstorming involves bringing a group of people together to work on one problem at the same time. It involves at least two people, and typically four to eight. A group of more than ten starts to become unwieldy. The group employs brainstorming to create a list of ideas or alternatives quickly.

Conduct Brainstorming with Equals

Having a manager present is not a good idea if the presence of the manager means that others will be hesitant to come up with "silly" ideas.

During brainstorming, you clearly state the problem that everyone will address. Then the group comes up with possible solutions or ideas. These are not to be evaluated or judged, initially—any and all ideas are considered valid, even if they sound "way out there." One or two people summarize each idea, in one or two words, at the front of the room. After a given amount of time (decided on beforehand) or when the ideas seem to have stopped, the group goes into synthesis and evaluation mode. For this process, a facilitator walks through each item on the list, combining items that say essentially the same thing, and asking the group to evaluate each item for desirability and feasibility.

Describe Design Considerations

Interface design does not happen in a vacuum. A variety of issues affect your design decisions: for instance, the type of hardware to be used or the physical environment of the users. During step two of analysis, you document the design issues as shown in Figure 11.2, including:

Technical considerations. Hardware, software, and platform issues that may affect design.

Style considerations. Issues or decisions that will affect the look and feel of the interface, for example, existing corporate guidelines.

Environmental considerations. Physical characteristics of the environment that may affect the interface, for example, the location of monitors on a factory floor.

Social considerations. Any factor that will affect the human relationships, for example, if the new system will introduce the computer into what was previously a human-to-human interaction.

Design Considerations for Speech Now

Technical

- Integration with existing document software
- Office users
  - Windows NT 4 operating system
  - Pentium III, 600mHZ, 128 MB RAM
  - 17" monitor at 600x800 resolution
- Remote users
  - Windows 98 operating system
  - Pentium III, 600mHZ, 128 MB RAM
  - 17" monitor at 600x800 resolution

Style

- Fits with MS Office 2000 suite
- Adheres to Windows operating system guidelines
- No existing corporate user interface guidelines

Environmental

- Fortune 1000 office environment
- Users will wear headsets
- Remote users will call in from home offices

Social

- New to the idea of issuing commands to the computer via speech

---

Figure 11.2 Design considerations example.

Identify User Groups and Characteristics

It's important to document user characteristics that will affect design decisions later in the design process. Not all users are alike; therefore, you must identify and categorize user groups and describe the characteristics that will be most important for interface design. The user matrix is a simple tool that describes each user group in detail. It also allows for comparison of user groups at a glance and is shown in Figure 11.3.

User Matrix for Speech Now		
	Office Operators (Primary)	**Home Office Users**	**System Administrator**
Frequency of use	Constant	Occasional to frequent	Infrequent
GUI experience	Medium	Medium to High	High
Task knowledge (dictating and proofreading with speech)	Low	Low	Low
Domain knowledge	High	High	High
Demographics	75% female Ages 18-60, median age 32 Some higher education	75% male Ages 25-40, median age 30 Most degreed	85% male Ages 25-35, median age 27 Technical education
Environment and conditions	Office cubicle Voice noise	Home office Quieter than corporate office	Technical support center Onsite support

User Matrix for Speech Now			
	Office Operators (Primary)	**Home Office Users**	**System Administrator**
Languages	English, Spanish, French (Canadian)	English	English
Experience with similar applications	None to little	None to little	Some
Key usability requirements	Ease of learning Ease of use	Ease of learning Ease of use	Ease of learning Ease of use

Figure 11.3 User matrix example.

Interviews

We rely heavily on interviewing in usability engineering. Even though most usability engineers recognize the limitations inherent in conducting interviews and the need to use other techniques (such as field studies), interviewing remains an important part of what we do. We interview users, project managers, programmers, and key stakeholders. We conduct these interviews throughout the design process: at the beginning for information gathering, during analysis and conceptual modeling, and during evaluation so that we continue to get feedback from key people during the design process. This allows us to re-iterate our design and improve usability.

We list here some guidelines for effective interviewing:

Plan your interview. Prepare your questions in advance. You want to use your time wisely, so decide beforehand what areas you will discuss.

Prepare your interviewee. Before you meet with the person you are interviewing, make sure they know what the interview is about, what topics will be covered, why you need this information, what they should bring with them, if anything, and what you expect their role to be during the interview.

Decide on a timeframe. Interview with a specific timeframe in mind. Let your interviewee know what it is. For example, "We're going to talk about the order processing task for the next hour." This helps keep everyone on task.

Interview one-on-one or in a small group. You can't conduct an effective interview with 15 people. Aim to have one or two interviewers and one to three interviewees at a time.

Take good notes. If you want to use the information you collect, you must take good notes. If there are more than two people involved, either as interviewers or interviewees, you may need to assign an interviewer to take notes. Consider audio- or videotaping the session, but realize that this can make interviewees nervous, and may affect the results of the interview.

Use the apprenticeship model. We have found the apprenticeship model to be useful in interviewing. This model is described in detail in Hugh Beyer and Karen Holtzblatt's book, *Contextual Design* (Beyer & Holtzblatt, 1998). In this model, the interviewer takes the role of the apprentice who is actively engaged in learning from the expert, the interviewee. This model seems to elicit the best information the fastest.

Ask open-ended questions that invite the interviewee to expand on their statements.

Phrase your questions carefully. The types of questions you ask and how you ask them can influence the answers you get. Ask open-ended questions that invite the interviewee to expand on their statements.

Stay in your role. During the interview, make sure you stay in your role as interviewer. Don't become the expert when you're not. Don't start designing the system or telling the interviewee how it should be.

Synthesize and summarize your notes. As soon as possible after the interview, summarize the important points. If you wait too long to review your notes, you will forget a lot of information and your detailed notes will not be as comprehensible.

Field/Contextual Studies

Conducting interviews provides valuable information, but there are flaws inherent in conducting interviews. During an interview, you are asking people to remember events, remember how they work, and articulate mental processes that may normally be performed without a lot of conscious thought. As a result, the answers may not be accurate. One of the best ways to get accurate information is to conduct a field study or contextual study in addition to or instead of interviews.

During a field study, you plan a trip to the location of an event or work that you are going to observe. Field studies imply observation, but can also include interviewing. The difference is that you go to the workplace or event, rather than bringing people to you. Field studies can reveal more accurate information because you are there to observe first-hand what really happens. You need not rely on someone to explain the process away from the work location or event.

Field studies can reveal more accurate information because you are there to observe first-hand what really happens.

The terms *contextual study* or *contextual inquiry* are used sometimes as synonyms for *field study*, although they can have a deeper meaning. Some usability engineers use *contextual study* to imply studying people in the context of where they work. In this sense, the term is the same as field study. When *contextual inquiry* is used, however, it sometimes refers to a specific method of inquiry described by Beyer and Holtzblatt in *Contextual Design*. The authors describe a detailed process not only of gathering information, but of analyzing the information to determine what information systems to build. In communicating with others, then, you should be specific and define how you are using the term. We usually use *study* to mean the broad idea of going out to a customer or user site, and save *contextual inquiry* for performing a full investigation as described by Beyer and Holtzblatt.

Here is a summary of guidelines for conducting field studies:

Prepare yourself. To make the best use of your time in the field, prepare ahead of time exactly how you will use the field study time. How many people do you need to meet with and observe? How much time will be spent observing and how much in discussion? What topics will you discuss? How much time will you realistically have with each person or group?

Make the best use of your observation. You may be able to conduct more interviews later, but this may be the only time you have to go out into the field. Make sure you leave plenty of time for observation.

Prepare your subjects. It is possible that the people you are going to observe have never participated in a field study. Before you go out, make sure you have explained to them what the study is about and what they can expect.

Set the tone and ground rules. Once you are at the site, reiterate the purpose and the ground rules with the participants. What do you want them to do? Are they supposed to talk to you while you are observing? If you are audiotaping or videotaping, can they ask you to stop the tape for any reason?

Choose an observation style. Decide ahead of time what the style of the study will be. Are you going to only observe? Observe and conduct an interview? It's often useful to use several methods.

Take good notes. If you want to be able to use the information you collect, you must take good notes. Consider having one person there just to take notes. Consider having two or more people take notes so they can be compared later. Consider audio- or videotaping the session.

Synthesize and summarize your notes. After the field study, summarize the important points as soon as possible.

User Narratives

It is often useful to describe user groups by describing a particular representative, but a fictitious, individual user, rather than the characteristics of the group. For example, here is a user narrative for the primary user group described in the matrix:

"Marianne is an office manager in a small engineering firm. She is 32 years old, and has a two-year technical college degree. She has been with the engineering firm for eight years and knows her job well. She has used computers for several years, and is familiar with Windows. She works in an office cubicle; the office is fairly noisy. English is her native language. She has never used speech software."

Narratives Make the User Present

In our experience, when teams develop user narratives, the user becomes more "real" and "present" during design. Team members will actually refer to and talk about "Marianne" as though she really existed. User narratives seem to keep the design process more user-centered.

Develop Current Task Analysis

Documenting the current tasks involves looking at how users do their current job in enough detail to provide the data you need to design a new interface. Task analysis provides the basis for deciding what the interface organization and conceptual design should be.

With speech interfaces, the new system is seldom a replica of the functions and tasks of the old work method. This new way of performing tasks is documented in later steps. First, it's critical to clearly understand the mental models users will bring with them to the new system. Users have built up certain ways of thinking about their work. You need to study and document these mental models, and take them into account when you design.

Document Task List

First, make a list of all the user tasks that relate to the software whose interface you are working on. We recommend that you limit your list to 20 or 30 items total. This means that for a large system, or complex tasks, you will combine small tasks into larger groups and list the groups only. Too long a list is unwieldy. For a small system, you may only have five or seven items on your list.

Consider using a task hierarchy to categorize tasks. Some systems may require only a simple list of tasks. Others may be more complex. A list of tasks and subtasks may be useful (or even just a simple categorization of tasks). You can use contextual studies, artifacts, and interviews in documenting the task list.

Analyze Current Workflow

The task list documents *what* work is being done with the current system. A workflow diagram describes *how* users are doing the work, as shown in Figure 11.4. It describes the process by detailing the tasks. By documenting and refining workflow, you will understand how users navigate through the current system. This information will be used in designing the new system. You can look for opportunities to leverage well-designed features of the legacy system. You can further improve the design by improving workflow and creating intuitive navigation. When you start working with future tasks, you will want to go into the detail of the workflow. However, the scope of analysis for workflow of current tasks is more critical for some systems than others. Some may require only a high-level analysis. As an interface designer, you need enough information to feel comfortable in understanding how users currently do their work so that you can improve the process by designing a more usable interface. Use as many levels of detail for workflow as needed for your project, keeping in mind that for future tasks you will go into even more detail.

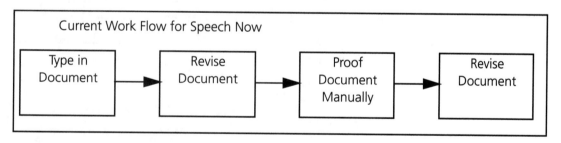

Figure 11.4 Current workflow example.

Develop Future Task Analysis

Moving from current tasks to future tasks represents a change from *what is* to *what will be*. This is a key point in the process and involves several steps, similar to the steps for developing the current task analysis.

Describe Problems and Opportunities

Once you have documented how work is currently done, you are ready to describe the changes to be made. Gather all problems and opportunities in a single document, called the Problems and Opportunities List. These can come from many sources. Write each problem or opportunity onto the current workflow. This combining the current workflow with the problems and opportunities is called the Problems and Opportunities Map. To come up with these problems and opportunities, you may want to use some of these techniques: brainstorming (described previously), a fishbone chart, or an affinity diagram (both of which are described next).

Fishbone Chart

A fishbone chart is a technique for diagramming the various factors that influence other factors or outcomes. It's called a fishbone because each part of the diagram looks like a bone from a fish. Altogether, the diagram looks like a fish skeleton, as shown in Figure 11.5.

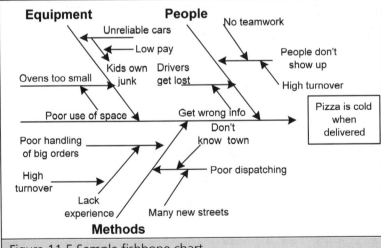

Figure 11.5 Sample fishbone chart.

Affinity Diagram

An affinity diagram is a technique for categorizing information. First you put each item of information on its own card or Post-it note. Then cluster the cards or Post-it notes that seem to "go together." You purposely do not come up with initial names for categories. The idea is to find the items that belong together and then later find a name for the group or category. Affinity diagrams, as shown in Figure 11.6, are useful for categorizing information, ideas, or tasks.

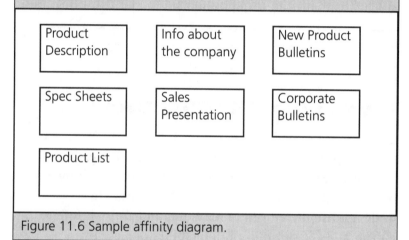

Product Description	Info about the company	New Product Bulletins
Spec Sheets	Sales Presentation	Corporate Bulletins
Product List		

Figure 11.6 Sample affinity diagram.

Create Task List

This is similar to the procedure you worked through in analyzing the current tasks. However, at this point you are creating new tasks that describe the future, called the Future Task List.

Analyze Workflow

Now you are ready to draw the future workflow. This workflow will describe what tasks users will do, and in what order, once the new system is in place. Starting from the current workflow, and building in the problems and opportunities you identified, you document the new workflow. Later, you will work with scenarios to elicit more details regarding workflow for different user groups and verify your analysis. Figure 11.7 shows the future workflow for our Speech Now interface.

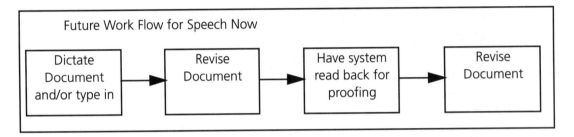

Figure 11.7 Future workflow sample.

Develop Usability Objectives

Earlier you defined high-level usability goals. Now is the time to specify what you mean by usable or user-friendly for this interface. Typical usability objectives include: ease of learning, rapid task performance, accurate task performance, perceived ease of use, and user preference. Figure 11.8 is a sample list of usability objectives.

Tasks (Measurable Behavior)	Criteria	Assumptions
Train system for personal speech	15 minutes	Use online coaching
Dictate one page of text	5 minutes	Support available
Listen to one page of text while making corrections and edits	10 minutes	Support available

Figure 11.8 Usability objectives list sample.

Revise Tools

You have now completed the analysis work and are ready
to make changes to the tools in any of the previous steps.
When you finish making any changes, gather all the tools
for all the steps into a deliverable: the analysis document.

Conceptual Model Design

A *conceptual model* can be thought of as a plan for how the
user will see the interface. It's a model of the interface, not
the underlying software structure. For users to predict
what will happen next and make appropriate decisions
about what to do next, they need a mental model of how
the software works. A conceptual model of the interface
conveys to users a working model that they can use to form
their mental model. The deliverable for this third phase is
the conceptual model design document and the steps
included in this phase are outlined in Table 11.3.

A conceptual model of
the interface conveys to
users a working model
that they can use to form
their mental model.

Software designers often jump immediately from existing
or proposed system design to detailed interface design,
translating the software professional's view of the system
(and jargon) into menus and prompts. Because the
interface is a direct translation of the system model, users
can't form a good mental model of how the system works
and how they should work with the interface to
accomplish their goals. They describe the interface as
"unfriendly."

Steps	Sub-Steps	Tools	Recommended Techniques or Comments
1. Describe user's interaction with new system	None	User scenarios and scripts	
2. Define objects	a. List candidates	Candidate objects list	Brainstorm Use card technique Use post-it notes
	b. Select major user objects	Major user objects list	
	c. Describe objects within system	Object matrix	
3. Design navigation		Window flow and/ or script flow diagram	
4. Revise tools and previous work, and develop a Conceptual Model Design Document		Analysis and design documents	

Table 11.3 Phase Three: Conceptual Model Design

Describe Interaction with New System

In this step, you use scenarios and scripts—a series of steps—to describe how users will do their work with the new software. To create scenarios and scripts, use your categorized user task list and workflow diagrams. Make sure in your scenarios and scripts that you adopt a user (not system) point of view.

Scenarios and scripts should

- Provide detail for each user task.
- Be in a prose or dialog format, and broken into steps.
- Include frequency information as a percentage. For example, note whether a particular step is performed 50 percent or 75 percent of the time. This allows you to optimize for the most frequent path.
- Specify modality. It's useful at this point in the analysis to note which tasks will involve what modalities. For example, some tasks may be speech only, others visual only, and others both speech and visual.

Figure 11.9 shows a sample scenario.

Create and Proof Documents

1. Dictate text into the word processor. This can be done using:

    speech only (30%)

    typing only (5%)

    or a combination of typing and speech (65%)

2. Visually proof as it appears on the screen (95%)

3. Have the computer read the text while visually proofing (50%)

4. Make corrections/revisions (60%)

5. Have the computer read again (10%)

Figure 11.9 Sample user scenario.

Scripts

Scripts are dialogs or conversations that users have with systems. They can be abstract and at a high level, or very specific, as in a prototype script. In a script, you show who is talking, followed by what they are saying.

> **Focus on Common Paths**
>
> It's often useful to focus first on common paths for your scenarios and scripts. Exceptions can quickly use up all your time, and you will find you have documented tasks that will happen only a small fraction of the time. Write your scenarios and scripts so that you have details for the common paths first. Then fill in the exceptions later. Use the 80 percent rule—first document what 80 percent of the users will be doing 80 percent of the time. Then document those tasks that will be done more than 50 percent of the time, but less than 80 percent. Lastly, make a pass to detail those branches that occur less than half the time.

Define Objects

User objects or *interface objects* are the pieces of your interface that users have to manipulate, either literally or figuratively, as they move through their workflow. These interface objects are usually related to (but not necessarily the same as) *underlying software objects*, or the objects described in the object-oriented (OO) analysis and design. Interface objects are objects in the representational world that you are creating with the interface. Interfaces without clear and obvious user objects are hard to design and hard to learn and use.

Interfaces without clear and obvious user objects are hard to design and hard to learn and use.

List Candidate Objects

In defining objects, begin with a list of candidates. A brainstorming session with members of the design team is effective for generating this list. Work with actual end users and subject matter experts as much as possible. Also, use your scenarios and scripts as a resource. Nouns indicate potential objects. Look at existing technical documentation of the system, including entity relationship diagrams and OO models, if they are available. If using technical documentation, be careful. Your focus is on identifying objects from a user's perspective. Technical documents are useful for brainstorming candidate objects, but must be tempered by a user-centered review.

Post-it Notes

Post-it notes are useful tools to have in your toolbox. We use Post-it notes to create affinity diagrams, list problems and opportunities, and create window and script flow diagrams. Post-it notes are useful because they can easily be picked up and repositioned.

Card Technique

Similar to an affinity diagram, the *card technique* allows you to cluster items that "belong together." One difference between the card technique and the affinity diagram is that the card technique allows you to name the categories as you proceed.

Select Major User Objects

Review your list of candidate objects and select the major user objects. Careful consideration needs to be given to the possible objects that users could manipulate during a particular task. Not all objects that users might interact with should be major user objects. It is critical that the interface design team decide which objects are the most important so that the design can be built around them.

Interface Objects vs. Programming Objects

The term *object* can be confusing. Here are some definitions and concepts that we find useful.

- We focus on interface objects. These are "things" that the user will actually manipulate—an invoice, a customer record, a hotel reservation, for example.

- Interface objects are not the same as programming objects. There is a relationship, but not exact. For example, Customer, Vendor, and Employee may have the same underlying programming object, but from the user's point of view these objects are very different.

- Once you pick interface objects that have importance and meaning for the user, and make them clear and identifiable, then your interface will be "intuitive."

- Keep the total number of interface objects in an interface to 15 or fewer. For a small application, seven is good. Some of your identified objects may actually be sub-objects or attributes, or different views of an object. For example, payment date may be an attribute of payment history, which is a sub-object of the customer object. Customer may have different "views," for example, a list of customers or details on customers.

- Design your windows/pages and navigation according to these interface objects and their views.

As you document your major user objects, choose object names carefully. See Figure 11.10 for an example. You are defining terminology that will be used throughout the interface. Make sure to get agreement on terms at an appropriate level for your project. Also, make sure that you adopt the user's terminology and not technical jargon.

Major User Objects for Speech Now

- Document
- Draft
- Final

Figure 11.10 Sample major user object list.

Describe Objects within the System

Once you have started to explore the objects and their relationships, create an object matrix to define additional information for each object as it will appear in the system. Your matrix should include a count for each object, as well as a list of the views and actions associated with each object. Figure 11.11 shows an example of this.

Design Navigation

At this point, your design includes all the requisite tasks and definitions of objects needed to begin developing navigation. As a designer, you have to answer the question, "How does the user navigate through the system?" To answer this question, create a navigation model.

If your interface involves auditory modalities, you will need a *script flow diagram*. The script flow diagram describes how the user moves through dialogs with the system. To create a script flow diagram from your scenarios, start at the beginning of a scenario and ask, "What dialog does the user need to have with the system to complete this scenario?" Draw a box representing a dialog, with arrows that show the order and relationship among the dialogs.

Object	Count	Views	Actions
Customers	Thousands	List, detail	Create new Edit Duplicate Inactivate Save Assign sales contact
Accounts	Thousands	List, detail, customer	Create new Edit terms Edit contact info Inactivate Save Assign sales contact Enter order Ship order Invoice for order View history
Items	Thousands	List, summary, detail	Create new Edit Inactivate Save Assign distributor View details

Figure 11.11 Sample object matrix.

If your interface involves visual modalities in addition to auditory, you will need to include *window flow diagrams*. The window flow diagram organizes objects and views, and defines how the user moves from one object to another. To create a window flow diagram from your scenarios, start at the beginning of a scenario and ask, "What object and what view are necessary for the user to take the steps described in this scenario? What object and view would come next according to the scenario?" Draw a box for each object-view combination, with arrows to connect the boxes in order. See Figure 11.12 for an example of a window flow.

If your interface includes both visual and auditory modalities, your navigation model will combine both window flow diagrams and script diagrams. Choose one type of box to represent a window and another to represent a dialog.

Window Flow Diagram for Checking Product Inventory

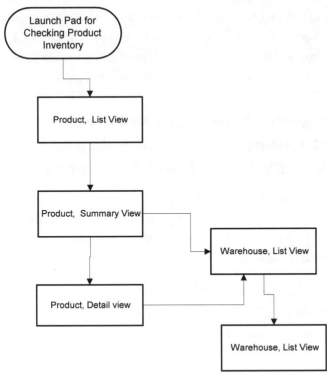

Figure 11.12 Sample window flow.

The navigation model gives you a bird's-eye view of the system. It shows the relationship between windows, between dialogs, and between windows and dialogs. Working from the scenarios in this way ensures that the navigation model supports the user's workflow. Since you use this navigation model to prototype the interface, you therefore ensure that the interface will match the way users do their work.

Flow-Charting

Whenever you need to show the movement through a sequence—for example, a series of steps to accomplish a task—a flow chart can be useful. There are formal notation schemes you can follow, or you can loosely create a flow chart by drawing boxes and using arrows to show the flow. We use flow charts to describe how users currently do their work, describe the future flow of work, and draw window and script flows.

Revise Tools and Previous Documents, and Develop a Conceptual Model Document

You have now completed the conceptual model work. You are ready to make changes to tools in any of the previous steps for this phase, or changes to the analysis information from phase two.

When you are finished making your changes, gather all the tools for all the steps of phase three into a deliverable: the conceptual model document.

Really Windows? And Dialogs?

Although we are using the terms window flow and dialog diagram, each box in the diagram may actually represent one window or dialog, part of a window or dialog, or even a collection of windows and dialogs. Because you have not tackled detailed design yet, you do not know how much will fit on a window or into a particular dialog. We are, therefore, using these terms loosely. You may come to realize later that one box contains multiple entities, or several boxes are combined into one.

Detail Design

The goal of the detail design phase is to use the analysis and conceptual model information to create actual windows and dialogs for the interface. During this phase, you create a prototype using storyboards, sketches, and online windows and dialogs. During this phase, you apply standards and guidelines. You also use heuristic reviews and walkthroughs with users and key stakeholders to get feedback and make changes to the interface. The steps and sub-steps and the necessary tools and techniques are highlighted in Table 11.4. The deliverable is the design document.

Steps	Sub-Steps	Tools	Recommended Techniques Comments
1. Determine scope for detail design	None	List of user scenarios	Select the breadth of the first detail design iteration
2. Create paper prototype	a. Create a storyboard	Storyboard	Storyboard
	b. Develop details	Window sketches and script dialogs Window and script descriptions Menus and toolbars, if any	
	c. Employ standards		Create or update standards as necessary
	d. Iterate window sketches and dialogs		
	e. Evaluate		Heuristic evaluation Walkthrough Usability testing
	f. Iterate design	Window sketches and dialogs	
3. Create design document	None	Design document	
4. Begin interface prototype	a. Create online prototype	Interface prototype	

Steps	Sub-Steps	Tools	Recommended Techniques Comments
	b. Evaluate		Heuristic evaluation Standards review Walkthrough Usability testing
5. Iterate design	None	Interface prototype	
6. Complete design document	None	Design document	

Table 11.4 Phase Four: Detail Design

Determine Scope for Detail Design

The first step in detail design is to decide which part or parts of the interface you are going to work on. If the system you are designing is large, you may want to limit the scope of phase four to a piece of the system. Repeat phase four as needed until the entire interface is designed.

Choose the scenarios, window flow diagrams, and dialogs that match the part you want to work on for this pass through phase four and make a list of user scenarios. This is where you select the breadth of the first detail design iteration.

Create Paper Prototype

To create usable interfaces you must be able to

- Iterate the design several times
- Get feedback early
- Create collaboratively rather than alone

Paper prototyping allows you to do these tasks, rather than creating windows and dialogs online immediately.

Create a Storyboard

A storyboard is a series of rough drawings or dialogs that correspond to a portion of your window flow diagrams or script flow diagrams. Storyboards are rough and easily changed. To create the storyboard, you need the scenarios, scripts, script flow diagrams, and window flow diagrams in front of you. Working from these tools, you will draw the series of windows that match the part of the window flow diagram you are creating, and type dialogs to match your scripts.

Develop Details

Once you have a storyboard for a set of windows and dialogs, you can iterate them by developing window and dialog details.

Employ Standards

Check your design at this point to be sure that it meets industry standards, as well as any corporate or project standards that exist. Update or create standards if you need to.

User interface standards are concise rules for design that can be followed by designers and developers with minimal interpretation. User interface standards provide system users with a more effective and productive interface. In addition, implementation of standards contributes to a more efficient software development process. Benefits of implementing user interface design standards include:

> **Reducing user interface design time.** Recurring design decisions, such as the graphic for a navigation toolbar

button, don't have to be discussed repeatedly for each new application or site.

Reducing development time. Standards allow the development of reusable class libraries. These class libraries can contain code that automatically supports guidelines.

Providing consistency. People concurrently use many internal applications as well as external applications. Developing consistent user interface elements and standards gives users confidence and causes less work-related frustration.

Reducing user-training time. Once users are familiar with one application, they will know how to use other applications.

Reducing user assistance development costs. User assistance can be more efficient if many user interface functions are consistent between applications.

Having standards in place and making sure they are used are two different things. Some standards are so well known that they are adhered to out of habit. Others are new and will not be followed unless people consciously remember to apply them. It's important that during the design process you perform standards reviews and change the interface to reflect the standards.

In the early part of conceptual model design, the team is focused on initial design work. Although it's useful for the team to know about the standards during this part of the process, it's not likely, or necessary, that they be conscious of them early in design.

As soon as the interface has moved past storyboarding and initial design, however, it's important that standards reviews be performed.

Just as it's hard to proofread your own writing, it can be difficult to review your own interface for a standards check. If you do your own review, make sure to have someone else review the interface as well. Do standards reviews on early prototypes, later prototypes, and after implementation. Any time someone works on the interface or iterates it once more, there is the chance that standards were not followed when incorporating the changes.

Iterate

Before windows and dialogs are coded, it's easy and inexpensive to iterate and make changes.

Evaluate

You need feedback from others about the prototype. Use a combination of heuristic evaluation, walkthroughs, and usability testing to get feedback from others.

Heuristic Evaluations: According to *Merriam-Webster's Collegiate Dictionary, heuristic* means "an aid to learning, discovery, or problem-solving by experimental and especially trial and error methods." A heuristic evaluation is an evaluation of an interface based on rules and principles that have been developed over time from experimentation and trial and error. To employ a heuristic evaluation, you must ask another interface designer or usability engineer go through your interface piece by piece and apply certain principles, rules, or laws: for example, the heuristics that we have covered in this book.

It's useful to have another person evaluate an interface you have been designing, since it's sometimes difficult to identify flaws when the design is your own.

Just as it's hard to proofread your own writing, it can be difficult to review your own interface for a standards check.

Before windows and dialogs are coded, it's easy and inexpensive to iterate and make changes.

Walkthroughs: One of the most common and useful techniques we have for improving an interface is the *walkthrough*. In a typical walkthrough, you take someone through the interface as though they were performing a task, although this is not necessary. You demonstrate windows and scripts to them, and ask for their comments. You would then ask them questions, if necessary, about their comments, and take notes on their feedback.

It's useful to conduct walkthroughs with a number of people: for example, users who have not been involved in the project or key stakeholders who may not be users but whose opinions are important. Domain experts, other interface designs or usability engineers, and technical experts or developers are also good people to ask because each of these groups will give you different feedback. All points of view are useful when deciding how to iterate or improve an interface.

Usability Testing: The goal of usability testing is to collect real data on real users in order to discover usability problems before software is released. Domain experts, interface designers, and programmers are not real users, and until real users are asked to do real tasks, the usability of a product cannot be adequately evaluated.

A usability test uncovers valuable information that is used to improve the interface design. The usability testing team should assume there will be usability problems. Even a system that is well designed and follows best practice will reveal some usability problems during testing, although these problems are usually small and easily fixed if best practice has been followed.

> Domain experts, interface designers, and programmers are not real users, and until real users are asked to do real tasks, the usability of a product cannot be adequately evaluated.

> The usability testing team should assume there will be usability problems.

Usability testing for software has established protocols, procedures, and methodologies that testing teams follow to ensure accurate and reliable data.

The following is a summary of usability testing tasks:

Usability testing project planning. Decide on testing goals, timetables, and members of the testing team. Write a preliminary test plan.

Decide on and prioritize usability specifications. Decide what to test, create usability specifications for those tasks, and prioritize them.

Decide on the user participants. Based on the goals of the project and what is to be tested, determine the characteristics of the user participants. Include a description of the desired participants, sub-groups, if any, and a participant matrix that shows how many participants are to come from each sub-group.

Schedule participants. Based on participant decisions, recruit and schedule participants.

Create participant descriptions. Once participants have been chosen, describe the actual participants.

Decide on and describe testing scenarios. Based on the usability specifications, decide on the exact testing scenarios to be used, including the order of the tasks.

Identify and describe testing specifications for prototype and test data. Describe the specifications for a prototype and sample data for the test scenarios to be completed.

Create a final testing plan. Create a final testing plan, including

- the objectives of the test
- a description of methodology
- a schedule of participants
- participant descriptions
- a description of testing scenarios
- a description of the testing location, facilities, and equipment

Prepare the testing materials. Prepare all the materials for the test, including

- the script for the participants (with any data they need);
- questionnaires or surveys
- thinking aloud instructions
- a briefing form for the tester
- observer forms and logging software
- a post-test interview form for the tester
- permission/confidentiality forms

Describe and prepare the testing location, facilities, and equipment. Describe your final decisions on the location, facilities, and equipment for each test. Prepare the facilities and all equipment for testing.

Test the prototype and test data. Test the prototype and test data against the script to make sure all parts of the system are working correctly.

Run a pilot. Conduct a pilot test in the actual facilities with a real end-user from the participant roster.

Conduct the usability tests. Conduct the actual tests with the participants.

Prepare your preliminary findings. Prepare a brief preliminary report of your findings immediately after the tests.

Analyze the data and prepare a final report. Perform a complete analysis and report. Create an excerpt videotape showing clips of the most critical findings.

Present and discuss your findings and recommendations. Present your findings to others, and decide on the next steps.

Create a Design Document

Once you have a paper prototype, you can begin your design document. The design document will be your final deliverable. Although you are not yet ready to complete it, you can begin it. The design document contains pictures and descriptions of each window and a script for each dialog. The purpose of creating a design document is to communicate to others the interface you have created.

Create an Online Prototype

Using an online prototyping tool, create a series of online windows and auditory scripts. The goal is to see what the windows will look like in a computer medium and to hear the dialogs.

Evaluate

Use one or more evaluation techniques to review the prototype in a computer medium: standards reviews, heuristic evaluations, walkthroughs, or usability testing.

> ### Prototype
>
> The term *prototype* has come to mean different things to different people. To a developer, a prototype is usually a robust working model. To an interface designer, a prototype often means a rougher earlier iteration. Both types of prototype are useful. An interface designer, however, wants to see or hear the design before too much time and money has been invested. Interface designers typically want to iterate and make changes. This means they will want their prototypes to be quick and changeable, and this usually means rougher and earlier.
>
> The purpose of the prototype is often different, as well, to an interface designer and a developer. The interface designer is testing interface ideas, conceptual models, metaphors, and the flow of the script or windows. The interface designer is less concerned with technical and implementation issues than the developer.

Iterate

Based on the evaluation, change and iterate the online prototype. It may seem that you are going through a lot of cycles of iteration. You are. Iteration is the key to usable interfaces. Every time you change the interface based on an evaluation, you are improving the interface. This is your chance to make changes before coding begins.

Complete the Design Document

Now you are ready to complete the design document as the final deliverable for this phase.

Iteration is the key to usable interfaces. Every time you change the interface based on an evaluation, you are improving the interface.

Implementation and Evaluation

With the completion of phase four and the design document, you have completed the interface design. You are ready to communicate the design to the programming team. During phase five, you formally evaluate the application and make your final iterations. Refer to Table 11.5 for a list of the tasks involved in this phase. The final deliverables are the evaluation documents, the revised design document, and the application.

Steps	Sub-Steps	Tools	Recommended Techniques Comments
1. Evaluate the application	None	None	Heuristic and standards review Walkthrough (optional)
2. Revise the design document	None	None	
3. Obtain user feedback	None	None	Usability testing Walkthrough (optional)
4. Iterate the design and update design document	None	• Next version of application • Revised design document	

Table 11.5 Phase Five: Implementation and Evaluation

Why a "Handoff" Doesn't Work

"Handing off" an interface to a programming team and then not being involved in its implementation is almost a guarantee of usability failure. You will need to stay involved as the interface is implemented. Here are some reasons:

Even if you do a good job with the design document, the programming team will have questions about the interface. You want to be available to them quickly so that they do not "guess" at the answer.

Technical and project issues come up during coding that may require changes to the interface. You want to be available to influence those decisions from a usability point of view.

Evaluate the Application

Evaluate the windows using one or more evaluation techniques, such as a standards review, heuristic evaluation, or walkthrough, discussed previously in this chapter.

Iterate the Design

Make changes to the application based on the evaluations.

Obtain User Feedback

In addition to evaluating the application, you are ready to do your final round of user feedback and testing.

Iterate the Design and Update the Design Document

Make your final changes to the application and create the next version of the application. Update the design document as necessary.

Interview with Nicole Yankelovich

Principal Investigator

Sun Microsystems Laboratories

Nicole Yankelovich is a principal investigator at Sun Microsystems Laboratories. Nicole established and managed the speech group at Sun Microsystems. Her background is in interface design research, including speech interfaces over the telephone and dialog design. In her interview, she describes some of her surprising results with usability testing of speech interfaces, and several of the usability engineering techniques they use at Sun to design speech applications.

What do you think are some of the interface challenges in speech applications?

Although I have designed a couple of multi-modal speech applications, my primary concentration has been on telephone-based applications. I think that the challenges are different, depending on your context. But in both contexts, the most difficult challenge is letting users know what they can say—letting them know the range of things they can say and where the limits of the application are.

The most difficult challenge is letting users know what they can say.

Talk some more about how you deal with that from an interface level.

Part of it depends on the constraints you have based on the technology you are using. My primary focus has been on using discourse cues in the prompts to constrain what people can say. That has some limitations. One of the techniques that I think is the most effective is the one that they use in Wildfire that I call "removable hints." It's a personalized approach where they keep track of how many times the user has successfully navigated a prompt. For the first, let's say, three times, they have hints on the prompt that suggest things you could say in response to the prompt. Once you have successfully navigated that prompt several times, those hints are removed, figuring that you know how to say it. If there is some piece of the interface you don't negotiate until a year down the line, since it's on a prompt by prompt basis, you would still get the hints on the prompts. This is a different approach from the expert/novice approach where a novice user gets lots of help but an expert doesn't. People can be a novice on parts of the system, and still be an expert on other parts.

Can you give me an example of a removable hint?

Here's an example from the Wildfire system that I wrote about in my 1996 *Interactions* article (Yankelovich, 1996). The first few times, the prompt from the computer with a hint in it would go as follows:

System: "Oh, hi! You have two new messages. The first is from Rich Miner."

I'd recommend saying, "What's-it-say, Describe-it, or Next-item."

After a few times the message would say instead:

System: "Oh, hi! You have two new messages. The first is from Rich Miner."

By that time you should have learned that you could say, "What's-it-say," "Describe-it," or "Next-item."

They design the prompts so that the hint is the second part and it can be removed, and the prompt will still make sense. It's a teaching technique, essentially.

I still think you need to use that in conjunction with some discourse cues, so that you phrase the prompt using the kind of language and sentence construct that you want people to reply with. That's what people do: they mimic the construct of the questioner.

By using these removable hints and the discourse cues, you're helping users know what's OK to say?

That's right. It's still a problem, because even with the removable hints there are some short cuts that they might be able to say. It's not realistic to think that you can give them suggestions of more than three or four possibilities, but at least they can get through the interaction.

What is the problem that you are trying to avoid?

Being able to predict what people are going to say makes your performance better.

Speech is so error-prone. You want to prevent people from speaking "out of grammar" if you're using a grammar-based system. But even with systems that are not grammar-based, being able to predict what people are going to say makes your performance better.

How do people react to these kinds of discourse cues or removable hints? Are they aware that their speech is being modeled or constrained? Do they mind that?

Oh, no. A lot my work has been based on the book *Media Equation* (Reeves and Nass, 1999). To me, all of their research indicates that people have "old" brains. Discourse is part of our old brain. It's part of the way our brain has developed to understand language, so if it seems natural, then people don't even notice. No matter how much you try to avoid designing personality into your system, people ascribe personality. My feeling is, you might as well take advantage of it rather than try to fight it. Tony Lovell did a brilliant interface design project. He was working with a constrained recognizer, not a grammar-based recognizer. His elegant design made the system seem so conversational even with a constrained recognizer.

> No matter how much you try to avoid designing personality into your system, people ascribe personality.

There are some other issues. There's the issue of people responding in human ways to the computer. One of the most startlingly findings that I had was in a usability study of our SpeechActs system. We were testing a mail and calendar application. Before this study, I had done a lot of usability testing of graphical interfaces. Users are much more tolerant of errors in graphical applications. If they get a dialog box and it says the same thing all the time, that is considered consistent. But in a speech application if your messages—not just your error messages, but any messages—are too repetitive, people get angry. Think about it: if I kept repeating the same thing to you, you would consider that hostile behavior. It amazed me at how upset people got, and how quickly.

> In a speech application if your messages—not just your error messages, but any messages—are too repetitive, people get angry.

So their expectations must be very different.

I think the way their brains process the verbal information is related to how they interact verbally. The only verbal interactions we have in our lives are with other people.

There's something wired in our brains; if you hear people say the same thing over and over, it's considered rude and uncooperative.

Not only is it annoying, users think the computer is not being intelligent. They actually take it personally.

It's an emotional response. Here's an example: In the first design, every time there was a recognition error, the system would say, "Sorry, please rephrase." After the third time the system said, "Sorry, please rephrase," people were visibly upset and angry. In response, we didn't change the performance of the system, we changed the error dialog. The first time the system just said, "Sorry." The assumption was that it was a recognition error caused, for example, by the person speaking too soon. If they just repeated what they said, there's a chance it would work the second time. If it didn't understand again, the system would say, "Sorry, please rephrase," because maybe they are talking out of grammar and they need to say it a different way. And the third time the system would say, "I'm having trouble understanding you. Try speaking clearly."

That's interesting. I always assumed that those multiple prompts were to give more information, but you are saying part of it is to say it in a different way.

It serves a dual purpose. You're both trying to correct the problem and you're trying to have the system act in a cooperative manner. When we changed the error dialogs, the people said the system was really good and cooperative. It was an amazing thing. To me, it brought home that you can't violate the discourse rules of a polite society. It's a combination of using proper language and some of the conventions that we've developed. People perceive that as cooperative behavior and they will put up with cooperative behavior. Even though in the end they weren't getting their task done any faster or better, their perception of the system was much more positive. We called those prompts "progressive assistance."

Designing a graphical interface and a speech interface are so different. When I started designing speech interfaces, I was frustrated because I didn't know what to draw. I was used to drawing storyboards! Designing a speech interface was tough. There still aren't any good tools to help you design a speech interface, but I finally came to a technique of writing out dialogs like you'd write for a play. I used to get my team to try out the script—we would do readings.

Hold auditions!

Sort of. Just having things spoken out loud was amazing. Some things were hard to say—they didn't flow, whereas written they sounded fine. The other aspect that's different is consistency. You would never dream of designing a graphical error dialog that was different every time it came up. I can't imagine designing anything like that. Graphical designers moving into speech have some different issues they need to think about.

Speech interface design needs to be a separate design effort. If you just tack it onto the graphical interface, your application is doomed to mediocrity if not failure.

What kinds of problems occur if people try and do that?

Techniques that work really well in graphical interfaces don't work well in speech applications. In the e-mail application we designed, listing message headers, senders, dates, and times are good techniques for a GUI application. But if you try to read that over the phone, it's a disaster. Text output is too slow. You need to come up with techniques for grouping messages, truncating what you say, picking out the pertinent information, and giving people summary information, rather than all the detail up front.

Speech interface design needs to be a separate design effort. If you just tack it onto the graphical interface, your application is doomed to mediocrity if not failure.

You have to structure the information differently if you want to present it orally.

You have to look at how people speak in the application domain. Even if you're adding speech to a graphical application, even if it's multi-modal, it's still important to understand how people talk about it

For every application I've designed, we've set up a situation in the lab where two people talk to each other.

You have to structure the information differently if you want to present it orally.

When you look at the whole UI design process, you have to do some sort of pre-design work before you start designing the application. You have to look at how people speak in the application domain. When we designed the calendar application, we did a field study of salespeople who called into their administrative assistant who maintained the calendar. They almost never talked about specific dates. The guys in the field didn't have a calendar in front of them, so they talked almost exclusively in relative terms. Relative dates are not even a concept that is in a graphical calendar. You don't discover that without doing some kind of a study of the language used in the domain. Just studying the graphical application isn't enough. Even if you are adding speech to a graphical application, even if it's multi-modal, it's still important to understand how people talk about it.

Talk to me about usability testing for speech applications. Would you want to test usability early with the speech equivalent of a paper prototype? What would that be?

I had no personal luck with any kind of a "Wizard of Oz" study (a testing technique that uses a human to simulate the role of the computer during testing), which would be the speech equivalent of a paper prototype. Some of the speech groups out there have some good tools for "Wizard of Oz" studies, and if we had those tools, I might reassess, but it's costly to develop them. You have to do a really good pre-design study. It's not just going out there and doing a field study. For every application I've designed, we've set up a situation in the lab where two people talk to each other. Sometimes it was two subjects, and sometimes it was an experimenter and a subject, but we tried to set up a situation that was as close to reality as possible. For example, with e-mail we set up one subject as the person who has the computer and e-mail in front of them and the other person is on the road with a telephone. And we said, "OK, call up this other person and have them read you your e-mail." That was all the instruction we gave. That mimicked the exact situation. We expected people to be calling from the road.

So you were using a person prototype instead of a paper prototype.

We called it a pre-design study. In another multi-modal example, we did a graphics editor with speech added, so you could use the mouse to "rubber band" out a rectangle. While you were doing that, you could say, "Make it red with a ten point blue border." We had an experimenter and subject in front of a computer with a graphics editor. The rule was that the subject could use the mouse within the drawing area, but the experimenter had to use the mouse for all the menus and tool selection. They passed the mouse back and forth. The subject had to somehow verbalize to the experimenter what they wanted done. We gave them a task, such as "draw your house."

My favorite application that we designed was called Office Monitor. It was a dummy that would sit in your office while you were out and take messages for you if people dropped by. It worked with a motion detector. So if someone walked into your office, it would detect movement and say, "Hi, are you looking for Nicole?" and go through a dialog. In the pre-design study, we did a survey of the building and found the three or four people who had the most visitors to their office. We said, "When you leave your office for more than an hour, give us a call." They would call and say, "I'm going out for an hour." We would run down and sit in their office and anyone that came by, we would take a message and we would record the conversation. One of the things we found was that the conversations didn't last more than 15 to 30 seconds. Trying to design a dialog that brief was a real challenge.

I do a pretty thorough job of these natural dialog studies. Then I go right to the dialog design. I'm blessed with a fantastic engineering team, so we're able to get the dialogs up and running pretty quickly. Rather than do any kind of "Wizard of Oz" study, we would implement the actual design. Everybody who works for me knows that they have to change things ten thousand times before we're done. We go from natural dialog study to implementation to usability testing, and then iterate like crazy. There's just nothing like trying it out with real people to find out all the ways you blew it.

> We go from natural dialog study to implementation to usability testing, and then iterate like crazy.

Are people as uniform with speech as with GUIs? With testing GUIs, you need four to six representative users to catch everything. Everybody after that does what everyone else did.

That's true in terms of the interaction. It's not true in terms of the recognition. You never really know what the recognizer is going to work for and what it isn't. The biggest frustration in designing speech applications is that you can do the best design in the world and somebody comes up with a voice that is not right for the recognizer and it doesn't work. It's demoralizing. For the very constrained applications that the vendors spend a lot of time training voice models for, it works pretty well. But for those of us using off-the-shelf voice recognizers who don't do any special voice modeling, it's still frustrating.

> The biggest frustration of designing speech applications is that you can do the best design in the world and somebody comes up with a voice that is not right for the recognizer and it doesn't work.

What about speech and handheld devices?

I don't know if it is going to fly. I think there are a lot of social reasons why that's not going to work. Do you really want to be walking down the street talking to your device?

This whole idea of talking to yourself—it's bad enough to be talking to yourself in your office, let alone out in public. There's a lot social stigma associated with that. Privacy is a huge issue, particularly if it's e-mail—you don't know the contents, and everyone can hear it. Having speech output is disruptive if everyone is working in an open office.

One problem with some multi-modal interfaces is that they're designed with speech in but no speech out. Wouldn't it be weird if I were talking to you and you were typing back at me? It seems that conversations need to have reciprocity.

Is speech mainstream yet and, if not, what will it take to get it there?

It's not mainstream yet and I think we are quite a ways from being mainstream. Microsoft is putting a lot of money into this area, though, so perhaps it'll happen faster than I think. We've seen some big breakthroughs in speech technology with continuous speech dictation systems. That's been a huge advance, but they still only work well for the people who speak in the right way and are very motivated. You can get speech to work well over the telephone for niche applications, but I don't see everyone interacting with their computer with speech for two reasons. One is the recognition technology, and two is that everyone thinks this is a big panacea—that everyone wants to sit down and talk to their computer. Speech is not the only issue. You've got to deal with language. Just because the computer understands your speech doesn't mean it understands your mind. That is a much bigger leap.

Do you think we'll get there?

It will be incremental. We won't suddenly see a product where you talk to your computer and it performs high-level conceptual agent actions. We'll see small applications

> Privacy is a huge issue, particularly if it's e-mail—you don't know the contents, and everyone can hear it. Having speech output is disruptive if everyone is working in an open office.

> Just because the computer understands your speech doesn't mean it understands your mind. That is a much bigger leap.

that do natural language inquiries. Speech is currently a better way to interact over the telephone than lengthy touchtone interfaces that exist for constrained applications, for getting stock quotes, interacting with your calendar, e-mail, voice mail. You can do an effective speech application like that, but to me that's not really mainstream. That's a long way away from everyone interacting with their computer using speech as a primary input mode.

Over the telephone is the best place to do speech, not on the desktop. I can't imagine why anyone would rather talk to their computer if they are able to type or use a mouse.

Summary

To ensure a usable product, you need to follow a process that stresses usability engineering techniques and steps.

Another aspect of best practice is making sure your design is accessible to all kinds of users, including those with disabilities. The next chapter focuses on universal access design.

Universal Design

"Hi, Grandma! It's me, Timmy, in 2036!
I'm using the video conferencing time
travel interface you just gave me
for Christmas!"

"It is our belief that computers do not just make people more productive, but that they have an almost magical way of increasing an individual's independence. Self-expression. Participation. Choices. And self-esteem."
Apple Computer's Disability Solutions Group

Universal design is the concept of designing products that are usable by all people, including people with disabilities. Part of a usability engineer or user interface designer's role is to act as an advocate for universal design, which will improve the overall usability of a product, as well as benefit users with disabilities.

The Audience for Universal Design

Approximately 10 to 15 percent of the population has an impairment that affects their ability to use consumer products safely or efficiently. This equates to about 30 million people in the U.S. Some people have impairments, or disabilities, from birth, while others acquire them through accident or disease. Many people are temporarily disabled during their lifetime and at some point we all face certain disabilities related to aging. Categories of disabilities we may face include

- visual impairments
- hearing impairments
- physical impairments
- cognitive and language impairments
- speech impairments

In addition, some people suffer from seizure disorders and others face multiple disabilities.

Assistive technology is specialized technology that accommodates users with disabilities. It is often discussed as being synonymous with universal design. While they are separate fields, they are closely related and have many goals and principles in common.

Assistive technology affects a small user group and tends to be expensive to develop because its costs are shared among a small population. For example, consider a paraplegic computer user who uses a "sip and puff" device to control their computer. The user blows air through a tube to produce Morse code that allows them to control their computer. This is an example of assistive technology. A speech-enabled GUI word processor may benefit a user with a visual or physical disability such as a repetitive stress disorder, but it's more an example of universal design than assistive technology. Other user groups benefit from its implementation as well. These concepts are often discussed under the general heading of accessibility. Refer to the resources on the World Wide Web listed here for more specific information about each of these areas of disability.

Universal design benefits people with disabilities, people without disabilities, and people who are temporarily disabled. Sometimes users may have trouble using products due to the environment or an unusual circumstance.

People who will benefit from universal design include

- a person on a noisy street who can't hear an ATM's voice response
- a person driving a car who has to make a phone call without looking at their mobile phone
- a person who forgot their glasses and is trying to read a subway schedule
- an elderly person
- a disabled person

Almost anyone will benefit from universal design.

Resources on the World Wide Web
www.trace.wisc.edu
www.w3c.org/wai
www.usdoj.gov/crt/ada
www.sun.com/access
www.ibm.com/sns
www.el.net/CAT/index.html
www.webable.com
www.eia.org/eif/toc.htm
www.lighthouse.org/print_leg.htm

Speech Technology and Universal Design

Speech technology can be used as an assistive technology, but it also has application for universal design. Consider a multi-modal GUI application. A person without a disability who may need to work in a hands-free manner for a specific task can use a multi-modal GUI application. A person with a visual or physical disability might use the application to perform the same task. There are many examples of universal design that employ speech user interfaces.

One early implementation of speech technology was a "smart house." Like the Hal2000 project described in chapter 7, this is a speech interface that lets users control most home electronic systems, such as lights, security, heating, and cooling. While this is a universal design concept for those who can afford it, it's also a blessing for people with severe physical disabilities. This technology allows such people to enjoy a level of independent living that would not be possible without speech recognition technology. As the baby boomer population ages, this technology may become more prevalent.

In addition to speech recognition, speech synthesis has implications for universal design and assistive technology. Consider a computer user whose voice may be unintelligible due to a disability such as cerebral palsy. They may be able to use text-to-speech technology to communicate verbally with others. If such applications were commonplace, even temporarily disabled users such as a person with laryngitis could benefit from the technology.

Blind users often rely on screen readers and speech synthesis. Internet e-mail has become one of the primary beneficiaries of speech synthesis. There are many applications available that read e-mail. This application was pushed forward by users who wanted their e-mail read to them over the telephone—a universal design concept—but it can benefit visually impaired users, as well.

Assistive technology has business implications for the labor market. There is a segment of the population that, because of their disabilities, has previously been unable to be part of the labor market. We were part of a program that involved mentoring physically disabled users in computer-based job skills. Using speech technology and other assistive technologies, our clients gained technical skills in programming and eventually obtained employment in the software development industry. With the current shortage of skilled workers in the labor market, it's important to take advantage of every opportunity to train skilled workers.

Accomplishing Universal Design

People with disabilities face the same usability issues as those without, and sometimes more. Whether we view them as issues of universal design or assistive technology, designing effective usable software requires following a good usability engineering process and paying attention to the principles of usable design. Employing speech input or output in an interface requires that a designer understand the users, their needs, their tasks, and their environment. In addition, an effective designer must understand the technology. Striving for a high level of usability will accomplish some, or even many, of the goals of universal design.

Specifically, designers must educate themselves on the principles, guidelines, and techniques of universal design. There are many resources available and information on universal design is increasingly available at trade shows, conferences, and professional development courses. Beyond employing these principles, guidelines, and techniques in design, it's critical that usability engineers test for universal design and accessibility. Evaluation is the key to assessing the level of a product's accessibility.

The Microsoft Windows Guidelines for Accessible Software Design (May 7, 1997, edition)

- Flexible, customizable user interfaces can accommodate the user's needs and preferences. For example, you should allow the user to choose font sizes, reduce visual complexity, and customize the arrangement of menus.

- Be compatible with accessibility aids, such as blind-access, screen magnification, and voice input utilities. This is achieved by using standard programming techniques and user-interface elements, or by supporting Active Accessibility.

- Support the user's choice of output methods through the use of sound and visuals and of visual text and graphics. You should combine these output methods redundantly or allow the user to choose his or her preferred output method.

- Support the user's choice of input methods by providing keyboard access to all features and by providing access to common tasks using simple mouse operations.

- Consistency with other Windows-based applications and with system standards makes it easier for users to learn and use the application. It also ensures that you support system accessibility features. For example, you should support Control Panel settings for colors and sizes and use standard keyboard behavior.

Printed with permission. For detailed guidelines and current information on accessibility, visit www.microsoft.com/enable

Justification for Universal Design

There are many reasons why it's important to include universal design concepts and accessibility in your design program and development effort.

- It allows you to comply with the Americans with Disabilities Act (ADA). This legislation requires that employers provide reasonable accommodation for employees with disabilities.

- It may also allow you to comply with sections 504 and 508 of the Rehabilitation Act.

- It allows you to comply with the United Kingdom's Disability Discrimination Act, which is similar to the ADA in the U.S. The Disability Discrimination Act legislation may soon be effective for the rest of Europe, as well.

- It allows you to prepare for compliance with pending changes to the Telecommunications Act, which may mandate specific levels of accessibility for applications on or distributed via the Internet.

"The power of the Web is in its universality. Access by everyone regardless of disability is an essential aspect."

Tim Berners-Lee, credited as the inventor of the World Wide Web

Section 504 of the Rehabilitation Act

"No otherwise qualified handicapped individual in the United States...shall, solely by reason of...handicap, be excluded from participation in, be denied the benefits of, or be subjected to discrimination under any program or activity receiving federal financial assistance."

Section 508 of the Rehabilitation Act

"Accessibility Requirements for Federal Departments and Agencies: Development, procurement, maintenance, or use of electronic and information technology: When developing, procuring, maintaining, or using electronic and information technology, each Federal department or agency, including the United States Postal Service, shall ensure, unless an undue burden would be imposed on the department or agency, that the electronic and information technology allows, regardless of the type of medium of the technology—

(i) individuals with disabilities who are Federal employees to have access to and use of information and data that is comparable to the access to and use of the information and data by Federal employees who are not individuals with disabilities; and

(ii) individuals with disabilities who are members of the public seeking information or services from a Federal department or agency to have access to and use of information and data that is comparable to the access to and use of the information and data by such members of the public who are not individuals with disabilities."

- It allows you to meet standards for usability published by the Human Factors and Ergonomics Society (HFES), American National Standards Institute (ANSI), and the International Organization for Standardization (ISO).

Industry Standards

For more information from HFES, ANSI, and ISO, go to these Web sites:

- www.hfes.org
- www.ansi.org
- www.iso.ch

- It may increase the market for your product by making it usable for an additional 30 million people in the U.S. and even more throughout the rest of the world.
- It's the right thing to do for both social reasons and for best practice toward achieving a high level of usability.

Summary

Designing products that are usable by all people, including people with disabilities, is part of making products usable. The legal and ethical justifications for universal design are substantial. In addition, with more than 30 million people in the U.S. facing certain impairments, there is a reasonable business justification for universal design for almost any product.

A History of Relevant Technology for Speech

**Any sufficiently advanced technology is
indistinguishable from magic.**
Arthur C. Clarke in **Technology and the Future**

Human-computer interaction (HCI) is a multi-disciplinary
field. This timeline is intended to provide a context for
developments in our industry and related communities of
practice. As with any discipline, those who are successful
stand on the shoulders of giants.

Time Period	Event
Circa 3000 B.C.	**Early Writing** Sumerians use pictographs as written language on stone. Not only do individual pictographs represent one or several words, but they contain phonetic implications to suggest pronunciation. Egyptian hieroglyphs further develop this concept. These are the first icons.
Circa 500 B.C.	**Writing on Paper** Paper scrolls replace stone tablets as a more convenient medium for recording information.
Circa 400 B.C. - 200 A.D.	**Primitive Calculators and Books** Primitive counting machines and calculators, such as the abacus in China as well as the similar Roman tools called calculi, were used. Various civilizations used manual calculators for mathematical calculations and application in areas such as trigonometry and astronomy. About 100 A.D. bound books replace scrolls and become the standard means of sharing information in Rome. In 200 A.D. the concept of zero comes into being in India, a significant mathematical event.
1455	**Printing Press Invented by Johann Gutenberg** Gutenberg employs metal castings for movable type and produces the first printed book, a Latin version of the Bible.

Time Period	Event
Early 1600s	**Manual Calculators** Scottish mathematician John Napier, inventor of logarithms, invents "Napier's Bones," a portable set of ivory rods used to perform calculations. A popular tool for performing multiplication and division, it was used in British schools as a math aid until the 1960s. In 1622, William Oughtred invents the slide rule, based on Napier's Bones.
1642	**Calculating Machines** Blaise Pascal invents the first calculating machine. His work is followed by Wilhelm Schickard and others.
Late 1700s	**Genesis of Synthesis** In 1773, the first attempts at speech synthesis were carried out by a professor of physiology in Copenhagen. He creates a machine that can produce vowels by connecting resonance tubes to organ pipes. In 1791, Wolfgang von Kempelen invents the first machine to produce entire words and sentences. His mechanical synthesizer is based on the human phenomena involved in speech production, including a bellows to simulate the human lungs and a reed to simulate the vocal chords. His machine is preserved in Munich's Deutsches Museum.

Time Period	Event
1801	**Foundation of Computer Programming** Frenchman Joseph-Marie Jacquard invents a loom that uses punch cards to create intricate patterns in fabrics. Jacquard's loom thus employs embedded sequential logic, which is considered to be the foundation of computer programming.
1822-1833	**Babbage's Engines** Charles Babbage creates a mechanical calculator called the "Difference Engine." This is followed by the first mechanical computer called the "Analytical Engine" which used punch cards to store data.
1835	**A Step Forward in Speech Synthesis** Joseph Faber improves on Wolfgang von Kempelen's work enough so that the machine was even capable of singing.
1836	**The First Software Program** The first software program is created, written for Charles Babbage's mechanical computer by Lady Byron, a British mathematician and Countess of Lovelace.
1837	**The First Long-Distance Communication** American Samuel F.B. Morse invents the telegraph, as do two British scientists working independently of Morse. A telegraph network quickly becomes the communication infrastructure in the U.S., foreshadowing the telephone network and Internet.

Time Period	Event
1877	**An Important Year for Auditory Inventions** The telephone is accidentally invented by Alexander Graham Bell while working on a machine designed to enable hearing-impaired people to hear sound. Thomas Edison invents the phonograph and creates the first recordings of sound.
1890	**A Step Forward in Programming** Hermann Hollerith extends punch card technology for his electric accounting machine.
1899	**The Foundation of Modern Sound Recording and Data Storage** Valdemar Poulsen creates the first magnetic recordings of sound, which pave the way for the modern recording industry as well as computer data storage.
1906	**Amplification of Audio** Lee De Forest invents the electronic amplifying tube which revolutionizes electronic communication. Amplified audio allows telephone networks to extend beyond just a few miles and creates the foundation for radio. Also marks the beginning of the end for the telegraph.
1911	**The Beginnings of Speech Recognition** Radio Rex is invented. Rex was a toy dog who would come out of his doghouse when called. He was also programmed to jump if he heard a loud noise.

Time Period	Event
1924	**IBM Founded** IBM is founded. Originally named Computing-Tabulating Recording Company.
1936	**Digital Computing** German Konrad Zuse claims to have developed the first binary digital computer.
1937	**Another Step Forward in Speech Synthesis** Riesz makes the first significant advances in speech synthesis since Wolfgang von Kempelen's work. Riesz creates a mechanical vocal tract nearly identical to the human structure.
1943	**The Beginnings of Artificial Intelligence** Warren McCulloch and Walter Pitts create a model of artificial neurons that would later become the first recognized work in artificial intelligence.
Mid-1940s	**The Era of Mainframe Computing** IBM produces its first computer, the MARK-I, at Harvard University in 1944. The ENIAC computer is created in 1946. It was the first mainframe computer to use vacuum tube technology.
1948	**The Transistor Is Invented** The transistor is invented in a Bell Telephone laboratory, making miniaturization of computer and audio technology possible. Later, in the 1990s, individual computer processors will contain more than 3 million transistors.

Time Period	Event
1949	**The Beginnings of Natural Language Processing** The initial concepts of natural language processing are developed when Claude Shannon and Warren Weaver compare languages to codes.
1950	**A Major Mainframe Computer Is Designed** Remington Rand creates the UNIVAC-I computer for the U.S. Census Bureau. Research and early development of speech recognition to control information systems begin this year.
1951	**The First Neural Network Computer** Minsky and Edmonds build a neural network computer.
1954	**Assembler Programming Language Is Created** Grace Hopper creates the Assembler computer programming language.
1956	**A Step Forward in Artificial Intelligence** Dartmouth College hosts a technology workshop whose members establish Artificial Intelligence as the name for their field. Members also develop a computer program that learns to play checkers at a competitive level.
1957	**A Step Forward in Natural Language and the Invention of the Integrated Circuit** Noam Chomsky's work in linguistics becomes the foundation for natural language processing systems.

Time Period	Event
	The integrated circuit is invented.
	Speech recognition research is conducted at IBM.
1959	**COBOL Programming Language Is Created** COBOL programming language invented by Grace Hopper.
Early 1960s	**The Beginnings of the Internet** The U.S. Department of Defense establishes the ARPANET, thus creating the infrastructure for the current Internet.
Middle 1960s	**Further Advance in Natural Language** A primitive machine translation assists in converting text from one language to another, based in part on Chomsky's theories.
1964	**IBM Demonstrates Speech Synthesis** A World's Fair exhibition features Shoebox, a spoken-digit machine created by IBM. Gene Amdahl designs several successful computer models for IBM. "Minicomputers" become commercially successful, gaining market share from mainframe computers.
1965	**Toward the Personal Computer** John Kemeny and Thomas Kurtz of Dartmouth College create the BASIC computer programming language.

Time Period	Event
1968	**The Computer Mouse Is Invented** The computer mouse is invented by Doug Engelbart. Originally called the "x-y position indicator" by Engelbart, a coworker coined the term that we now use for the device. Stanley Kubrick's film *2001: A Space Odyssey* popularizes the notion of speaking computers with the character HAL-9000.
1969	**C Programming Language Is Created** UNIX operating system and the C programming language are created by AT&T.
Early 1970s	**Advances in Computing and Natural Language Processing** The floppy disk is invented for computer data storage. Intel produces the first microprocessor and progenitor of the modern Pentium chip. Natural language processing systems are created in research and industrial environments with modest success. The American Rehabilitation Act of 1973
1974	**The Era of the Personal Computer Begins** The ALTAIR becomes the first microcomputer commercially available.

Time Period	Event
	Xerox establishes the Palo Alto Research Center (PARC) in the early 1970s, which ultimately leads to the first personal computer graphical user interface. Their Alto computer, released in 1974, incorporates innovations such as a GUI, modeless functionality, and multitasking. However, priced at $20,000, it is unable to be sold to a mass market. PARC also invents Ethernet technology.
1975	**DOS Is Invented** Disc Operating System (DOS) is invented for Intel-based microcomputers.
1977	**Sound Cards Introduced for Microcomputers** Apple II produces the first sounds from a microcomputer. It uses an alphaSyntauri sound card to create simple crashes and battle noises in fantasy games.
Late 1970s	**Progress in Speech Synthesis and Personal Computing** The Speak and Spell children's toy by Texas Instruments becomes the first major commercial success of speech synthesis. MIT develops a text-to-speech system, or "screen reader," called MITTalk that allows computers to speak unrestricted text. Apple's Lisa computer introduces the concept of "dragging" in a GUI. The computer sells for about $10,000. VisiCalc is released. Invented by Dan Bricklin and Robert Frankston, it's the first computer spreadsheet.

Time Period	Event
1980	**Klatt's Article on Synthesis** Dennis Klatt publishes an article titled "Software for a Cascade/Parallel Formant Synthesizer" which provides the development concepts for intelligible speech synthesis at a reasonable price.
Early 1980s	**Beginning of Microsoft and Progress in Other Technology** In 1981, Bill Gates buys DOS from Seattle Computing for $50,000 and renames it MS-DOS. Concurrently, Gates licenses a version of the operating system to IBM for its line of PCs, which are released this year as well. Stanford University develops FM synthesis and sells the technology to Yamaha Corporation. Artificial Intelligence in computing enjoys a resurgence as DEC develops the first expert system to become commercially successful.
1984	**Apple Macintosh** The Macintosh computer is created by Steve Jobs and Steve Wozniak for Apple Computers. It incorporates the first Graphical User Interface available to the general public.
1985	**Microsoft Windows** Windows operating system is released by Microsoft.

Time Period	Event
Mid-1980s	**Advances in Speech Technology** PC "screen readers" released by IBM become commercially available, making PCs readily accessible to visually impaired users for the first time. The military conducts developmental experiments using speech recognition of pilot's voices to control avionics.
1987	**Audio for PCs** AdLib offers an inexpensive sound card for IBM PCs which becomes the standard sound card for video game programmers. Soon CreativeLabs supplants AdLib's market leadership with the SoundBlaster, which remains the industry standard soundcard through the 1990s.
1988	**Object-Oriented Programming** Steve Jobs, having left Apple to start NeXT, Inc., releases development tools that allow programmers to create object-oriented applications for his NeXTSTEP operating system. Although the company is ultimately unsuccessful, this marks an innovation in software programming for PCs.
Late 1980s	**Progress in Speech Technology** IVR systems become pervasive interfaces to business information systems in the U.S. Speech recognition employed in the software prototype TANGORA, a listening typewriter, is developed by IBM. This is ultimately the foundation for ViaVoice.

Time Period	Event
1990	**Microsoft Advances Audio for PCs** Multimedia PC, or MPC, specifications are released by Microsoft. All MPC personal computers come with sound cards and speakers as standard equipment. Microsoft also releases an API that allows third-party developers to create speech-based applications for Windows.
1990	**A Major Step for Accessibility** The Americans with Disabilities Act (ADA) is enacted by Congress and signed into law.
1992	**Microsoft and IBM** Windows 3.1 is released by Microsoft. IBM introduces its Speech Server Series, its first dictation system.
1993	**Web Browsing and Handwriting Recognition** MOSAIC is created by Marc Andreesen. It's the first "browser" for the World Wide Web. Apple releases the Newton, a personal digital assistant (PDA). It's a mild commercial success that serves to popularize handwriting recognition.
Early 1990s	**Rapid Progress in Speech Technology** Scotland's Dundee University demonstrates synthesized speech capable of emotional connotation through prosodic manipulation.

Time Period	Event
	AT&T makes MailTALK available, allowing subscribers to call a mailbox via telephone to listen to their e-mail as read by a TTS system. The Microsoft Research organization is founded. Projects include research in spoken technology and natural language. In 1993, the IBM Personal Dictation System is released for OS/2 and becomes the first commercially available speech recognition product for PCs. However, the requirement of specialized hardware limits its success. Also in 1993, Apple releases PlainTalk for the Macintosh operating system, making speech recognition and synthesis extensions available to third-party developers. DragonDictate, a discrete recognition application, is released for the Windows operating system by Dragon Systems in 1994. It relies only on standard PC sound cards and is a mild commercial success. IBM establishes a speech business unit to expedite commercial speech product development.
1995	**Windows 95 and WebTV** Microsoft releases Windows 95. WebTV is introduced.

Time Period	Event
1996-1997	**Speech Technology Becomes Practical for Retail Applications** The first computer operating system with built-in speech recognition and navigation is released: OS/2 Warp 4 by IBM. MedSpeak/Radiology is released by IBM. This is the first continuous speech recognition, speaker-independent product available for PCs, but is useful only to a specialized market. NaturallySpeaking by Dragon Systems becomes the first PC-based continuous speech recognition application released for the home and small office computing market. It is immediately followed into the market by IBM's ViaVoice.
1998	**Changes in the PC Market** Netscape is purchased by America Online. Microsoft releases Windows 98. Apple releases the iMac and sells 800,000 computers within a year. Approximately 78 million voice mailboxes exist in the United States.

Time Period	Event
1999	**Convergence and Rapid Progress Continue** Microsoft announces that substantial functionality for speech recognition, speech synthesis, and natural language querying will be part of Microsoft Windows 2000. Apple announces it will release OS X late in the year. Voice recognition will be a built-in feature. Intel releases Katmai, a major advance in processing. Its speed promises to alleviate the bottleneck in digital audio processing. This will allow for improved continuous speech recognition and response time. America Online announces a partnership with DragonSystems. They promise to include continuous speech recognition functionality in this year's new version of the America Online software for e-mail, Internet chat rooms, messaging, and Web browsing. A telephony workshop is held for leading experts in speech recognition. The consortium addresses issues of telephony and e-commerce. Their goal is to promote telephone speech recognition as a supplement to Internet e-commerce. A $199 computer is released. Called the iToaster, it connects to a television and includes a modem, Internet software, and basic home office software. The world's smallest Internet server is announced. Called the iPick, it's a computer that can fit on a match head. The anticipated market price, including software, will be $1 when it reaches mass production.

Time Period	Event
	The U.S. Justice Department pursues landmark antitrust case against Microsoft. Microsoft is declared a monopoly by judge Thomas Penfield Jackson, who states, "Most harmful of all is the message that Microsoft's actions have conveyed to every enterprise with the potential to innovate in the computer industry." Microsoft CEO Bill Gates responds by stating, "If you want to look at what's great for consumers, you have to look at our work and the work of our partners over the last 20 years."

Interesting Web sites

- **Napier's Bones Web site**: www.cee.hw.ac.uk/~greg/calculators/napier/about.html

- **MIT Wearable Computing Project**: wearables.www.media.mit.edu/projects/wearables/timeline.html

- **Virginia Polytechnic Institute's History of Computers site**: ei.cs.vt.edu/~history/index.html

- **Comp.speech Internet newsgroup's Website**: www.speech.cs.cmu.edu/comp.speech

- **Dennis Klatt's History of Speech Synthesis**: www.cs.indiana.edu/rhythmsp/ASA/Contents.html

- **A History of the Internet**: lcweb.loc.gov/global/internet/history.html

Glossary

acoustic cues. Sounds that help a listener filter invariants (noise) in coordination with lexical information. For example, the suprasegmental phonemes.

affixes. Bound morphemes that modify meaning, such as by changing person, gender, tense, or number. For example, prefixes and suffixes are affixes.

affricatives. Complex sounds that are initially a stop but become a fricative, such as *ch* in *chill*.

agglutination. Concatenating morphemes to create a new word.

allophones. A subclass of phonemes that have a variation based on the sound resulting from a puff of air being released when the sound is made.

amplitude. The loudness of a sound, determined by the size of its wavelength.

articulation. The expulsion of air from the oral cavity.

assertion. Information that the speaker assumes is new to the listener or justifies emphasis.

assistive technology. Specialized technology that accommodates users with disabilities.

asynchronous communication. Communication where the receiver actually receives the message at a time different from its transmission time. For example, e-mail and voice mail.

attack. The point in time when a sound begins.

auditory icon. A non-speech audio signal that is based on a real world sound. For example, the sound of a police siren that conveys an emergency.

auditory user interface (AUI). An interface that relies primarily or exclusively on audio, including speech and sounds, for interaction.

barge-in. A technique that allows users to interrupt the computer and to take control or go on to the next step.

bound bases. Base morphemes that must be combined with other morphemes to extend meaning. For example, *cran* in *cranberry.*

channel. The medium used to transfer the message.

coarticulation. A neighboring phoneme that affects the articulation of another phoneme.

command-and-control. A speech application that allows you to speak commands to the computer that are then acted on, rather than issuing commands by typing or clicking a mouse or pointing device.

compression. A contraction in a sound wave where the air particles are compressed.

concatenated synthesis. Computer assembly of recorded voice sounds to create meaningful speech output.

conception. The stage of communication where the communication is begun or conceived.

connotation. The suggestive meaning of a word.

constrained speech. A speech technology that limits users to certain words or phrases to improve recognition and performance of the system.

continuous recognition. A speech technology that allows a user to speak to a system in an everyday manner without using specific learned commands and without pausing.

contracted forms. Bound morphemes that are shortened when combined with another morpheme: for example, we will contracted to we'll.

cycle. The distance between a peak (highest point) and a trough (lowest point) in a sine wave.

decay. The part of a sound right after the maximum volume has been reached.

decibel. A ratio used to describe the change in loudness.

decoding. The stage of communication when the receiver decides on the meaning of a message that has been received.

demi-syllable. Half of a syllable either from the beginning of the sound to its center point or from the center point to the end of the sound.

denotation. A literal, or dictionary, definition.

dictation. Speech technology that allows the user to enter text using speech input rather than a keyboard.

diphone. The transition between two phonemes. A unit of acoustic data comprised of two phonemes recorded from the center point of one phoneme to the center point of the next phoneme.

diphthong. A combination of vowel sounds. For example, *oy* in the word *toy.*

discrete recognition. A speech technology that recognizes a limited vocabulary of individual words and phrases spoken by a person.

disfluencies. Parts of human speech that do not flow and are hard for a computer to interpret. For example, *umm* or *uhh.*

dynamic range. The difference between the lowest and highest amplitude that a sound card can manage; measured in decibels.

earcon. An auditory icon that has a meaning: for example, the sound of corn popping means "please wait."

encoding. The stage of communication when the sender chooses the specific words, phrases, and sentences to convey the most precise meaning of the message.

enrollment. A reading of text provided by the manufacturer during installation of a speech software application.

envelope. A graph that describes the attack, decay, sustain, and release of a sound.

feedback. A transmission regarding a message that was just received. A feedback message allows the receiver to clarify or gather additional information.

formant synthesis. A set of phonological rules to control an audio waveform that simulates human speech; machine-generated speech.

free morphemes. Bases that can have other morphemes or affixes attached to extend meaning; opposite of bound bases.

frequency pitch. The number of cycles a wave completes in one second.

frequency response. The range of frequencies that a sound card can manage.

fricatives. Sounds created by a narrowing of the vocal tract, such as the initial consonants in *fit* or *sit*.

fundamental wave. A sound's lowest frequency.

generative notation. A system of diagramming linguistic structure based upon Noam Chomsky's work in *Syntactic Structures*, published in 1957.

glides. Consonant sounds that either follow or precede a vowel. They are distinguished by the segue from a vowel and are also known as semivowels. For example, the initial consonants in the words *yet* and *wool*.

grammar. A set of rules describing the technical structure of language.

harmonics. The additional frequencies of a sound besides its fundamental wave or lowest frequency.

Hertz (Hz). Cycles per second.

homophones. Words that have the same pronunciation but differ in meaning. For example, *there* and *their*.

human-computer interaction (HCI). The branch of human factors that deals with improving the interaction between humans and computers.

human factors. Taking the human being (the user) into account during design.

immediate constituent diagramming. A technique to conduct surface structure analysis.

infrasounds. Sounds below what the human ear can hear, that is, below 20 Hz.

interactive voice response (IVR). Talking to computers via telephone.

interface. The part of technology that people interact with, including hardware components such as keyboards, mice, or keypads; or software components such as a screen, window, page, sound, or voice.

invariants. Noises in an acoustic signal.

language. A system of rules which relate sound sequences to meanings.

lexicon. The total stock of all morphemes in the language.

linguistics. Rules defining sound sequences and their meanings.

liquids. Sounds produced by a complexity of phenomena with the tongue raised high. For example, the initial consonants in words such as *like* or *rut*.

message. The information transmitted in a communication.

modality. The reception of communication through a single sensory organ.

morphemes. A combination of phonemes that create a single distinctive unit of meaning; the minimum unit of meaning in a language.

morphology. The study of word structure.

nasals. Sounds that are similar to stops, but are voiced: for example, the initial consonant in *might* or *night*.

natural language. A speech technology that uses the languages spoken and written by a given culture for speech input and output rather than using a specialized technical syntax.

noise. An undesired sound.

non-speech audio. A sound that is not speech.

normalization. An editing procedure that converts abbreviations into full alphabetical forms.

orthography. The act of spelling words.

parsing. A computer operation that filters the antecedent and responds to a discrete command.

peaks. The part of a sine wave that shows a compression; the part of the sine wave curve that is the highest over the center line, or normal atmospheric pressure; at the peak the pressure is the greatest.

phase. The interaction of two simultaneous sine waves to create a composite sound wave.

phoneme. A single distinctive speech sound of a language; the primary unit.

phonetics. The area of phonology that notates variations in pronunciation of vowels and consonants.

phonology. The study of language sounds and how they are created by humans.

pitch. See **frequency**.

polarity. A description of how a microphone was designed to sense sound coming from different directions: for example, an omnidirectional microphone responds to sound from all directions.

pragmatics. The linguistic subfield that studies language usage; relates the intended or interpreted meaning of a message to the context in which it was spoken.

prosody. Characteristics of human speech, including pitch, intonation, and duration, that provide additional meaning to communication.

psycholinguistics. Relating language structure to the psychological processes involved in encoding, speaking, decoding, and comprehending language.

rarefaction. An expansion in a sound wave; during expansion there are fewer air particles, so they are more "rare."

receiver. The person who receives the message.

reception. The stage of communication when the receiver acquires a transmission.

resolution. Measurement of the quality a sound card output; the number of bits reflects the quality, or depth, of sound.

sampling rates. How often a sound is captured.

semantics. The study of the meanings of words and communications.

semiotics. The study of how humans perceive communication through their sensory organs.

sender. The person transmitting a message.

S/GUI. An interface that includes speech, but is joined by other interface forms, usually visual, such as a GUI window or a Web page.

signal-to-noise ratio. The ratio of the desired sound to the undesired sound or sounds.

sine waves. In speech technology, increases and decreases in atmospheric pressure over time.

sound. A vibration in an elastic medium at a frequency and intensity capable of being heard by the human ear.

sound pressure level (SPL). The range between the threshold of sound, or softest sound heard by the human ear, and the threshold of pain, or loudest sound we can hear without experiencing pain.

speaker-dependent. Speech systems that require the user to complete an enrollment process. The application optimizes for that person's voice and speech patterns.

speaker-independent. Speech systems that are designed to work for multiple users and do not use enrollment to personalize the application.

speech recognition. Technologies that enable computers or other electronic systems to identify the sound of a human voice, separate that sound from noise in the environment, and accept the messages from the voice as input for controlling the system.

speech synthesis. The technologies that enable computers or other electronic systems to output simulated human speech.

stops. Consonant sounds where the airflow is halted during speech: for example, the initial consonants in the words *pit* or *pop*.

supposition. Information that the speaker assumes is part of the listener's prior knowledge of the world.

suprasegmental phonemes. Sounds that augment phonemes; sounds that occur over, or during, other phonemes and include intonation, stress, tone, and juncture.

surface structure rules (phrase structure rules). Definitions of the phrases in a sentence, such as noun phrases, verb phrases, and prepositional phrases.

sustain. The part of a sound after the initial decay of maximum volume until the sound is reduced to silence.

synchronous communication. Communication where the sender and receiver are communicating directly with one another at the same time: for example, a face-to-face meeting or phone call.

syntax. The study of sentence structure.

telephony. To send and receive voice messages via telephone lines.

text-to-speech (TTS). Text data that is output as speech.

timbre. The tonal character of a sound; tonal color.

transducers. Devices that change one form of energy into another: for example, a microphone.

transmission. The stage of communication when the sender selects a channel and transmits, or broadcasts, the message.

trough. The part of the sine wave where the air pressure is the lowest and where the expansion, or rarefaction, is the greatest; the lowest part of the curve below the center line that represents normal atmospheric pressure.

ultrasounds. Sounds above what the human ear can hear: for example, above 20,000 Hz.

universal design. Designing products that are usable by all people, including people with disabilities.

Wizard of Oz. This technique is named after the movie in which the characters thought they were talking to a great and wonderful being, but really it was a hidden human making the controls of a machine work; in the Wizard of Oz technique, a human makes the "computer" work which allows testing of technologies that are either not yet available, or just being conceptualized.

word spotting. A technique used by some discrete recognition applications to provide an illusion of continuous speech.

Resources

In this section we list several resources by topic. The resources include books, articles, organizations, and Web sites.

Speech Research

American Voice Input/Output Society (AVIOS). AVIOS is a not-for-profit society dedicated to disseminating information about real-world applications that use speech technology. They publish the International Journal of Speech Technology (IJST).

Peggie Johnson
AVIOS
P.O. Box 20817
San Jose, CA 95160
408-323-1783
avios@aol.com

www.avios.com/page_welcome_to_web2.htm

Balentine, Bruce and David P. Morgan. 1999. *How to build a speech recognition application*. San Ramon, CA: Enterprise Integration Group, Inc.

Barrass, Stephen. Auditory Information Design. http://viswiz.gmd.de/~barrass/thesis/#Demos

Berger-Liaw Neural Network. 1999. www.usc.edu/ext-relations/news_service/releases/stories/36013.html

Carey, Stephen. 1998. *A beginner's guide to the scientific method*. Boston: Wadsworth.

Cohen, P.R., and S.L. Oviatt. 1994. "The role of voice in human-machine communication," Chap. 3 in *Voice communication between humans and machines*. Edited by D. Roe and J. Wilpon. Washington, DC: National Academy of Science Press.

Dobroth, K. 1999. "Practical guidance for conducting usability tests of speech applications." Paper presented at the annual meeting of the American Voice I/O Society.

Dobroth, K. 1998. "It's both what you say and how you say it: The role of prosody in prompt design." Paper presented at the annual meeting of the American Voice I/O Society.

Dobroth, K., D. Karis, & B. Zeigler. 1990. "The design of conversationally capable automated systems." Paper presented at the 13th International Symposium on Human Factors in Telecommunications, Turin, Italy.

Dobroth, K., B. Zeigler, & D. Karis. 1989. "Future directions for audio-interface research: Characteristics of human-human order-entry conversations." Paper presented at the annual meeting of the American Voice Input/Output Society, Newport Beach, CA.

Gardiner-Bonneau, Daryle, ed. 1999. *Human factors and voice interactive systems*. Boston: Kluwer Academic Publishers.

International Academy for Auditory Display (ICAD) Web site. www.santafe.edu/~icad/

Internet Telephony magazine. www.internettelephony.com

Kamm, Candace. 1994. "User interfaces for voice applications," *Voice communication between humans and machines*. Edited by D. Roe and J. Wilpon. Washington, DC: National Academy of Science Press.

Karat, John, et al. 1999. "Speech user interface evolution," Chap. 1 in *Human factors and voice interactive systems*. Edited by Daryle Gardiner-Bonneau. Washington, DC: National Academy of Science Press.

Karis, D. & K.M. Dobroth. 1995. "Psychological and human factors issues in the design of speech recognition systems." In A. Syrdal, R. Bennett, and S. Greenspan (Eds.) *Applied Speech Technology*, Boca Raton, FL: CRC press.

Karis, D. & K.M. Dobroth. 1991. "Automatic speech recognition over the public switched telephone network: Human factors considerations." *IEEE Journal on Selected Areas in Communication, 9(4)*, 574-585.

Klatt, Dennis. Web page on the history of speech synthesis. www.cs.indiana.edu/rhythmsp/ASA/Contents.html

Mané, Amir, Susan Boyce, Demetrios Karis, and Nicole Yankelovich. 1996. "Designing the user interface for speech recognition applications," Presented at a workshop of the ACM SIGCHI Conference, 1996. www.acm.org/sigchi/bulletin/1996.4/boyce.html

Oviatt, S.L. November 1999. "Ten myths of multimodal interaction" *Communications of the ACM*, 42 (11).

Raman, T.V. 1997. *Speaking computer*. Boston: Kluwer Academic Publishers.

Silverman, K.E.A., et al. TOBI: A standard for labeling English prosody. In *Proceedings of the 1992 International Conference on Spoken Language Processing (ICLSP)*, Banff, Alberta, Canada, October, 1992, 867-870.

SpeechLinks: A speech recognition and speech technology hyperlinks page. www.speech.cs.cmu.edu/comp.speech/Section6/speechlinks.html

Stifelman, Lisa J., Barry Arons, Chris Schmandt, and Eric A. Hulteen. 1993. *VoiceNotes: A speech interface for a hand-held voice notetaker*. www.media.mit.edu/~lisa/interchi93.html

Yankelovich, Nicole. November/December 1996. "How do users know what to say?" *ACM Interactions*, (3) 6. Sun Microsystems, Inc. Sun Microsystems Laboratories. www.sun.com/research/speech/publications/acm-interactions-1996/Interactions.html

Yankelovich, Nicole, Gina-Anne Levow, and Matt Marx. 1995. "Designing speechacts: issues in speech user interfaces." *CHI '95 Proceedings*. www.acm.org/sigs/sigchi/chi95/Electronic/documnts/papers/ny_bdy.htm

Guidelines

Ameritech Phone-Based User Interface Standards: Dialogue Design. www.ameritech.com/corporate/testtown/library/standard/pbix4.html

Apple Computer, Inc. 1992. *Macintosh human interface guidelines*. Reading, MA: Addison-Wesley.

Creative Labs' developer relations site. http://developer.soundblaster.com/

McCormick, Bill. March 1995. *"Building a better script."* 13 guidelines for IVR scripting. www.genfax.com/bldivr.html

Windows user experience: Official guidelines for user interface developers and designers. 1999. Redmond, WA: Microsoft Press.

Speech and Sound Technology

Baber, Christopher, and Janet Noyes. 1993. *Interactive speech technology: Human factors issues in the application of speech input/output to computers*. London: Taylor & Francis.

Bartlett, Bruce, and Jenny Bartlett. 1998. *Practical recording techniques*. Boston: Focal Press.

Center for Computer Research in Music and Acoustics. A history of digital synthesis. www-ccrma.stanford.edu/~jos/kna/kna.html

Cook, Perry R., ed. 1999. *Music, cognition, and computerized sound*. Cambridge, MA: MIT Press.

Engdahl, Tomi. Digital signal processing Web page. www.hut.fi/Misc/Electronics/dsp.html

Lemmetty, Sami. Home page. He is a researcher at the Helsinki University of Technology Laboratory of Acoustics

and Audio Signal Processing. www.acoustics.hut.fi/
~slemmett/index.html

Microsoft Web site on microphones. http://microsoft.com/
iit/documentation/mikes.htm

The Microsoft Windows Guidelines for Accessible Software
Design. May 7, 1997 edition. www.microsoft.com/enable

Moscal, Tony. 1994. *Sound check: The basics of sound and sound
systems*. Milwaukee, WI: Hal Leonard Publishing Company.

Sirota, Warren. 1995. *Making music with your PC*. Rocklin,
CA: Prima Publishing.

Syrdal, Ann. 1995. *Applied speech technology*. Boca Raton, FL:
CRC Press.

Voice extensible markup language. www.voicexml.org

Waugh, Ian. 1997. *Making music with your PC*. Kent, UK: PC
Publishing.

Speech Vendors

Apple's speech offerings. www.apple.com/macos/speech/

AT&T Advanced Speech Products Group. www.att.com/
aspg/

Dragon NaturallySpeaking. www.naturalspeech.com

IBM ViaVoice. www.ibm.com/software/speech/dev/

Java. http://java.sun.com/marketing/collateral/
speech.html

L & H VoiceXpress. #, www.lhs.com/speechtech/embdprod.asp

Lucent's Speech Technologies Group. www.lucent.com/speech/

Microphones. All about microphones. www.microphones.com/

Microsoft. http://research.microsoft.com/srg

Microsoft Speech Products. http://microsoft.com/iit

Microsoft Speech Technology Group. Research and development of spoken language technologies. www.research.microsoft.com/research/srg/

Phillips Speech Processing Web page. www.speech.be.philips.com/

SpeechDepot: a speech developer community sponsored by Unisys and Microsoft. www.speechdepot.com/

Sun speech products. http://java.sun.com/products/java-media/speech/

Wilcox's Commercial Speech Recognition Web page. www.tiac.net/users/rwilcox/speech.html

Natural Language

Dr. Dodd's Natural Language Speech Input and Output Web page. www.geocities.com/CapeCanaveral/4355/natlanpage1.htm

Experiments in integrating speech recognition and natural language processing. yara.ecn.purdue.edu/~harper/nsf-mine.html

Long, Byron. May 1994. Natural language as an interface style. www.dgp.toronto.edu/people/byron/papers/nli.html

Microsoft. http://research.microsoft.com/nlp

Microsoft Natural Language Group. www.research.microsoft.com/nlp/

Natural Language Processing Group at the Information Sciences Institute of the University of Southern California (USC/ISI). www.isi.edu/natural-language/nlp-at-isi.html

Language

Akmajian, Adrian, et al. 1997. *Linguistics*. Cambridge, MA: MIT Press.

Chomsky, Noam. 1957. *Syntactic structures*. The Hague: Mouton.

Cole, Ronald A., ed. 1980. *Perception and production of fluent speech*. Hillsdale: Lawrence Erlbaum Associates.

Frauenfelder, Uli, and Lorraine Komisarjevsky Tyler, eds. 1987. *Spoken word recognition*. Cambridge, MA: MIT Press.

Hayes, Curtis, Jacob Ornstein, and William W. Gage. 1997. *The abc's of languages & linguistics*. Lincolnwood, IL: NTC Publishing Group.

International Phonetic Association Symbols. www2.arts.gla.ac.uk/IPA/ipa.html

Miller, Joanne L., and Peter D. Eimas, eds. 1995. *Speech, language, and communication*. Boston: Academic Press.

Pickett, J.M. 1999. *The acoustics of speech communication*. Boston: Allyn and Bacon.

Usability Engineering/ Interface Design

Association of Computing Machinery. Special interest group for Computer-Human Interaction prints the proceedings of their conference. The following years' proceedings have several papers on speech interfaces:

>   ACM SIGCHI Proceedings 95. 1995. New York, NY: ACM Press
>
>   ACM SIGCHI Proceedings 96. 1996. New York, NY: ACM Press
>
>   ACM SIGCHI Proceedings 97. 1997. New York, NY: ACM Press
>
>   ACM SIGCHI Proceedings 98. 1998. New York, NY: ACM Press
>
>   ACM SIGCHI Proceedings 99. 1999. New York, NY: ACM Press

Allen, C. Dennis. 1995. Succeeding as a clandestine change agent. *Communications of the ACM*, 38 (5).

Bias, Randolph G., and Deborah J. Mayhew, eds. 1994. *Cost justifying usability*. Boston: Academic Press.

Bringhurst, Robert. 1997. *The elements of typographic style.* Point Roberts, WA: H & M Publishers.

Collins, Dave. 1995. *Designing object-oriented user interfaces.* Redwood City, CA: Benjamin/Cummings Publishing Company.

Communications of the ACM. Published by ACM. 212-626-0500 for subscription information. New York.

comp.human-factors. An interface design news group.

Cooper, Alan. 1995. *About face: The essentials of user interface design.* Foster City, CA: IDG Books.

Dayton, Tom, et al. July 1993. "Skills needed by user-centered design practitioners in real software development environments." Report on the *CHI '92 Workshop. SIGCHI Bulletin*, 25 (3).

Eriksson, Hans-Erik, and Magnus Penker. 1998. *UML toolkit.* New York: John Wiley & Sons.

Fernandes, Tony. 1995. *Global interface design.* San Diego: AP Professional.

Furgeson, Eugene S. 1993. *Engineering and the mind's eye.* Cambridge, MA: MIT Press.

Galitz, Wilbert O. 1997. *Essential guide to interface design.* New York: John Wiley & Sons.

Genter, Don, and Jakob Nielson. August 1996. "The anti-mac interface." *Communications of the ACM*, 39 (8).

Horton, William. 1994. *The icon book.* New York: John Wiley & Sons.

IBM. 1992. *Object-oriented interface design*. Carmel, IN: QUE.

Insensee, Scott, and James Rudd. 1996. *The art of rapid prototyping*. Boston: International Thomson Computer Press.

interactions Magazine. Published by ACM. 212-626-0500 for subscription information.

Itten, Johannes. 1975. *Design and form*. New York: Van Nostrand Reinhold.

Itten, Johannes. 1970. *The elements of color*. New York: John Wiley & Sons.

Jordan, Patrick W., Bruce Thomas, ed., and Bernard A. Weerdmeester. 1996. *Usability evaluation in industry*. Bristol, PA: Taylor & Francis.

Kano, Nadine. March/April 1995. "Putting on an international interface." *Microsoft Developer Network News*, Bellevue, WA: Microsoft.

Kay, David C., and John R. Levine. 1995. *Graphic file formats*. New York: Windcrest/McGraw Hill.

Kidder, Louise H., and Charles M. Judd. 1986. *Research methods in social relations*. New York: Holt, Reinhart and Winston.

Lakoff, George, and Mark Johnson. 1980. *Metaphors we live by*. Chicago: The University of Chicago Press.

Lutz, Ronald A. 1991. *Applied sketching and technical drawing*. South Holland, IL: The Goodheart-Willcox Company.

Shneiderman, Ben. Web page for his book. *Designing the user interface: Strategies for effective human-computer interaction.* www.aw.com/dtui

Shneiderman, Ben. 1997. *Designing the user interface: Strategies for effective human-computer interaction.* Reading, MA: Addison-Wesley.

SIGCHI (Special Interest Group for Computer-Human Interaction), Association for Computing Machinery, 11 West 42nd Street, New York, NY 10036, 212-869-7440. www.acm.org/sigchi/chi98

Trower, Tandy. 1994. *Creating a well-designed user interface.* Produced by University Video Communications, directed by Tandy Trower. 64 min. Videocassette.

Tufte, Edward R. 1998. *Visual explanations.* Cheshire, CT: Graphic Press.

Usability Professionals Association, Cindy Clark, 230 East Ohio Street, Suite 400, Chicago, IL 60611-3265, 312-596-5298, Fax: 312-644-8557. office@upassoc.org, www.upassoc.org

Weinschenk, Susan. October 1995. "Intelligent GUI design: Six critical mindset shifts." *Data Management Review,* 5 (9).

Weinschenk, Susan, Pamela Jamar, and Sarah C. Yeo. 1997. *GUI design essentials.* New York: John Wiley & Sons.

Wenger, Etienne. 1998. *Communities of practice.* Cambridge, England: Cambridge University Press.

Wiklund, Michael E., ed. 1994. *Usability in practice.* Boston: Academic Press Inc.

Zetie, Carl. 1995. *Practical user interface design*. London, UK: McGraw Hill Book Company.

Usability Testing

Dumas, Joseph S., and Janice C. Redish. 1994. *A practical guide to usability testing*. Norwood, NJ: Ablex Publishing Corporation.

Mack, Robert L. 1994. *Usability inspection methods*. New York: John Wiley & Sons.

Rubin, Jeffrey. 1994. *Handbook of usability testing: How to plan, design, and conduct effective tests*. New York: John Wiley & Sons.

Trochim, William M.K. 1999. *The research methods knowledge base*. Ithaca, NY: Cornell University.

Winograd, Terry, and Fernando Flores. 1987. *Understanding computers and cognition*. Reading, MA: Addison-Wesley.

Human-Computer Interaction

Amheim, Rodolf. 1969. *Visual thinking*. Berkeley, CA: University of California Press.

Anderson, John R. 1985. *Cognitive psychology and its implications*. New York: W.H. Freeman and Company.

Baecker, Ronald M., Jonathan Grudin, William A.S. Buxton, and Saul Greenberg. 1995. *Human-computer interaction: Toward the year 2000*. San Francisco, CA: Morgan Kaufmann.

Helander, Martin. 1997. *Handbook of human-computer interaction*. Amsterdam, The Netherlands: North-Holland.

Johnson, Steven. 1997. *Interface Culture*. New York, NY: HarperEdge.

Norman, Don. 1988. *The design of everyday things*. New York, NY: Basic Books.

Norman, Don. 1992. *Turn signals are the facial expressions of automobiles*. Reading, PA: Addison-Wesley.

Norman, Don. 1993. *Things that make us smart*. Reading, MA: Addison-Wesley.

Preece, Jenny. 1994. *Human-computer interaction*. Reading, MA: Addison-Wesley.

Salvendy, Gavriel, ed. 1997. *Handbook of human factors and ergonomics*. New York: John Wiley & Sons.

Sanders, Mark S., and Ernest J. McCormick. 1993. *Human factors in engineering and design*. New York, NY: McGraw Hill.

Wickens, C. 1984. *Engineering psychology and human performance*. Columbus, OH: Merrill.

Analysis for Interface Design

Beyer, Hugh, and Karen Holtzblatt. 1998. *Contextual design*. San Francisco: Morgan Kaufmann.

Carroll, John M., ed. *Scenario-based design*. New York: John Wiley & Sons.

Hackos, JoAnn & Ginny Redish. 1998. *User and task analysis for interface design*. New York: John Wiley & Sons.

McGraw, Karen L., and Karan Harbison. 1997. *User centered requirements: The scenario based engineering process approach*. Mahwah, NJ: Lawrence Erlbaum Assoc.

Wixon, Dennis, and Judith Ramey. 1996. *Field methods casebook for software design*. New York: John Wiley & Sons.

Universal Access

Americans with Disabilities Act (ADA), Sections 504 and 508 of the Rehabilitation Act. www.usdoj.gov/crt/ada

Center for Accessible Technology Web site for universal access. www.el.net/CAT/index.html

IBM. Web site for universal access. www.ibm.com/sns

IBM. Special Needs Systems Web site.
www.austin.ibm.com/sns

Lighthouse International's Web site for universal access.
www.lighthouse.org/print_leg.htm

Microsoft Accessibility home page. www.microsoft.com/
enable

Public Service Commission of Canada. Web site on
designing universal Web pages. www.psc-cfp.gc.ca/dmd/
access/welcome1.htm

Sun's Web site for universal access. www.sun.com/access

University of Wisconsin universal design Web site.
www.trace.wisc.edu

WebAble Web site for universal access. www.webable.com

World Wide Web Consortium's Web site on universal
design. www.w3c.org/wai

Appendix D

Bibliography

The American heritage talking dictionary 3rd ed. [CD-ROM]. Cambridge, MA: Softkey.

American National Standards Institute (ANSI). www.ansi.org

Apple's speech offerings. www.apple.com/macos/speech/

AT&T Advanced Speech Products Group, www.att.com/aspg/

Bailey, Robert. 1982. *Human performance engineering.* Upper Saddle River, NJ: Prentice-Hall.

Bates, Regis, and Donald Gregory. 1998. *Voice and data communications handbook.* New York: McGraw-Hill.

Berger-Liaw Neural Network. 1999. www.usc.edu/ext-relations/news_service/releases/stories/36013.html

Beyer, Hugh, and Karen Holtzblatt. 1998. *Contextual design*. San Francisco: Morgan Kaufmann.

Bias, Randolph G., and Deborah J. Mayhew, eds. 1994. *Cost justifying usability*. Boston: Academic Press.

Boyce, Susan. 1999. Spoken natural language dialogue systems: User interface issues for the future, Chap. 2 in *Human factors and voice interactive systems*. Edited by Daryle Gardiner-Bonneau. Boston: Kluwer Academic Publishers, pp. 37-61.

Brassard, Michael, and Diane Ritter. 1994. *The memory jogger II*. Lawrence, MA: GOAL/QPC.

Chomsky, Noam. 1957. *Syntactic structures*. The Hague: Mouton.

Cohen, P.R., and S.L. Oviatt, 1994. The role of voice in human-machine communication, Chap. 3 in *Voice communication between humans and machines*. Edited by D. Roe and J. Wilpon. Washington, DC: National Academy of Science Press, pp 34-75.

Computer Telephony Magazine. www.computertelephony.com

Cooper, Alan. 1999. *The inmates are running the asylum*. Indianapolis: Sams Publishing.

Crystal, David. 1987. *The Cambridge encyclopedia of language*. Cambridge: Cambridge University Press.

Dragon NaturallySpeaking.
www.naturalspeech.com

Dumas, Joseph S., and Janice C. Redish. 1994. *A practical guide to usability testing*. Norwood, NJ: Ablex Publishing Corporation.

Edgar, Bob. 1997. *PC telephony*. New York: Flatiron Publishing.

Fernandes, Tony. 1995. *Global interface design*. San Diego: AP Professional.

Gardiner-Bonneau, Daryle, ed. 1999. *Human factors and voice interactive systems*. Boston: Kluwer Academic Publishers.

Gates, Bill. 1995. *The road ahead*. New York, NY: Penguin USA.

Hackos, JoAnn, and Ginny Redish. 1998. *User and task analysis for interface design*. New York: John Wiley & Sons.

Hayes, Curtis, Jacob Ornstein, and William Gage. 1997. *The abc's of languages & linguistics*. Lincolnwood, IL: NTC Publishing Group.

Human Factors and Ergonomics Society (HFES).
www.hfes.org

IBM ViaVoice. www.ibm.com/software/speech/dev/

International Organization for Standardization (ISO). www.iso.ch

International Phonetic Association Symbols, www2.arts.gla.ac.uk/IPA/ipa.html

Isaacs, Alan, John Daintith, and Elizabeth Martin, eds. 1996. *The Oxford concise science dictionary.* New York: Oxford University Press.

Java. http://java.sun.com/marketing/colateral/speech.html

L & H VoiceXpress. www.lhs.com/, www.lhs.com/speechtech/embdprod.asp

Long, Byron. 1994. *Natural language as an interface style*, Unpublished. www.dgp.toronto.edu/people/byron/papers/nli.html

McGraw, Karen L., and Karan Harbison. 1997. *User centered requirements: The scenario based engineering process approach.* Mahwah, NJ: Lawrence Erlbaum Associates

Merriam-Webster's collegiate dictionary 10th ed. 1993. Springfield, MA: Merriam-Webster.

Microsoft. http://research.microsoft.com/nlp, http://research.microsoft.com/srg, http://microsoft.com/iit

The Microsoft Windows Guidelines for Accessible Software Design. May 7, 1997, edition. www.microsoft.com/enable

Miller, G. 1956. "The magical number seven, plus or minus two: Some limits on our capacity for processing information." *Psychological Review* 63: 81-97.

Miller, Joanne. 1995. *Speech, language, and communication*. Boston: Academic Press.

Moscal, Tony. 1994. *Sound check: The basics of sound and sound systems*. Milwaukee, WI: Hal Leonard Publishing Company.

Nielsen, Jakob. 1994. *Usability engineering*. San Diego: AP Professional.

Phillips speech products. www.speech.be.philips.com/

Reeves, Byron & Clifford Nass. 1996. *The media equation: How people treat computers, television, and new media like real people and places*. Stanford, CA: Cambridge University Press.

Roe, David B., and Jay G. Wilpon, eds. 1994. *Voice communication between humans and machines*. Washington, DC: National Academy of Science Press.

Rubin, Jeffrey. 1994. *Handbook of usability testing: How to plan, design, and conduct effective tests*. New York: John Wiley & Sons.

Salvendy, Gavriel, ed. 1997. *Handbook of human factors and ergonomics*. New York: John Wiley & Sons.

Sanders, Mark S., and Ernest J. McCormick. 1993. *Human factors in engineering and design*. New York: McGraw-Hill.

Shneiderman, Ben. 1997. *Designing the user interface: Strategies for effective human-computer interaction*. Reading, MA: Addison-Wesley.

Silverman, K.E.A., et al. 1992. TOBI: "A standard for labeling English prosody." *Proceedings of the 1992 International Conference on Spoken Language Processing (ICLSP)*, Banff, Alberta, Canada, October, 1992, 867-870.

Stifelman, Lisa J., Barry Arons, Chris Schmandt, and Eric A. Hulteen. 1993. VoiceNotes: A speech interface for a hand-held voice notetaker. *Proceedings of INTERCHI, ACM.* New York.

Sun speech products. http://java.sun.com/products/java-media/speech/

Syrdal, Ann. 1995. *Applied speech technology.* Boca Raton, FL: CRC Press.

Voice extensible markup language. www.voicexml.org

Weinschenk, Susan, Pamela Jamar, and Sarah C. Yeo. 1997. *GUI design essentials.* New York: John Wiley & Sons.

Wickens, C. 1984. *Engineering psychology and human performance.* Columbus, OH: Merrill.

Wood, Larry. 1996. The ethnographic interview in user centered work/task analysis. *Field methods casebook for software design.* Wixon, Dennis and Judith Ramey, eds. New York: John Wiley & Sons.

World Wide Web Consortium. www.w3.org/

Yankelovich, Nicole. 1996. "How do users know what to say?" *ACM Interactions* 3 (6), November/December 1996. Sun

Microsystems, Inc. Sun Microsystems
Laboratories, www.sun.com/research/
speech/publications/acm-interactions-1996/
Interactions.html

INDEX